PRESUPPOSITIONS OF INDIA'S PHILOSOPHIES

PRENTICE-HALL PHILOSOPHY SERIES

Arthur E. Murphy, Ph.D., Editor

PRESUPPOSITIONS OF INDIA'S PHILOSOPHIES

KARL H. POTTER
Department of Philosophy
University of Minnesota

GREENWOOD PRESS, PUBLISHERS
WESTPORT, CONNECTICUT

The Library of Congress has catalogued this publication as follows:

Library of Congress Cataloging in Publication Data

Potter, Karl H
Presuppositions of India's philosophies.

Original ed. issued in series: Prentice-Hall philosophy series.
Bibliography: p.
1. Philosophy, Indic. I. Title.
[B131.P6 1972] 181'.4 72-6843
ISBN 0-8371-6497-4

Originally published in 1963
by Prentice-Hall, Inc., Englewood Cliffs, N. J.

Reprinted with the permission
of Prentice-Hall, Inc.

First Greenwood Reprinting 1972

Library of Congress Catalogue Card Number 72-6843

ISBN 0-8371-6497-4

Printed in the United States of America

FOR TONI

PREFACE

It may appear presumptuous for a Westerner to set himself the task of explaining Indian philosophers. And, indeed, if the aim here were the reconstruction of the actual thought processes of the philosophers of India, then surely the best person to write such a book would be an Indian. However, the reconstruction attempted here is not psychological but philosophical; we are not concerned with what passed through the minds of Indian philosophers, but rather with the *presuppositions* of India's philosophies. I attempt to identify criteria of success and failure in Indian philosophizing, to indicate on what grounds certain ideas can be recognized as relevant or true and others rejected as irrelevant or false. I do not claim that all Indian philosophers, or even any one of them, would in fact put these criteria in just the way I have put them, though I do claim that there must have been a general commitment to these criteria by those who have written works of philosophy in India.

My critics will say that I am imposing Western assumptions about the nature of philosophy upon an Indian tradition that is differently oriented. I can only say that I have tried my best to avoid doing so. I have tried to identify the assumptions implied in the traditional commitment to freedom (*mokṣa*) as the ultimate goal of human striving, a commitment which seems, upon examination of the sources, to be evident. My argument here is that the criteria of success in Indian philosophizing are derived from this commitment, that good reasons in philosophy stem more or less directly from the basic requirement that truth is that the recognition of which leads to freedom. This orientation is not peculiarly Indian, but it is typical of Indian thought. Although Sanskrit has no term equivalent to our English word "philosophy," the various words that do define the scope of what has come to be called "Indian philosophy" are understood by Indians in a context dominated by the orientation toward freedom.

There is, on the other hand, another respect in which my Western bias may be said to show through, and that is in the large amount of space devoted to what I call "doubts." Indian tradition appears to draw no very sharp distinction between thinking directed toward an understanding of oneself preparatory to one's achievement of greater freedom and thinking directed toward an analysis of the nature of the not-self, that is, the world, or, if you like, reality. In order to explain how speculative thought about the nature of things is related to the orientation toward freedom, I have been forced to the conclusion that speculation becomes relevant because of men's doubts that freedom is possible of attainment. I must confess that I can appeal to no direct textual confirmation of this explanation; I cannot point to a text in which a classical Indian philosopher explicitly says that he is racked by doubts about the possibility of freedom and therefore proposes to embark on speculation. Nevertheless I believe that such doubts are presupposed by the very fact that a large proportion of Indian thought is speculative in the extreme. The alternative explanations of which I can think are precluded by strong evidence. Speculative philosophy is obviously dominated by the orientation toward freedom, as can be seen by the tendency of philosophers to begin their works by pointing out the elements of causal chains culminating in release from bondage. Therefore it cannot be supposed that speculation in India is just a different inquiry altogether from self-understanding and control, a divorce that is at least plausible in assessing some Western forms of speculation. Nor can it be thought that all speculative philosophers in India conceive of speculation as itself a path to freedom, for several schools of Indian philosophy declare that a successful analysis of the nature of things, though it may be a necessary condition for the realization of freedom for some people, is not a sufficient condition for anyone. I am therefore forced to conclude that speculation is relevant in Indian thought as the antidote to lack of faith in the availability of freedom for man. There is plenty of indirect evidence to bolster this interpretation, as the reader will discover.

Finally, I may be thought to be Westernizing Indian thought in my choice of what falls within the scope of this work. It is true that I do not discuss some of the texts that are clearly dominated by the commitment to freedom, specifically such ancient text as the Upanishads and such more recent ones as the Purāṇas and the devotional hymns of South Indian mystics. I do not deny that these texts are philosophical. But I have chosen to devote my efforts to an understanding of *speculative* philosophy, and this admittedly because of the link on which I have just commented between speculation and the doubt about freedom's availability. This choice is in part dictated by my conviction that it is the speculative portions of Indian thought that are particularly relevant to Western interests, but it is also dictated by the conviction that it is those same portions that must come once again to be relevant to Indian interests. Even if the doubts of which I speak were not explicitly recognized by the ancient Indians, the impact of Western culture upon India could not help but raise them now. If Indian thought has any future, I maintain that it must be in the direction of dealing with the skepticism and fatalism now creeping into Indian thinking through Western channels. Therefore, my emphasis here is not merely a function of my bias as a Western philosopher or even as a Western man. Rather is it due to my concern lest a valuable and important set of answers to doubts that are becoming worldwide be lost for want of careful exposition and analysis.

This, then, is my defense of the peculiar kind of approach I here make to Indian philosophy. It differs from that of other contemporary writers on Indian thought because I think that not only is classical Indian philosophy still relevant today but more specifically that it is its technical aspects that are most crucially relevant. I do not believe that others have been of this opinion. Most recent exponents of Indian metaphysics and epistemology tend to lack the investigative temper, to be content to say what the classical authors believed without feeling it necessary to ask why they believed it, what the beliefs presupposed, or whether or not the arguments those authors gave are sound.

I have many to thank who have in one way or another helped in the preparation of this volume. The opportunity for writing it came in the form of a Fulbright grant for research in India during the year 1959–1960, and I must first thank Dr. Olive Reddick and her staff for allowing me to do the things I felt necessary to best carry out my project. I have also to record a special debt of gratitude to Mr. Chadbourne Gilpatric and the Rockefeller Foundation for inviting me to organize a series of discussions among American philosophers concerned with Indian thought which took place in Minnesota and Massachusetts during the year 1957–1958. It was from the stimulation provided by these discussions that some of the most important ideas for the book developed.

Among my Indian friends I hardly know how to choose those who have helped me most, since all have been so kind in giving of their time and thought to the problems with which I have been concerned. I think, among many others, of Professor T. R. V. Murti of Banaras Hindu University and Professor Kalidas Bhattacharya of Visvabharati University, who made very helpful general suggestions. Mr. Anthony J. Alston and Mr. Sibajiban Bhattacharya read portions of my manuscript and gave me valuable suggestions on several important details, as did Dr. Mary Runyan, Dr. Stephen Hay, and, on the other side of the ocean, Professor Daniel H. H. Ingalls, Professor David White, and Dr. Reginald Allen. I wish in particular to thank Professor Carl Wellman of Lawrence College for his painstaking examination and criticism of a large portion of the manuscript.

I wish to acknowledge with thanks permission granted by George Allen & Unwin Ltd. and the Macmillan Company, on behalf of Professor T. R. V. Murti, to reproduce brief passages from his book *The Central Philosophy of Buddhism.*

To my wife, finally, I owe a great debt for her constant good judgment, which has tempered my excesses and kept me on fruitful paths.

KARL H. POTTER

Minneapolis, Minn.
February 13, 1962

TABLE OF CONTENTS

5

GOOD REASONS IN PHILOSOPHICAL DISCUSSIONS 56

Perception. *Inference.* Tarka. *Verbal authority* (śabda). *Miscellanea.* *Conclusions.* *Exercises on inference.*

6

FREEDOM AND CAUSATION 93

A fresh classification of philosophical systems. *Causal chains.* *Causal models.*

7

WEAK DEPENDENCE RELATIONS 117

Inherence: The Nyāya-Vaiśeṣika dependence relation. *Similarity: The Buddhist dependence relation.*

8

THE JAIN THEORY OF RELATIONS 145

9

STRONG DEPENDENCE RELATIONS 150

Pariṇāma *or transformation as the dependence relation.* Vivarta *or manifestation as the dependence relation.* *Conclusions.*

10

NEGATION AND ERROR 186

Left-hand theories. *The center.* *Right-hand theories.* *Conclusions.*

11

LEAP PHILOSOPHIES 236

12

CONCLUSIONS AND OUTSTANDING PROBLEMS 257

SOME SUGGESTIONS FOR TEACHERS 261

Pronunciation.

BIBLIOGRAPHY 265

INDEX 271

1

FREEDOM AND ITS CONDITIONS

To understand the philosophy of a culture we must come to some understanding of its ultimate values—of what is of paramount importance in the lives of the people of that culture, of what are the highest ideals of its wisest men. To understand European thought, it is imperative to realize that throughout the history of our tradition there has been a regular commitment to some notion of a highest good which is the ultimate desideratum of a human being, the perfection, within human limits, of man's nature. This idea of the Good (as Plato called it) or of moral perfection has for the most part been dominant in the reflections of our wisest thinkers; where other values were suggested as paramount, we witness regularly a return to this conception of a supreme ethical norm.

The Platonic notion of human nature presupposed that man's nature was limited, that his perfection consisted in the control of the passions by the intellect, so that the reasoned life was the best life, balance of soul was of the essence, and this balance was defined in terms both of the encouragement of the rational faculty and the discouragement of the appetites. When one had reached the state of balance so attractively described by Socrates in such dialogues as the *Republic,* there was no farther to go; one had reached the limits of man's capabilities. And the main stream of philosophers throughout the history of European and Western thought has agreed essentially with Plato in granting to self-knowledge and self-control through reason its claim to be the ultimate source of any happiness within man's reach. In their various ways, the most influential philosophers—Aristotle, Aquinas, Descartes, Locke and Hume, Kant and, in our own day, Russell—have affirmed this view of man and agreed that morality, the highest value for him, lies in the exercise of his reason and the subjugation of his passions.

This is not to say that there have not been great thinkers who have dissented. Some have questioned the priority of moral value, or rationality, to other sorts of value. There is, particularly in recent thought, a tendency to resist the classical penchant for seeing aesthetic and scientific value as subsidiary to virtue. In addition, there have been those, such as Nietzsche and before him medieval mystics such as Eckhart, who questioned the supremacy of moral values on the grounds that there are other values beyond good and evil. One is tempted to forget that—running as an undercurrent throughout the history of Western philosophy—there is a strand of thought which glorifies spontaneity and growth, which looks ahead to man's eventual success in overcoming the bonds which make him temporarily less than divine, and which sees no exercise of power of which man is not in principle capable.

The dissenters are frequently treated as the representatives of evil advice, voices seductive and dangerous, to be silenced by good reasons or bad but at any rate to be silenced somehow—so that values which are taken to sustain the society should not be corrupted. The result has been that the defenders of the supremacy of values other than moral ones have been pictured by the proponents of reason in exceedingly prejudicial fashion: either they have been dismissed with little or no hearing, or they have been represented in influential writings in distorted ways, or they have been associated by implication with unpleasant social practices and institutions. This misrepresentation has not been deliberate, at least not always. Those who were responsible for it frequently acted from what we consider the purest of motives, if not from the clearest of insight. But the fact that we call their motives pure only underlines our bias in favor of taking rationality as the highest norm. We weep for Socrates, defender of reason, damned by the citizens of Athens on the trumped-up charge of corrupting the youth, but do not bother to investigate Nietzsche, damned without examination by the citizens of the modern world on the trumped-up charge of being responsible for Hitler. We want to think that Socrates was right and Nietzsche, or at least the Nietzsche we've been told about, wrong. Plato attacks the Sophists—who believed that man was the measure of all things and that ultimate value lies in the maximization of his capacity to control himself and his environment—by producing in the *Republic* a Thrasymachus whom Socrates catches in the grossest sort of mistakes, who preaches that might makes right where what he should say, if his case were allowed to be made properly, is that might, though it does not make right, is a part of man's self-realization, a sign of improvement though not a sufficient condition for perfection. Many of us tend to think that positivism and by association modern empiricist philosophies of science are shallow because they insist in distinguishing norms from facts and persist in ignoring, for purposes of their investigations, the ethical and religious implications of their discoveries. In short, the main stream of Western thinking elevates rationality at the expense of power, whether the claim of power be defended in a limited framework as it is by the pragmatists and the champions of applied science or whether it be defended as an overriding norm, as it was by the antinomian mystics, by Nietzsche and by Bernard Shaw.

In introducing Indian philosophy to Western audiences it has been fashionable either to avoid all discussion of ultimate values or else to gloss over the fact, unpalatable to the main stream of Western thinkers, that Indian philosophy *does* in fact elevate power, control, or freedom to a supereminent position above rational morality, shrouding this difference in a mist of vague platitudes about the unity of all religions and peoples and the *moral* preferability of seeing Indian and Western thought as one, whether they really agree or not. Indian philosophers have themselves been responsible for this latter fashion, but it is important to note that they have not been Indians trained in traditional Hindu ways and governed accordingly, but rather Westernized Indians, speaking and writing in Western languages, who wish to be heard in the Western community of scholars and to be accepted among them. The traditional Indian scholars have infrequently been heard on this point, a result not only of the language barrier, but also of their lack of interest, in keeping with their heritage, in proselytizing or in seeking favor as if that were of importance in itself.

Nevertheless, for better or worse, the ultimate value recognized by classical Hinduism in its most sophisticated sources is not morality but freedom, not rational self-control in the interests of the community's welfare but complete control over one's environment—something which includes self-control but also includes control of others and even control of the physical sources of power in the universe. When, in the Bhagavadgītā, Arjuna complains to Krishna that if he fights his kinsmen he will destroy the foundations of a moral society, Krishna answers that it is more important for Arjuna to be himself than to be a cog in the social machine; he must fulfill his capacities as a man of certain gifts, a warrior, not necessarily by inciting wars but at least by meeting the challenges of war when it arises. By doing so he enhances his control; he comes to be not dictated to by circumstances, but master of them.

There can really be no doubt about the supremacy of control and freedom over morality among Indian ideals in the mind of anyone who has read the tales of ancient India or who has studied *yoga* or who has read about the attributes of the good teacher (*guru*) in Indian sources.

The man of control is celebrated in various ways within traditional literature. Professor Van Buitenen has emphasized, for instance, that in the fascinating stories of ancient and medieval India "the ideal type of man . . . is endowed with a particular quality of spirit which we can perhaps best paraphrase as presence of mind. [This quality] . . . is the articulation of a constant cagy awareness of what is going on, the refusal to permit oneself to be distracted momentarily, the preparedness and collectedness of one's faculty of discrimination and decision. It is what the philosophic psychology calls *buddhi,* which comprises both this wide-awake vigilance and the capacity for immediately acting upon what comes within its purview. This faculty is the hero's principal weapon in the struggle for survival."[1] The path of the hero in the struggle referred to is frequently a bloody one, and sometimes marked by activities which we might regard as immoral in someone else, but in him these acts are merely the manifestation of a superior spirit and not to be judged by standards inappropriate to his stature.

The same sort of thing is said in different connections about the true *yogi. Yoga,* cognate to English "yoke," carries the meaning of "discipline," i.e., "self-control." In the Bhagavadgītā we read:

> The undisciplined man has no *buddhi,*
> And the undisciplined man has no power to produce anything.[2]

Of the *yogi,* the disciplined one, we hear

> What is night for all beings,
> Therein the man of restraint is awake;
> Wherein (other) beings are awake,
> That is night for the sage of vision.[3]

Once again we perceive the value placed upon superior awareness, discrimination, and the ability to decide and act appropriately in situations where others find themselves at a loss. We know, too, that the *yogi* is one who seeks to pass "beyond good and evil," that the injunctions of the Vedas which prescribe morally correct actions do not apply to the true *yogi*,[4] and that it is accepted in many circles that the path of the saint may well involve him in external behavior which in others would be highly inappropriate.

The traditional ideal of the *guru* or teacher, better called "spiritual advisor," also follows the same pattern. That those only are fit to guide who have gained mastery of their subject is a commonplace requirement; but the relationship of the student to his *guru*, an especially intimate one, requires the teacher not only to have mastered the variety of subject-matters included in the "curriculum" but also, and more important, to have such insight and superior awareness—coupled with the ability to carry out the decisions that insight dictates—as to be always cognizant of his pupil's innermost needs as well as master of the exactly appropriate ways of satisfying them. It is no wonder, with this ideal in mind, that the gifted teacher remains in contemporary India a figure highly fitted in the mind of the community to take on the added burdens of political leadership. Nor is it any wonder that, in the light of the correspondence we have noted between hero, saint, and teacher, the men who appeal to Indians as leaders have been respected and revered as being at one and the same time all three. Because of their superior understanding, such men are held to be worthy of everyone's trust and allegiance, even despite apparent external inconsistencies in their behavior.

The hero, the *yogi*, and the *guru* exemplify superior mastery of themselves and their environment; they, among men, most closely approximate the ideal of complete control or freedom. We shall have more to say about this ultimate value of complete freedom shortly. First, however, it will be helpful to ask what, according to classical Indian ways of thought, constitutes the path by which ordinary men mature toward this superior state.

FOUR ATTITUDES

In dealing with the process of maturing, the ancient Indians had recourse to a series of notions frequently called, in contemporary accounts of them, "the aims of life." The Sanskrit terms for these notions are *artha, kāma, dharma,* and *mokṣa*. The proper understanding of the meaning of these terms, though essential for understanding Indian philosophies, is by no means easy.[a]

To call these four things "aims" suggests that they are *states* of control toward which one aims. Now in some sense perhaps the last of the series, *mokṣa* or complete freedom, is a state, but the sense in which this is so is one which makes it inappropriate to apply the same description to the other three. There is no state of *artha,* of *kāma,* or of *dharma* which a man may come to realize and rest in. Rather these terms are to be construed more subtly, perhaps as attitudes or orientations.

Artha is usually said to have to do with material prosperity. *Kāma* has to do with sexual relations—and incidentally with aesthetic value. *Dharma* is said to have to do with one's duty to family, caste, or class. It is certainly not at all easy to see the underlying rationale for this list, and calling them attitudes or orientations may not seem in any very evident fashion to help us understand the notions better. Nevertheless, if we take time to explore the concepts, I think the reader will see why calling them attitudes is perhaps the least misleading way of assessing them.

Consider first the kind of attitude one tends to take toward material objects that one has to handle from day to day in the routine of making a living—say, toward the door to one's office. How concerned are we for the door? That is to say, do we identify ourselves with the door and care what happens to it? Yes, but minimally. We care that the door opens and shuts when operated. We may care what it looks like, that it not have an unpleasant appearance. Beyond that, it would not occur to most of us to have a concern for the door. It is, therefore, an object of minimal concern for us, and it is the attitude of minimal concern which is the attitude marked out by the word *artha.*

Now such an attitude can, in principle, be taken toward any item in the world. Most men take an attitude of minimal concern toward some animals, or even all animals. Most of us take this attitude toward some men, reserving our attitudes of more intimate concern for relatives and close friends. A few men have no friends, and treat their relatives impersonally. There have even been cases where we might be justified in suspecting that a man has taken an attitude of minimal concern toward

[a] The reader will search in vain in Indian texts for the precise explanation I am about to offer of these four terms. Nevertheless it is my firm belief that my explanation communicates the spirit which pervades talk of these four "aims of life," and it is this spirit that I am primarily interested in getting across here. My purposes will be served as long as the explanation I give is not incompatible with the tenor of the Indian texts, and I believe it satisfies this requirement.

himself, although this has an air of paradox about it; nevertheless, one who kills himself in a fit of despair may well be thought to have, at least at the suicidal moment, considered himself as of minimal concern.[b] When the Indians have said that *artha* has to do with material prosperity, I think they have had in mind that those things which are manipulated in making a living, including in some cases men or even oneself, that *those* things are typically things we take an attitude of minimal concern toward. But it is the kind of attitude that the Indians were interested in, and the identification of this attitude by reference to material prosperity was merely a convenient way of marking down contexts in which this attitude is most frequently taken. It is not a defining characteristic of the attitude of minimal concern, *artha,* that it be directed toward those things with which we come in contact in our search for material prosperity, although it is in fact true that we tend to see this attitude exhibited frequently toward those things.

The attitude one tends to take toward those to whom one is passionately attracted has a very distinct feel from the attitude of minimal concern. Again, one may take this attitude of *kāma* or passionate concern toward anything in the world. The little girl who hugs her teddy bear takes it toward an inanimate object, while the grown man who loves a woman passionately takes it toward an animate one. Again, it is possible to take this attitude toward oneself, as may be the case in narcissism. The mark of this attitude is an element of possessiveness in the concern one has for the object of one's attentions, coupled with a partial identification of oneself with that object. In the *kāma* relationship one depends upon the object that is loved and therefore guards it jealously, restricting if need be its habits or wishes (if it has them) in one's own interest. This is also true, to be sure, of the *artha* attitude, for one who takes an attitude of minimal concern toward a thing may guard it jealously and not hesitate to restrict its habits or wishes. But in the *kāma* attitude, unlike the *artha* one, there is a feeling that at some moments, at any rate, one is enlarged by becoming one with the loved one or thing. The little girl projects herself as the teddy bear and talks and feels on its behalf and receives satisfaction therefrom, as does the successful lover who in making love projects himself as the beloved and acts, for the moment, as if he were she or the two were one. Again it is paradoxical to speak of

[b] I do not, however, wish to argue whether this is the proper way of explaining any suicide's attitude toward himself, for it may also be that a suicide has such intense concern for himself that, considering his self as independent of his body, he does away with the latter in the interests of the former.

the narcissist projecting himself into himself—at the least this seems to involve two uses of the word "self," for the self that projects is distinct from the self into which it is projected. But the paradox will be recognized, I think, as reflecting something essentially true. As before, when the Indians describe *kāma* in terms of sexual relations they do not mean to restrict the operation of this attitude to just those objects with which one can come into a sexual relationship, but are rather pointing to sexual relationships as typically involving instances of the taking of this kind of attitude.

When we turn to the *dharma* notion, we find again that it is an attitude which the term has primary reference to. It is an attitude of concern greater than that involved in *artha* or *kāma*. In taking the *dharma* attitude one treats things commonly thought of as other than oneself as oneself; not, however, in the way that the *kāma*-oriented man treats himself—in a spirit of passion and possessiveness—but rather in a spirit of respect. That is, not only do we in the *dharma* orientation project ourselves into others, but we do so with a certain conception of ourselves which precludes either using others as the *artha*-oriented person does or depending on them as the *kāma*-oriented person does. It is customary to render *"dharma"* as "duty" in English translations of Sanskrit works dealing with the "aims of life." This rendering has the merit that it suggests, following Kant's use of the word "duty," the crucial aspect of respect for the habits and wishes of others. It has the drawback, however, that it suggests to many people a rather stiff, perhaps even harsh, attitude, from which one tends to withdraw to something halfway between possessive love and "righteous" minimal concern. As a result, there is a supposed irreconcilability between an ethic of passionate concern for others and an ethic of duty which operates independently of concern for others. But we need not wish this difficulty upon Indian thought; *"dharma"* does not mean "duty" in any sense of lack of concern for others—quite the opposite. The attitude of *dharma* is an attitude of concern for others as a fundamental extension of oneself. To see more clearly what this means we do well once more to appeal to examples.

Like the others, the *dharma* attitude can be taken toward anything, but the Indians mention certain things in the world as being more frequently its object. The attitude of a wise and loving mother toward her child is a case in point: the mother is concerned for her child as a fundamental and (within this orientation) indistinguishable part of herself. Her own self is enlarged by this identification. But since she respects herself—i.e., she respects her own habits and wishes, unlike one who takes an *artha* or *kāma* attitude to himself—she must also respect her child's habits and wishes, so that she neither uses the child for her own devices nor does she depend on the child in the way the passionate lover depends on his beloved. This is because the child is part of herself within this orientation. And generally speaking, since Indians have a strong feeling for the sacredness of family ties, relations of parent to child and grandchild, of child to parent and grandparent, are primary areas where one may expect to find the attitude of *dharma* exemplified. Not far removed, too, are the relations between oneself and the rest of one's clan, or caste, or class. Here, too, one may hope to find *dharma* instanced, although all too frequently—especially in this day and age, so degenerate according to classical Indian tradition—one will be disappointed.[c]

Before we turn to the final "aim of man," we would do well to examine the evidence for my contention that *artha, kāma* and *dharma* are best considered as attitudes and that this conception does justice to Indian ideas. There are various facts which it seems to me can only be explained if we construe these three "aims of life" as attitudes. For one thing, it explains why the Indian can point to certain kinds of objects or relations in the world and say "these are *artha,* or *kāma,* or *dharma* objects, i.e., objects which are relevant to those aims of life," and still go on to recommend, as he does, that one *ought* to treat all objects in the *dharma* spirit, as extensions of the self. This would be impossible if the scope of the term *dharma,* for instance, precluded by definition one's taking objects like doors or the people one buys from and sells to in the *dharma* spirit. Thus, these three terms are not to be thought of as essentially applying to a certain range of objects or relations, but rather as being most frequently exemplified in ordinary life in that range and therefore identifiable by reference to it. It is as if I should identify my car as the one that is usually found in a certain parking-place; it wouldn't follow that if one found it somewhere else, it wouldn't be my car. To identify something is not necessarily to specify any defining characteristics.

Another bit of evidence to suggest that I am on the right track is to be found in the fact that the Indians—rather cruelly, I suspect we think —distinguish the relationship of man and wife from that of parent and child. It is not that one ought not to treat one's wife in the *dharma* manner, since of course one ought; it is rather that one is more likely to

[c] According to Hindu tradition, we live in *kaliyuga,* the fourth and most degenerate of the four eras into which each creation-cycle is divided.

identify oneself in the *dharma* manner first with the members of the family in which one is brought up or whom one brings up, and only subsequently with others, including one's wife. This certainly can and will be questioned by Americans, who believe that marriage is as noble a challenge as that raised by family ties. Yet there is something to be said in the Indians' favor here, and it is that since the most engrossing aspect of marriage for many people at least for the first few years is the sexual one, and since the sexual relationship so easily tempts one to take *kāma* attitudes, it is perhaps not the area of relations in which one will most easily be able to take a *dharma* attitude. For most people, it is not easy to love with concern though without passion; many do not even think it worth trying to.

But most important, I do not see what else these terms can mean if they do not refer to attitudes. They do not refer to states, in any commonly recognized sense of the term; states are the sorts of things people are *in,* and one is never in a state of *artha* rather than *kāma;* instead, he takes *artha* attitudes toward some things in his environment and *kāma* attitudes toward other things. They do not refer to objects, or classes of objects, or relations or classes of relations, as has been argued above. They are "aims of life," I conclude, just in the sense that they represent capacities for taking things in a certain way. This is what I have in mind in calling them attitudes.

The route to superior control, to the fourth and most worthwhile kind of attitude, *mokṣa* or complete freedom, lies in the mastery of attitudes of greater and greater concern coupled with less and less attachment or possessiveness. In fact, the fourth orientation is well understood by extrapolating from this route. In moving from *artha* to *kāma,* we move from lack of concern to concern, and from more attachment to less. *Mokṣa* or freedom is the perfection of this growth. When one attains freedom, he is both not at the mercy of what is not himself, that is to say, he is *free from* restrictions initiated by the not-self, and he is also *free to* anticipate and control anything to which he turns his efforts, since the whole world is considered as himself in this orientation. The freedom-from corresponds to his lack of attachment, and the freedom-to to his universal concern. It will be my task in the next few chapters to show in more detail the ways in which the Indian philosophers approach this grand conception of complete freedom. In doing so, I shall try to build a conceptual bridge from our conventional attitudes about the non-perfectibility of man to the Indian attitudes about man's perfectibility.

BONDAGE AND *KARMA*

At every moment in life a man faces specific challenges which test his freedom. The function of the "aims of life" categories can easily be interpreted as a way of distinguishing varieties of such life-challenges by reference to the kinds of attitudes men are regularly called upon to grow up to. Every man is faced with challenges arising from his relationships with impersonal objects and people in business, with adored objects, with family and close friends, and each time we become conscious of these challenges, as we do when we find time in this busy world to reflect about ourselves, we are forced to recognize inadequacies in our responses to the challenges which continually face us. These inadequacies reflect, in Indian terminology, our bondage (*bandha*).

The world of natural objects binds us, for example, through the physiological tensions resulting from the absence of goal objects that can satisfy basic and derived biological drives. The world of the passions binds us because of the emotional tensions which result from lack of reciprocation, as well as from our own excesses. And the inner world of our own personal being binds us through the psychological tensions resulting from a lack of self-understanding manifested in irrational fears, partial withdrawal, or rationalization. The human being faces challenges on many fronts, challenges the meeting of which may help to free him from bondage. Challenges may be met in various ways: by birth, when one is born into a prosperous family or society; by social action, when the community works together to improve the general standard of living; by the application of scientific techniques which remove the threat of disease and other sources of natural calamity. But though these forces can certainly help a man get into position to grow toward freedom, discipline is still required on his part in order to overcome habits. To help man become free from the general conditions which breed bondage is the goal of science and technology and the social advances that we claim bring us freedom, but more subtle challenges lie underneath the surface, challenges not so easily met by those techniques. These more subtle challenges arise from the habits themselves, which continue after the conditions that engendered them have been removed and which engender new habits which in turn must be removed somehow. This round of habits breeding habits is a part of what is called in Sanskrit *saṃsāra,* the wheel of rebirth, which is governed by *karma,* the habits themselves.

To succeed in the affairs of the world requires the building of habits on a man's part, habits which enable him to overcome the obstacles which lie in the way of material success. If one is to succeed in the business world, one must learn certain skills—reading the stockmarket accurately, buying and selling appropriately. One must also, to take a more fundamental aspect, learn certain habits of mind, learn to leave aside extraneous considerations, learn perhaps a certain ruthless way of abstracting from situations in order to see clearly where advantage or disadvantage in one's financial pursuits lie. These habits, necessary to success in business, constitute a source of bondage. For as one becomes more and more successful through the development of these habitual responses, he tends to become less and less capable of adjusting to fresh or unusual contingencies. Insofar as this hardening of habits does take place, one comes to be at the mercy of his habits, as he will find out to his dismay when a fresh or unusual situation does occur. And to be at the mercy of one's habits is to be out of control, that is to say, in bondage.

Again, consider the man who successfully woos and wins a mate. He has made himself more attractive to his wife by the acquisition of pleasing traits of character—not necessarily by conscious design, but rather as a way of dealing with one of life's challenges in a natural fashion. Yet those traits which appeared pleasing to the young lady become habitual in him, and he drifts into routine ways of pleasing her. The result is the dulling of his perception of the beauties of the intimate relationship of marriage through insufficient resiliency in response to its ever-new developments. This inflexibility once again constitutes bondage; it renders a man unable to respond emotionally to some degree, and this is a limitation of his freedom. He has lost control of the sources of attractiveness within him; his *buddhi,* his discrimination and power to act appropriately and incisively, has been muddied over by habit.

In both these cases we can clearly see, I think, a constant source of tragedy and frustration in life as we know it. In each case, a man of perfectly good will seeks success with respect to a challenge, and in each case he fails despite his best efforts—even though he appears to have achieved his goal—because habits of mind and action are set up within him through his apparent success which, as it develops, he is unable fully to control. Western modes of thought offer expression of this source of frustration in the fatalism of the ancient Greeks, in the doctrine of original sin, in the "hedonistic paradox." In India the cause of this type of failure is *karma,* also sometimes identified with *avidyā* or "ignorance," more precisely "want of discrimination and insight." Indian philosophy is particularly mindful of this source of failure. *Karma* is described in the philosophy of the Jains, for example, as a kind of dirt which accretes to the otherwise pure *jīva* or self by virtue of one's actions. This dirt clouds, i.e., restricts, the self in its activities, and regulates the behavior of that *jīva* in the next life—until it is worn off by time and replaced by newer *karma*. In the Bhagavadgītā the dirt is described as being of three kinds—practically transparent (*sattva*), translucent (*rajas*), and opaque (*tamas*).[5] One may think of these as types of habits: good habits, whose nature is to lead us toward real rather than apparent control; habits neither enlightening nor debilitating; bad habits, which hold us in a low stage within an orientation. The point at present is just that each of these types of habits—good, bad, or indifferent—binds a man as surely as another.

To put the point another way: man finds frequently and much to his dismay that success in itself does not necessarily enlighten him. Nor do suffering and frustration enlighten by themselves, despite some who have made the claim that they do. I use the term "enlighten" deliberately, for the truly free person, the soul which has been stripped of its *karma* and its load thus lightened, is precisely the truly free, masterful, powerful, controlled-and-controlling Self[d] which constitutes the real, though usually hidden, goal of our attempts to meet challenges. Full lifetimes of experience, containing both success and failure in abundance, are still not a sufficient condition for complete freedom. Something more is needed.

With bondage one cannot remain permanently satisfied. Bondage breeds frustration and sorrow. This is the kernel of the first of the Buddha's four noble truths—"All is *duḥkha*," i.e., frustration, sorrow.[e] More experience, as long as it bears the seeds of more bondage, will at best enable us to substitute more positive capabilities for present incapacities and to substitute transparent dirt for opaque. But by itself it cannot remove bondage altogether. For that, special methods must be found.

[d] I shall sometimes capitalize "Self" to make it clear that I am talking of the potentially perfected self and not the bound self. Sanskrit sometimes makes the distinction by two different words: *ātman* (Self) and *jīva* (self).

[e] The usual translation of *duḥkha* as "pain" is misleading since its connotations in ordinary English are narrower than those intended by the Buddha. The Buddha included, for example, "not getting what one wishes" as *duḥkha*. Cf. *Source Book,* p. 274.

THE DISTINCTION BETWEEN *DHARMA* AND *MOKṢA*

"All very well," you may say, "as far as the limitations contained in the attitudes of minimal concern or even passionate concern, but what about the third kind of attitude, *dharma,* in which one respectfully identifies all else as a part of oneself? Why is not this your complete freedom? How does it differ from *mokṣa?*"

To see the difference, let me first suggest the kind of frustration which even a man who has attained *dharma* experiences. What we have said of *dharma* is that a person who has this attitude perfectly, who has mastered the challenges it generates, is one who respects all his environment as himself. This is possible, it was noted previously, only if one respects oneself, but in the notion of respecting oneself there still lurks the possibility of habituation. To see this we may discuss the notion of *resignation*.

The minimally concerned man is resigned most completely, resigned to be at the mercy of a large part of his environment. Complete resignation is at the opposite pole from complete freedom. The passionately-oriented man is farther up the ladder because he is not resigned to some part of his environment, that part he passionately loves or hates. He is less resigned, because more concerned, and therefore more confident of his ability to realize himself in those moments when his self identifies with others. But it is this very passion which betrays him, for although it leads him to identify completely for the moment, it is undisciplined and partial and so breeds habits which lead to frustration, as has been suggested in the previous sections.

Now the man of *dharma,* the respectful one, has largely overcome the resignation to others typical of minimal concern, but he has not mastered the challenge of finding a proper balance between the extremes of passionate identification on the one hand and non-concern on the other. He tries to find that balance, but finds it by resigning himself to his conception of himself! The man of *dharma* sees the importance of treating others as himself, but fails to generate the kinds of real concern which the man of passion has at his most glorious moments. He sees himself as respecting others, as bound by the concept of duty toward others. However, he has not mastered himself, for his conception is not based upon a spontaneous feeling. His posture is not natural, not spontaneous; he is being governed by principles, and is resigned to the principles which govern him, instead of mastering himself to such an extent that he lives those principles without having to stop and consult them. In more subtle ways, then, he is not one with himself but still split into many parts, some controlled and others controlling. And this split nature gives rise to frustrations. The man of *dharma* is a more complex case than the others; his tragedies, like Hamlet's, are profoundly moving, and the answers to his difficulties are not easy to discover. No wonder most men, American or Indian, are willing to concede that there are no solutions to his difficulties and that he should be satisfied to know that he is the best of us all, a virtuous man.

But the wisest men of India do not concede that there are no solutions to the dharmic man's difficulties. They place no ceiling on man's capacities and oppose resignation of all kinds. The dharmic man's trouble is that he is a spectator of himself, a slave to his conception of himself, lacking the creative drive to fashion a spontaneous and unique way of life not subject to the limitations of common custom and morality. To counteract this trouble, the philosophers of India recommend undertaking a discipline leading to renunciation, which is different from resignation. Through renunciation of the fruits of one's actions, they teach us, a man of *dharma* can perfect himself and remove the sources of all frustrations.

RENUNCIATION AND RESIGNATION

One remarkable paradox about complete freedom, noted in various religious traditions,[f] is that in external appearance the man who is completely free, the *mukta,* resembles if anything the man who is least free, the man of minimal concern. The difference lies in their attitudes. Where the man of minimal concern is resigned, the free man has renounced.

The crucial difference between these two polar attitudinal concepts is that while the resigned man doubts his ability to master that which he is resigned to, the man who renounces is confident of his ability to gain that which he renounces but finds more mastery—greater freedom—in meeting the challenge of not exerting his power for gain. The man who renounces has faith in his powers, while the resigned man does not have faith and doubts his capacity to effect all that he wishes. Faith, that is to say the faith born of the conviction that one is capable of mastering a

[f] See, for example, Søren Kierkegaard's description of the "man of faith" in *Fear and Trembling,* Anchor Books A–30, New York, 1954, pp. 49ff. Kierkegaard's use of the word "resigned"—or at any rate his translator's use—is clearly different from mine, however.

challenge, is a necessary condition for renunciation; without faith, a refusal to exert one's powers is called resignation, not renunciation. And that which signifies lack of faith is doubt, that doubt born of an inadequate conception of self, a conception of self as broken off from others and from the world in which we live in some way that sets limits on man's capacities in general. This doubt is manifested inwardly as fear, the fear that one is at the mercy of some or all of one's environment since it is irradicably other than oneself and thus incapable of being brought under control.

But what is the magic of renunciation that enables it to enlarge one's capacities beyond their apparent limits? First, we had better be clear about what it is that one renounces. One does not, by renouncing, give up his ability to exert a certain capacity that he knows he has, but rather chooses not to be attached to whatever gain or loss might result from exerting that capacity. Attachment breeds bondage, habits which control the self and limit its freedom.

This is Krishna's message to Arjuna in that most important of Indian texts on renunciation, the Bhagavadgītā. It is not altogether easy for us, raised in a tradition emphasizing man's limitations, to understand Krishna's teaching. But if one keeps in mind what I have just said about renunciation and resignation, the meaning, I think, becomes clearer. Arjuna is visited by doubts and fears; he finds himself about to enter into a war against his relatives and friends, and he worries about the effect this war will have on his society.

> Evil alone would light upon us,
> Did we slay these (our would-be) murderers.
>
> . . . . For how, having slain our kinsfolk,
> Could we be happy, Mādhava?
>
> . . . . Upon the destruction of the family, perish
> The immemorial holy laws of the family;
> When the laws have perished, the whole family
> Lawlessness overwhelms also.
>
> Because of the prevalence of lawlessness, Kṛṣṇa,
> The women of the family are corrupted;
> When the women are corrupted, O Vṛṣṇi-clansman,
> Mixture of caste ensues.
>
> . . . . By these sins of family-destroyers
> [Sins] which produce caste-mixture,
> The caste laws are destroyed,
> And the eternal family laws.

When the family laws are destroyed,
  Janārdana, then for men
Dwelling in hell certainly
  Ensues; so we have heard. . . .[6]

But Arjuna is not worried about the right things, as Krishna points out in the following chapters. He fears that the wrong *results* will accrue from his exerting what is in his power, i.e., to kill his kinsfolk. Therefore he throws down his weapons and refuses to fight. But Krishna explains to him that the more important choice he has to make is not between fighting and not fighting, but between attaching himself to the fruits of fighting and not attaching himself to those fruits.

There is no possibility of choice between acting and not acting.

For no one even for a moment
  Remains at all without performing actions;
For he is made to perform action willy-nilly,
  Everyone is, by the Strands that spring from material nature.[7]

The "Strands" (*guṇa*) is Krishna's way of referring to the bondage of habits, which (as was pointed out previously) breed ever-anew in a circle of rebirths. Whatever one does, or whatever one refrains from doing, is an action, and unless it is an act of renunciation it is bound to breed *karma,* bondage and frustration. Arjuna thinks, as it is natural to think, that his choice is between one action and another, each with its frustrating consequences. He can either kill family and friends, which leads to hell as he has just pointed out, or he can refuse to fight and, as Krishna immediately suggests, lose his self-respect and that of others by failing to exert his capacities as a warrior. The fruits of either course lead inevitably to sorrow. But Arjuna thinks wrongly; he has failed to consider the more important choice, between acting attached to the fruits of his action and acting unattached to those fruits. This choice is more important precisely because bondage is a necessary condition for sorrow, and non-attachment, i.e., renunciation, removes the necessary condition for bondage. No attachment, no bondage; no bondage, no sorrow—once one believes this to be the case, and has faith in his capacity to discipline himself to non-attachment, it should be clear that this choice supersedes the choice between two unpleasant courses of attached action.

But one does not renounce the fruits of one's capacities for action merely by refusing to exercise those capacities. Why does Krishna advise Arjuna to fight? It is because only by disciplining himself through the non-attached exercise of a capacity that he believes himself to have can Arjuna grow into greater freedom. Arjuna is a warrior, indeed the best bowsman in the land, as we are told in the Mahābhārata epic of which the Bhagavadgītā is but an episode. He has achieved already one important condition for renunciation, namely faith in his own capacity to do something successfully: Arjuna does not doubt that he can kill many of his kinsfolk with a flick of his wrist. The important thing is not the effect of this ability, but Arjuna's faith in it. Krishna urges him to act upon that faith but without attachment to the results. If Krishna should try to discipline himself by the other course, i.e., by retiring from battle, he would not be acting upon faith in his ability and would soon be led into frustration once more.

> Now, if thou this duty-required
>   Conflict wilt not perform,
> Then thine own duty and glory
>   Abandoning, thou shalt get thee evil.
>
> Disgrace, too, will creatures
>   Speak of thee, without end;
> And for one that has been esteemed, disgrace
>   Is worse than death.[8]

The point is not what others would think of Arjuna (though undoubtedly Krishna uses this as a kind of persuasion); it is rather what Arjuna is going to think of himself. Disgrace is worse than death for someone like him because by it he loses faith in himself.

This is not, however, to say that for someone else, differing in personality from Arjuna but placed in his circumstances, Krishna would have offered the same advice. The reason why Arjuna cannot unattachedly withdraw from the battle field is that he is who he is, a warrior with a certain personality makeup, a set of habits already formed. Someone whose personality differed might well discipline himself more appropriately by withdrawing; for him, disgrace is either not forthcoming, or if it is, he has faith in his capacity to disregard it—it is not worse than death for him. And now we can see very clearly that self-knowledge is a necessary condition for renunciation and eventual complete freedom: it is necessary to have knowledge of one's personality makeup, of one's capacities at a given moment, so as to choose the appropriate role within which to renounce and thus become free.

But many readers find Krishna's teaching selfish, indeed callous, since, they claim, it sacrifices the lives of others to the self-advancement of one man, Arjuna. These critics, of course, do not share Krishna's presuppositions. They refuse to admit that there can be anything more important than the result of prolonging the life of more people. Krishna's position is simply that ultimate values do not rest in the fruits of actions, on results such as the winning or losing of wars or the killing or nonkilling of people, but rather in freedom alone, which is not a result at all but an attitude. Now of course the issues involved in this confrontation of Krishna's philosophy and that of such critics are many and complex; we cannot try to discuss them all. But we can point out that, once Krishna's presuppositions about the possibility and ultimate value of freedom is accepted, and freedom is interpreted as maximum concern in the fashion I have explained, then the critics can themselves be criticized for taking their stand on the ultimate fragmentedness of human nature, on the impossibility of attaining freedom. For if freedom is possible, then men have it in their power to be concerned for each other lovingly yet disciplinedly, spontaneously yet responsibly. If freedom is worthwhile everyone has a stake in everyone else's advancement, for to help another become more concerned for yourself is at the same time to help yourself become more concerned for him.

Krishna's philosophy, then, encourages the development of mutual concern between one self and another in order that each may eventually reach *mokṣa*. But the realization of this kind of freedom appears to require a continuity of self through time, or between selves across space, which strains a Westerner's credulity. There is no more dramatic difference between the Western tradition's characteristic philosophy of limited human capacities and the Indian's belief in the unlimited potentialities of man than the one we have arrived at.

TRANSMIGRATION

Westerners, then, may be tempted to dismiss Krishna's advice, and the philosophy that stands behind it, because they want no truck with the doctrine of transmigration. Is it not too easy for an Indian, who holds such a belief, to think lightly of taking a human life? And is not a Westerner—for whom such an idea is silly, or at least unfashionable—therefore justified in paying no further attention to what Krishna is saying?

Now it is true that transmigration is a typically Indian belief, but it is worth asking whether, even if it is not accepted, Krishna's arguments are not still powerful. I think one does not need to assume transmigration in its bald aspects—i.e., the view that an individual soul is reborn in another body after death—in order to justify them. Once one has accepted the ultimate value and the possibility of attaining freedom, then it seems to me the conclusions drawn in the Bhagavadgītā follow whether transmigration is brought in or not.

Of course, Krishna seems to appeal to transmigration in his opening words, when he indicates that there is no point in mourning those whom Arjuna might kill, because

> . . . not in any respect was I [ever] not,
> Nor thou, nor these kings;
> And not at all shall we ever come not to be,
> All of us, henceforward.
>
> As to the embodied [soul] in this body
> Come childhood, youth, old age,
> So the coming to another body;
> The wise man is not confused herein.[9]

But I fear his intentions at this point have been regularly misunderstood by Western readers, confused as they are by the many-sidedness of the Bhagavadgītā's functions. For Krishna is not saying that the acceptance of his views is dependent upon the prior acceptance of the special theory of transmigration, but rather that the general theory that the good of all of us is found in the freeing of any of us is what the wise man knows, and therefore he knows that

> Dead and living men
> The [truly] learned do not mourn.[10]

If one who listens to Krishna believes in the special theory of the transmigration of the soul from one body to another, as many Indians profess to, then they are that much better off, for the peculiarly Western reaction of pity for the necessary loss of life of others is one that they will not be visited with. And furthermore, when addressing an orthodox Hindu such as Arjuna—who presumably is aware of, and perhaps even in a way believes, the special theory—one way of persuading him to think more clearly is to remind him of this belief and thus to avoid an extended discussion of what is, for him, not an important consideration. Arjuna is not visited with an attack of pity for his opponents at the outset; one of the remarkable facets of his opening speech for Western readers is his singular lack of pity—he worries about everything else but the pain he may inflict upon those he wounds or kills. It is therefore not appropriate for Krishna to give him an extended answer intended to alleviate worries about the pain he might produce. For other people, it is extremely important to do so; it is the pain one causes others that most worries a Christian, or indeed a Buddhist or a Jain, when he considers what to do in Arjuna's case. And for them, an appeal to the special theory of transmigration would be pointless.

But it does not follow that an appeal to the general theory that the good of all is found in the freeing of some does not constitute an important kind of answer. And this general theory, while it does not specifically imply that one soul transmigrates into another body (though it is not incompatible with that special theory), does imply that in an important sense some of each of us is to be found in some of all of us, and that therefore when a man's body dies some part of him lives on in those who survive him. Furthermore, if this is accepted as an implication of the primacy and possibility of freedom, it also follows that in a given instance it may not be most to the benefit of either everyone or anyone that more people's bodies live rather than less, since in a given instance the weight of the *karma* on the souls of all (for on this view if one is bound all are) may be more profitably attacked and removed if the *karma* is located in fewer bodies rather than in more.

Nevertheless, the feeling that this is a callous philosophy remains for many despite these considerations. It is significant, however, that the two philosophies of life in India which reacted against Hinduism—Buddhism and Jainism—did not reject even the special theory of transmigration; it was not on the grounds of their failure to believe in transmigration that they emphasized the virtues of compassion (*karuṇa*) and non-violence (*ahiṃsā*). Rather, they accept the general theory which I have just outlined, but balk at concluding that *anyone,* Arjuna or anyone else, is ever put in a position where producing more pain in someone or something is more contributory to total freedom than producing less pain. Their emphasis on these virtues takes the form of a doctrine that the discipline involved in avoiding the production of pain in others, which is to say in oneself, constitutes a part of anyone's path to complete freedom. This emphasis is not inconsistent with Krishna's general theory; it *is,* however, incompatible with his specific advice to Arjuna. The issue between Hinduism and the Buddhists and Jains on ethics is just the issue between those who believe one must sometimes fight to defend one's freedom and those who believe that freedom can only be won by never fighting; it is the issue between activism and pacifism. But on the basic postulation of ultimate values, Hinduism, Buddhism and Jainism are united: complete freedom is the only thing worth striving for, and complete freedom means maximum concern with minimum attachment.

THE NECESSARY CONDITIONS OF FREEDOM

Next I wish to gather together and develop some hints that have been dropped in previous pages about what must be the case in order that freedom be taken seriously as the ultimate value by a man. That is to say, I shall now try to review what are the necessary conditions for faith in the ultimacy of freedom, in the unlimited capacities of all men to achieve spontaneous identification with all else.

One necessary condition for faith in the ultimacy of freedom is the belief that freedom is not only logically possible but *actually* possible, i.e., that at least one route is open which a man can find and travel to complete freedom. There must be one route for every man, but not necessarily the same route. That is, either there is one route which each and every man can find and travel on to freedom, or else there are several routes on which men with different personality characteristics can travel—as long as for each and every man there is a route. But this belief in turn has its necessary conditions.

In order to believe that there is a route for any given man, I must presuppose that the notion of a "route" means something; that is, I must believe that certain conditions which are part of the defining characteristics of a "route" can be satisfied. A route is, first, something that a man can be "on." Secondly, it is something which has stages—if only the two stages of "not there yet" and "arrived." If I doubt that a man can ever be "on" a route. then I doubt that freedom is actually possible; the same is true if I doubt that there is any distinction between "not there yet" and "arrived." The experiential counterparts of these intellectualistically expressed doubts are certain fears—the fear that men are never on their way to anything, and the fear that the best there is is what we have already, with all its frustrations.

Supposing that I am free from such doubts, I must further believe that each and every man is in a position from which he can get himself onto an appropriate route and stay on it. Every man either is already on such a route or must be able to bring it about that he gets on it; and once on it, he must be able to see to it that he doesn't get off. To believe this is not, of course, to believe that every man is on an appropriate route now or to predict that once on no man will ever lose his way: it is just to believe that it is within man's control to see to it that these things come about. The enemy of this belief is doubt about man's capacities to bring things about, and the correlative fear is the fear that nothing one does makes any difference in any respect that matters.

But the belief in a man's ability to get on and not get off a route presupposes two more beliefs—one is the belief that there is a sufficient condition for getting on and not getting off, and the other the belief that man is free enough from external influences so that he can bring about a sufficient condition for getting on and not getting off his route. The twin doubts pertinent to this set of conditions are, on the one hand, skepticism, the doubt that events are regularly connected and consequently that there is a sufficient condition for getting on and not getting off, and on the other hand, fatalism, the doubt that man is free from a predestined fate determined by impersonal forces independent of his control. The parallel fears are, on the one hand, the fear that nothing one can do can bring about a hoped-for result, and, on the other, the fear that nothing one can do can alter what is bound to occur.

Going back to the first necessary condition, which was that one must believe that at least one route is open whereby men can travel to complete freedom, we can next note another important presupposition which is a necessary condition in turn for the first one, distinct from the conditions already mentioned. This presupposition is the belief that renunciation constitutes a route to the removal of bondage—i.e., to complete freedom—which does not in turn breed more bondage. Complete freedom is the removal of all *karma;* and if one believes that no real distinction can be found between renunciatory routes and routes of activity or resignation which beget partial freedom, one is necessarily in doubt about the possibility of attaining complete freedom. The correlative fear here is, I suspect, one which most of us are prone to: the fear that whatever one does will bring about results to which he will be subject willy-nilly, that either one takes active interest in the results of his actions ("attaches himself to them") or one resigns himself to whatever the consequences of his actions may be, and that there is no other alternative to these two.

Now as I argued in my review of Krishna's advice to Arjuna, renunciation must be with respect to the fruits of actions of which one is the master and which one is capable of performing successfully—otherwise to give up attachment to fruits is resignation, not renunciation. Therefore a necessary condition for the belief that renunciation constitutes a route to complete freedom is the belief, not only that there are actions which men are capable of performing successfully, but also that each man is capable of knowing which actions he is capable of performing successfully. If a man could not know which actions he is capable of performing successfully, he could not knowingly renounce the fruits of those actions; if he could not knowingly renounce the fruits of those actions, he could only gain freedom by accident, which is to say he could not find a route. The doubt here concerns man's ability to know himself; and the fear correlative to it is the fear of the absurd within man, the fear that there is something irrational that is natural to man such that his capacities in any particular situation as well as in general cannot be gauged, by himself or by any other.

In succeeding chapters I shall be concerned to show how the doubts and fears which threaten to undermine these necessary presuppositions of one's faith in complete freedom can be addressed and perhaps set to rest. Roughly, there are two branches of presuppositions which must be defended; first, the branch leading from the notion of a "route" to the requirements of freedom to and freedom from; second, the branch leading from the necessity that there be renunciation as well as activity and resignation to the necessity of the possibility of self-knowledge. I shall take up the latter branch first, and try to show how it can be argued that self-knowledge is possible, and how the Indians think about renunciation (Chapters 2 and 3). Then I shall turn to the former branch, the branch which, so I shall argue, gives the rationale for speculative philosophy in India, and after reviewing the generation of the problems and discussing the methods of reasoning adopted in India for handling those problems (Chapters 4 and 5), I shall spend the major part of this volume discussing the problems themselves as they are treated within the various systems of Indian thought.

NOTES

Where complete data are not listed, references are to the editions and translations given in the Bibliography under the rubric mentioned in the footnote.

1. Hans van Buitenen, "The Indian Hero as Vidyādhara," *Journal of American Folklore,* 71:306 (1958).
2. *Bhagavadgita* (II.66), p. 28. My translation.
3. *Bhagavadgita* (II.69), p. 28.
4. *Bhagavadgita* (IV.22), pp. 46–47; (IX.30), pp. 94–95.
5. See *Bhagavadgita,* esp. Chapter XIV, pp. 134–144.
6. *Bhagavadgita* (I.36–44), pp. 10–13.
7. *Bhagavadgita* (III.5), pp. 32–33.
8. *Bhagavadgita* (II.33–34), pp. 20–21.
9. *Bhagavadgita* (II.12–13), pp. 16–17.
10. *Bhagavadgita* (II.11), pp. 16–17.

2

KNOWING ONESELF

If we can show that it is possible to have self-knowledge, i.e., knowledge about one's capabilities in particular situations, we will remove one source of doubt concerning the possibility of finding a path of renunciation. Since this book is an inquiry into the presuppositions of Indian philosophy, it does not seem out of place to offer an independent investigation of this problem, even though little if any philosophical literature from classical Indian sources deals directly with it. As we shall see in Chapter 10, epistemological problems within the Indian systems are primarily extensions of metaphysical ones and concern what causes our knowledge when, for instance, we know incorrectly. The problems of saying how we know, of describing the knowledge process, are lumped in Indian philosophy under the general rubric of *nyāya,* the study of the *pramāṇa*s. In Chapter 5, we shall describe the Indian approach to these problems; at the present I merely remark that the theory of Indian logic is oriented for the most part toward an exposition of the proper method to be used in metaphysical investigations, not specifically as used in personal introspection. As a result, I have to go my own way here, taking my cue from the fact (to be demonstrated later) that the method of any thinking for an Indian philosopher is the familiar method of hypothesis and verification.

The problem of this chapter is, then, to explain how self-knowledge is as possible as any knowledge about the world, and to show that judgments to the effect that renunciation is possible with respect to the fruits of a certain kind of action are just as open to verification and falsification as any other assertions. And so, indeed, are judgments that a certain discipline leads toward freedom for a given individual.

The topic of this chapter may have some interest for contemporary philosophers independently of any value it may have for the exposition of Indian thought, for it addresses a problem currently under heavy discussion, namely the question whether moral reasoning is or is not to be conceived analogously to reasoning about matters of fact. I should say, on this question, that the answer to it depends upon what use one intends to make of moral reasoning. If one is in doubt about the ultimate value of freedom (or any other candidate for ultimacy) and wishes to use reasoning to ascertain its claims, then this is, it seems to me, a different use of reasoning than our use of it to aid us in discovering what we ought to do in order to realize an ultimate value already discovered. To ascertain what is the ultimate value, one searches for the presuppositions of his most firmly held beliefs, and the search comes to an end, perhaps, when he arrives at beliefs which cannot practically be doubted (like *cogito ergo sum*). But, supposing one has discovered that freedom, say, is the ultimate value, he may still be doubtful about his ability to discover what line of action in concrete situations maximizes that ultimate value. Since it is commonly supposed that scientific reasoning requires an unbiased, value-free attitude, it is natural to question whether reasoning appropriate to discovering facts is also appropriate for discovering how one ought to behave. My purpose here is precisely to show the doubtful reader that empirical reasoning is appropriate for discovering the proper action in concrete situations, and that, because it is, there is no reason to doubt—on these grounds, at least—the possibility of a man's using reason to discover an appropriate path of renunciation. Granted that he cannot use reasoning of this sort unless he has faith in some ultimate value, still it can be shown, I think, that if he has such a faith he can use reason to realize that value.

THE IDENTIFICATON OF APPROPRIATE CHALLENGES

A key concept for my discussion is that of a challenge. A challenge is a felt tension in a situation. Let me emphasize several things in this definition. First, a challenge is a *felt* tension. Psychologists tell us that we are subject to many tensions which lie below the threshold of consciousness. Such tensions will not constitute challenges unless we are in some fashion aware of them. Psychoanalysis has made it its business to raise such unfelt tensions to the status of challenges on the supposition that a person can address himself profitably to a challenge but not to an unconscious tension. However, the term "conscious" is ambiguous, for it can mean either "aware of" or "explicitly aware of." That is to say, we can be aware of a tension without being explicitly aware of the circumstances which generate that tension—circumstances which may include the nature of the self, one's purposes, the exigencies of the situation, etc. Thus I have avoided the terms "conscious" and "unconscious" in my definition; what I intend by "felt" is mere awareness, not explicit awareness.

Continuing the examination of our definition, note next that a challenge is a felt tension *in a situation*. What is meant is that to be a challenge a felt tension must occur in a context, that is to say, it must be felt to occur in a context. The person challenged must be aware not only of his dissatisfaction but also of more: he must consider himself as in a situation. Now the situation he thinks himself in may not be at all what others think him in; we shall consider that fact in a moment. But the tension must be felt as arising out of something given to him by the world in which he finds himself; it is, in other words, a real tension as opposed to an imagined one insofar as the person believes himself to be seriously involved in an actual situation.

Finally, what constitutes a "tension?" A tension is a disparity between one's capacities and his performance or expected performance. It implies one's failure to control what he has the capacity to control, though one is not usually clear about one's capacities when one feels a tension. The disparity between possible and actual is the source of discomfort, frustration, and dissatisfaction—to a greater or lesser degree depending on one's sensitivity, i.e., his awareness and involvement.

A challenge, then, is a felt tension in a situation. Now in many situations there are several challenges arising from the disparity between our various purposes in life and our inability to satisfy them all at once. We find, through experience, that some of these challenges lead to dead-ends, whereas others lead to greater ability in facing future challenges; responding to certain challenges disciplines one toward greater control, while responding to others does not. Part of the problem of deciding what to do—the problem to which I am arguing empirical reasoning is applicable—is to tell which challenges are appropriate, i.e., are likely to lead on to greater control and eventual freedom.

It should be clear from anyone's experience that one cannot hope to discover which challenges are appropriate from the "feel" of tensions alone, i.e., without careful thought. Of course, that is the way many of us in fact try to identify appropriate challenges—but we all too frequently fail. The more we learn about the world and about men, the more we realize how utterly men can be fooled by their intuitions. And since this is so, and since it matters greatly to us which challenges we choose to respond to, we are left with no other option than to try to sharpen our understanding of the situations which engender those challenges.

The appropriateness or inappropriateness of a challenge is a function, then, of our *assessment* of situations. An appropriate challenge is a felt tension which stems from an adequately and accurately judged situation; an inappropriate challenge is a felt tension which stems from an inadequately or inaccurately judged situation. Self-understanding, which requires the recognition of appropriate challenges, depends on the correct assessment of situations, i.e., on discrimination (accuracy) and awareness of the full nature (adequacy) of the situation.

But, as we mentioned before, the situation one thinks himself in may not in fact be the one others think he's in. The term "situation," as used here, has meant the context one feels oneself to be in and not the so-called "external situation" which would constitute the subject-matter of a description by an impartial onlooker. Does not a "correct" assessment require just such an impartial point of view?

This is a crucial question, upon the answer to which a great deal depends. It is tempting to identify discrimination and awareness—accuracy and adequacy—with the recognition of *all* the facts of that "external situation" I just spoke of. That is to say, one may be tempted to think that there are just two ways of failing to assess a situation correctly—first, by failing to see that besides facts A, B, and C there is also fact D to consider; second, by failing to see fact A, for instance, as not really one fact but two or more. The assumption implicit in this way of putting things is that in any situation there are just so many facts, and that the clue to understanding is to analyze the situation until just that number of facts are discriminated. Error in judgment, on this view of understanding, always consists in not speaking strictly enough; vagueness and ambiguity are the only enemies we need consider. The resolution of problems of the kind we face is to be gained, on this view, by assuming the stance of the impartial observer; when all sources of bias and confusion have been removed, the true number of facts will lie spread out before one.

The crucial question is whether this is the proper way to understand understanding. There can be no doubt that one way of going wrong in assessing a situation is by allowing bias to obscure a relevant distinction, but it does not follow that this is the only way of going wrong. Furthermore, one wonders whether it is possible or advisable to discriminate *every* factor in a situation. If this is what "speaking strictly" is to mean, surely it goes too far. If one speaks strictly enough, language and thought become impossible.[1] Understanding is not only a matter of distinguishing, it is also a matter of classification—and all classification is for some purpose or other. Hence we cannot hold to the doctrine of the impartial observer.

Understanding a situation—or the world—is like making a map. If the thing to be mapped is curved, like the earth, and if the map is to be flat, then there is no one projection which does not distort, i.e., which does not overlook some distinction which may be reflected in another projection. Consequently, geographers conclude that in order to get on with their business they will have to make do with different projections for the various purposes for which maps need to be constructed, whatever they may be. If one is interested in navigating a ship, certain projections are awkward which may be useful in other respects, say, for reflecting the relative sizes of land-masses. Whichever purpose we are interested in, the crucial considerations of other purposes are overlooked for the moment. Factors which are pertinent for one purpose are not relevant for another. A purpose, that is, provides a criterion of relevance for mapping, which is to say that it endows with value certain features and renders other features negligible as long as that purpose is paramount. In mapping the earth, there are, depending upon our purposes, certain judgments we care about reflecting or translating into map-terms and others that we don't care about. The appropriate projection for a given purpose is one which accurately translates into map-terms the judgments about which we care; if it distorts the others, that doesn't matter, since we have no need for them.

The situation in understanding ourselves must, I suggest, be conceived analogously. We normally assess challenges for a purpose, but we do not care about every fact that could be distinguished concerning the challenges; we only care about those facts which are relevant to our purpose.

In that case, it will be said, there can be no ultimate value, since there is no way of understanding independent of our various and conflicting purposes. This is why one is moved to defend the doctrine of the impartial observer, who abstracts his notion of understanding from all purposes whatsoever. We fear that to settle for a variety of purposes, each generating its own map, would breed relativism in values and irresponsibility in morals as a result of our inability to compare any value against a more ultimate one. But the objection misses fire. For to deny that there is any one map which will translate all the judgments people might care about consonant with all the purposes they have is not to deny that there is an ultimate value which stands atop a scale of values or purposes and provides a check against irresponsibility. Such an ultimate value is indeed itself a purpose, the supreme purpose. The map which it generates will select certain features and thereby distort, just as other maps do, but this will not affect its supremacy. If freedom is the supreme purpose, it is so, not because it generates a completely adequate and accurate map of every last detail that might be mapped in some other projection, but because it is the purpose to which men discover themselves to be most ultimately committed. The free soul is not the impartial observer but the completely committed observer. There is all the difference in the world between these two.

But we are investigating the use of reasoning by one who is not completely free, who is only partially committed. He comes to situations with certain purposes—usually several—the adoption of any of which involves partial commitment to complete freedom. Each of these several purposes engenders a criterion of relevance which sets aside certain factors in the situation as among those about which he does not care. He tries to map the situation in accordance with this criterion, and if his map is accurate and adequate, he will be able to recognize the appropriate challenges and distinguish them from those which are not appropriate. An appropriate challenge, remember, is just a felt tension which arises in an accurately and adequately assessed situation. There may be several appropriate challenges in a given situation. But adequacy and accuracy have essential reference to a criterion or criteria of relevance arising from whatever purpose(s) one is committed to. The situation cannot be divorced from those purposes; indeed, the purposes are an essential part of the situation itself.

VERIFICATION AND FALSIFICATION OF ROLES

There is a further move one must make after he has correctly assessed a situation. I shall call it the verification or falsification of a role. It should be distinguished from the earlier move, the assessment of situations and of the appropriateness or inappropriateness of a challenge. The earlier move had to do with one's judgment that a felt tension arose from an accurately and adequately understood situation. Frequently challenges which are felt as pressing disappear or change under closer scrutiny of the situation. For example, someone who feels a tension arising from the disapproval of another directed toward himself will frequently find that the challenge disappears upon discovering that the other doesn't really dislike him but has some secret trouble of his own. Alternatively, since one's purposes are part of the situation (as was just pointed out) a re-assessment of one's purposes can remove tensions; so can clearer understanding of the criterion of relevance arising from a purpose. What has been removed in each of the instances is a source of erroneous understanding of the situation. Correction of this sort of error results in abandonment of the challenge as it comes to be seen as irrelevant to the situation more fully understood. Speaking in terms of our definition, there is no longer a challenge, since there is no longer a felt tension.

Verification of roles is another thing. Just as it makes little sense to deliberate about the truth or falsity of meaningless noises, so it makes little sense to experiment with challenges recognized as inappropriate. But once a challenge is thought to be appropriate (granting that one may still be wrong about this), the next thing the seeker for freedom wishes to discover is whether responding to it will in fact lead him toward his desired goal, complete freedom, along a path of increasing control.

To discover this, one must experiment. Since the judgment "meeting this challenge will lead to greater control" is a prediction, one expects that experimentation will be in order. There are two ways in which one attempts to assess challenges in this connection. One can either commit himself overtly to the challenge with whatever consequences its falsification may entail, or one may experiment in the imagination. In either case, one comes to assess what I call a *role*.

A role is a picture one has of oneself as oriented by a challenge. It is to be distinguished from the picture others have of one, or the picture an impartial observer might have. In verifying or falsifying a role, we use our imagination to construct the role and then judge whether the fulfilment of that role will lead to greater control. If when carefully considered it appears to do so, the role is verified; if not, it is falsified.

The analogy with scientific reasoning is close, but there is one apparent difference. When the scientist talks about verification and falsification, he has in mind the actual confrontation of his hypothesis with certain events. When I talk about verification and falsification here, I mean either the actual confrontation of a role with certain concrete actions in fulfilment of the role, or the rehearsal of such confrontation in one's mind. Thus it might appear that I will count an apparent verification or falsification as a real one, where the scientist insists on an actual confrontation.

In fact, however, I don't think the scientist insists on an actual confrontation in most cases. My inquiring man might, after all, insist on a crucial experiment in every case before he satisfied himself that his role was verified, but he knows that in practical affairs he cannot wait upon such developments; that is why he introspects and tries to imagine what would happen if he adopted a certain role. The scientist, too, must judge concerning the verification or falsification of many hypotheses without waiting for a crucial experiment. Crucial experiments are the exception rather than the rule. What the scientist typically does is to reason back from what would be the case if thus and so should occur until he finds a necessary condition for it which contradicts something highly verified already; then he concludes that his hypothesis won't do. Direct confrontation is very hard, and only in a few celebrated cases has it been possible. Indirect verification, which is the normal kind, consists in being satisfied after enough reasoning coupled with enough testing that no contradiction with established facts can be found. It is then a matter of words whether you want to call the more normal procedure "verification" or only "apparent verification"; in any case, it's all that one is likely to be able to achieve except in the unusual case.

How is one to tell whether fulfilment of a given role leads to greater control or not? What does one look for? This is the hardest sort of thing to describe in detail. Generally, and all too vaguely, we can perhaps say this: greater control arises from stretching one's capacities in answer to the exigencies of appropriate challenges. What one tries to see when verifying a role is whether that role opens up further appropriate challenges. One tries to imagine the kinds of situations adoption of this role will lead to, and the kinds of challenges which are appropriate to those situations. Furthermore, one tries to see whether those situations are composed of the same old challenges repeating themselves, or whether the role under perusal will lead to a reorganization and reorientation of one's view of things. One seeks, in short, for a foreglimpse of growth.

It is easier, perhaps, to talk about how roles are falsified. If one can foresee that a role will lead to hardening of habits, to repetition of similar situations similarly constituted—so that the givenness of the situation overpowers one's ability to maneuver in it—he has falsified the role. Or if one sees the role as leading to situations which engender no recognizable challenges at all, falsity again will be suggested—because the resulting situations are too easily mastered, growth hampered, and the personality atrophied, spontaneity will be lost. On the other hand, one may find that adoption of a given role promises to lead to challenges which are inappropriate because they are clearly beyond one's capacity, and this will also be reason to reject it.

There are limits to this procedure. It is hard to see very far along a route marked out by a role, for if it continues very far it presupposes change and maturation on one's own part, and what seems impossible or unfruitful now may well seem possible or fruitful then. But these are limits in practice, not in principle. The same kinds of difficulties limit the natural scientist in his attempts to predict future occurrences.

What happens to a role when it is falsified? We can see now that a falsified role stems from a challenge which, though apparently appropriate to the situation one is in, nevertheless engenders roles leading to inappropriate challenges. For example, if one feels the disapproval of his teacher and in fact has correctly assessed the situation, he may feel challenged to do something to please the teacher; but imaginative projection of the role of teacher-pleaser may appear to lead to too easy mastery of the challenges involved in the classroom situation (let us say); the role is thus falsified. On the other hand, he may also feel challenged to do better work, and this role may appear to be verified as far as he can tell. As a result he will adopt the role of working harder, rejecting the role of pleasing the teacher. What is interesting here is that in the very act of committing oneself to a role one revises the structure of his purposes. The result is that in retrospect, from the point of view of the new purposive structure, the challenge which engendered the falsified role no longer seems appropriate. That is to say, a falsified role now leads to a later revaluation of the challenge from which the role arose, just as a future inappropriate challenge leads to a present falsified role. There is a precedent for this in what we know about empirical knowledge. When an empirical proposition is thoroughly verified, it tends to become logically true—i.e., implied by the very meanings of the words in it—and its negation becomes logically contradictory. Our language habits change in the light of experience. These two phenomena are not unrelated; in science, and indeed in any kind of seeking for understanding, the conceptual scheme—that part of our knowledge which constitutes the conditions of significance—is relative to our purposes, and as these purposes are modified, clarified and extended, propositions which were false become insignificant; in this manner we hoist ourselves by our bootstraps, as it were. Likewise in improving ourselves, in the search for self-understanding and eventual freedom, we must use a scheme dictated by our present purposes to gain purchase on future possibilities, and as we grow, our purposes become more profound, so that types of challenges which were previously open to us as appropriate become irrelevant through deeper insight.

In all this it may be possible to see a connection with the description of complete freedom given in the first chapter. The process of growth carries with it, we have just finished saying, clarification and deepening of purposes together with a firmer conceptual scheme, a scheme or map in which ultimately all challenges become inappropriate. Such a state of experience coincides with complete spontaneity—since the scheme is completely the result of one's own activities of verification and commitment—together with perfect discipline—since within the perfected scheme there is no inappropriate course possible, and so no choice of roles. The saint is at the same time completely controlled by his scheme, and yet completely in control of it—not in the sense that he is likely to reject it, but in the sense that it is completely his—he created the scheme through his verificatory activities.

When may a man be said to know himself? Using the terminology I have developed in this chapter, we can say that he knows himself when he has identified and committed himself to roles which are constantly verified, or alternatively, when his conceptual scheme regularly yields the correct directions as to how to proceed. When a man can consult his understanding of himself and count upon the answers he gets to guide him into roles which in their turn will be verified, he can be said to know himself correctly.

It may be thought that this stage of self-improvement coincides with that of complete freedom, so that self-knowledge necessitates renunciation. But the two stages do not coincide, and furthermore self-knowledge is a necessary but not a sufficient condition for complete freedom. A man may know himself very well, may be armed with a set of roles which is highly verified, and still not be spontaneous; he may still be attached to the satisfaction born of his achievement, and so subject to challenges. The completely free man, though he has an armory of roles at his disposal, is free from challenges, is unattached to his achievement and so responds spontaneously though in a disciplined manner to situations as they arise.

The man who knows himself but is not completely free still has challenges, since he feels tensions; the saint is without challenges, and feels no tensions. We must now explore renunciation, which separates the former sort of man from the latter.

NOTES

1. R. Crawshay-Williams, *Methods and Criteria of Reasoning,* London: Routledge and Kegan Paul, Ltd., 1957, pp. 143–154.

3

RENUNCIATION, THE PATH TO FREEDOM

Supposing that the doubts about man's ability to know himself have been laid to rest, what other sources of doubt contribute to the fear that there is no such thing as renunciation as distinguished from resignation, and so no such thing as a route to complete freedom? Another source of doubt is that renunciation in fact always involves either action or inaction, and since both action and inaction breed *karma,* the path of renunciation will not constitute a route to complete freedom.

PATH PHILOSOPHY

Unlike the material of the previous chapter, the discussion of the nature of renunciation and the various paths to complete freedom occupies a prominent place in Indian philosophical texts. I shall call this phase of Indian thought "path philosophy." Some of India's greatest philosophical names are path philosophers and little more; this category includes Patañjali. author of the *Yogasūtras,* for example; in recent times, Mahatma Gandhi might be considered solely a path philosopher. Others, among them those counted by Indians as the greatest of all, are both path philosophers and speculative philosophers, men such as Śaṃkarācārya and Rāmānuja, as well as Gautama Buddha. There are also those who have very little to say about path philosophy, contenting themselves with an examination of speculative issues. The distinction is, needless to say, not hard and fast; nevertheless, I think these two phases of Indian thought should be distinguished, though they cannot be separated.

In this chapter I shall first review what has been said about the way in which renunciation can be distinguished from resignation and from attached action. Then I shall review the major types of paths recognized by the path philosophers of India, and discuss their interrelationships.

The doubt we are addressing here is whether it is possible to avoid the workings of the Law of Karma by renunciation. In one way, this is a question which belongs to speculative philosophy and will be under discussion in the chapters following this one. But there is another sense in which it is not a speculative question but a practical one. The speculative question is about the nature of the universe: is the universe such that the Law of Karma can be avoided at all? The practical question, however, is this: granted that the universe is such that the Law of Karma can be avoided in principle, is there in practice any route which can be shown to avoid the Law? In other words, it might be admitted that in principle there is nothing to prevent a person's achieving complete freedom through avoidance of the Law of Karma, but one may still fear that in fact every path which promises to take a person there is such that no one can utilize it.

Now it is hard to answer such fears until the basis for them is made clear. A person may fear that there is no path for *him,* and the only sure way to resolve that fear is for him to project roles, verify them, and progress to the point where he can see a role which constitutes a path of renunciation. A person may, on the other hand, fear that there is no path for *anyone,* and one may try to assuage that fear by describing a path for someone, not necessarily himself. That is what the path philosophers do.

A path, remember, is a role which leads, not merely to verification and more challenges, but to complete freedom. We have indicated already that there are requirements which a person must satisfy to be ready to get on a path. A person who is ready to get on a path is sometimes called an *adhikārin* by Indian path philosophers. The *adhikārin* must have considerable experience in getting to know himself, for he has come a long way in the search for freedom. In the course of this experience, he will have gained a great deal of confidence in his ability to meet challenges, choose roles, and master situations. Part of the source of the fear we are here addressing stems from the fact that the person who fears is inexperienced in solving the more ordinary problems involved in becoming an *adhikārin*.

But there is a more disturbing source of the fear in question. It was pointed out in Chapter 1 that the difference between the man of *dharma* and the man of *mokṣa* is that the former sees himself as respectful while the latter simply *is* respectful, spontaneously and without overt effort. If renunciation really will lead an *adhikārin* from *dharma* to *mokṣa*, it must somehow produce spontaneity where there was none before. Worse yet, the very training of the *adhikārin*, emphasizing as it does self-knowledge, has bred in him habits of introspection, habits which seem to be intractably opposed to spontaneity of expression. How does a path of renunciation eliminate the source of the *karma* which is entailed by our self-awareness?

The Indian path philosophers are by no means agreed about the theory of paths. One point on which everyone agrees, however, is the importance of nonattachment[a] to the fruits of actions as the core of renunciation. To see why this is a crucial movement in the process toward freedom, we may revert to a previous discussion concerning habits and bondage. We saw that as one succeeds in gaining control over nature, over others, and over himself, one inevitably runs the risk of being bound by his own success. One who can manipulate the things of this world is tempted to use his ability to gain more goods, and so falls into bondage to the very ability which could be used by him as a lever toward self-improvement; the thing that is lacking in him is the right attitude toward wealth, namely, nonattachment to its presence or absence. Likewise, one who by his attractive personality can wield control over other human beings, who is loved by many, is tempted to use this ability for the gratification of his desires; he once again lacks the right attitude of nonattachment to the fruits of his ability. And finally, even one who has mastered himself, who has self-knowledge and self-control, may fall prey to the error of pride, and become self-satisfied and content in his own righteousness. Once again the source of error is a lack of the right attitude, for the proud man is here, perhaps without himself knowing it, forming a picture of himself which gives him a false sense of security and contentment—false because it habituates him to ruts which rob him of resiliency in novel situations. The antidote to this is

[a] *Vairāgya* or *virakti*—literally, "without passion." These terms are variously translated. I think "nonattachment" is the least misleading and shall use it hereafter.

once more nonattachment to the satisfaction he derives from his ability to form this picture.

Does the maxim that one should not be attached to the fruits of a given activity mean that one should not think about what results it leads to? Are we being advised to avoid anticipating the results of our actions? It is worth noticing the ambiguity of the word "anticipate." When we look forward to something "in anticipation," we are clearly attached to what we look forward to, since we shall be disappointed if it fails to materialize; however, if I say that I anticipate that my action will lead to a quarrel it doesn't necessarily follow that I want one. The attitude of nonattachment is firmly opposed to the first sort of anticipation but is in no sort of opposition to the second. To be nonattached does not mean to become blind to the outcome of one's actions; on the contrary, one does not have full control over a contemplated kind of action until one has correctly predicted its results. That is why freedom *to* is so important, as we shall see.

The Bhagavadgītā is a veritable bible of nonattachment. In the early portions of the Gītā the practice recommended for the attainment of this attitude is called "action discipline" (*karmayoga*). But according to the Gītā, it is not the only discipline; there are several others to which it gives due attention in later chapters. These disciplines, whose relationships with each other are understood differently by different philosophers and are referred to in different times and by different men in different works under different names, can be collected into a few major families, however. The account of them which is to follow should in no way be taken as an exact or exhaustive summary of this side of Indian philosophy, but merely as a gathering of the basic materials needed for further study.

PATHS TO FREEDOM

What we are about to discuss are the various ways in which the attitude of nonattachment can be acquired and stabilized through practice and discipline, that is, those practices which constitute various paths of renunciation. The immediate purpose of renunciatory activities is to stabilize oneself in nonattachment, to train oneself so that one is never tempted to desire the fruits of his actions. One thereby comes to learn not to identify oneself with a certain role in the world, or as an ego with such-and-such a type of personality; one comes to see himself as not limited by the accidental features of his existence here and now.

There are some philosophers, as we shall see, who think that this last-mentioned awareness or insight must be achieved through a special path after nonattachment has been mastered, but most path philosophers are pretty well agreed that both the attitude of nonattachment and the discrimination of the unconditioned Self are the immediate conditions of freedom. I shall first try to identify the major types of renunciatory activity, and subsequently discuss the problem of their interrelationships.

1. *The Path of Activity* (*karmayoga*). This path is marked by the energetic performance of certain kinds of action as a means to attainment of nonattachment. In its traditional form it relates primarily to the performance of those sacrificial rites prescribed by the ancient texts of India for purificatory purposes. These texts are collectively known as the Vedas. In the Vedas we hear of three distinct kinds of action: optional actions (*kāmyakarma*), which have certain specified results which seem at the moment to be desirable; prohibited acts (*pratiṣiddhakarma*), which have untoward results and are to be avoided; and required acts (*nitya-* and *naimittika-karma*), which one must perform, as failure to do so means demerit. Some philosophers hold that freedom can be achieved by one who is properly prepared just by avoiding the first two types of acts and faithfully practicing the third type. The activities which comprise this third type constitute the various forms of worship practiced by devout members of the Hindu community; both daily and seasonal rites are included. Many of these activities are or were literally renunciatory in character (i.e., they involved giving up food, clothing, etc.) and in any case all were to be practiced in a reverent spirit.[1]

2. *The Path of Devotion to God* (*bhaktiyoga*). This path involves taking a less formal attitude toward ritual than does the previous one, and a more intensely personal attitude toward devotion. Whereas in performing works in a sacrificial spirit the emphasis was partly on the efficacy of the works, in this instance the emphasis is wholly on the efficacy of the spirit of worship itself. And while in the ancient Vedic sacrifice the atmosphere was purposeful, serious, and formula-bound, in the more recent *bhakti* forms of worship the atmosphere is playful, random, and expressive. The devotee is encouraged to find spontaneous means for expressing his devotion; the ritualist is bound by the conventions of the sacrifice in which he is partaking. It is to impassioned devotees that we owe much of the sublime poetry and religious literature of India.

3. *The Path of Knowledge* (*jñānayoga*). Some philosophers make a distinction within the sacred scriptures, the Vedas, between the portion

which gives injunctions and directions for performing religious activities (*karmakāṇḍa*) and the portion, most importantly including the end of the Vedas, called Upanishads, which does not enjoin but describes or points out the ultimate nature of things (*jñānakāṇḍa*). It is held that hearing (*śravaṇa*), thinking about (*manana*), and constant and repeated meditation upon (*nididhyāsana*) the latter section of the Vedas constitutes a distinct path to liberation. Another word used frequently in connection with this path is contemplation (*dhyāna*). In Buddhism one hears often about insight (*prajñā*). There are other words for this kind of knowledge. Exactly what is characteristic of knowledge, e.g., what is known, will be under discussion in later chapters.

The unifying feature of all the types of paths that have been distinguished is that they serve the function of bringing the freedom-seeker's attention to focus upon some aspect of things which does not arouse desires. Preferably it should be a single point. It perhaps doesn't matter so much what that point is, as long as it does not distract him from his as yet unstabilized nonattachment.

The function of the discipline which any path performs is thus to keep one's attention pin-pointed on something which is not capable of provoking his desires, so that he learns to move easily with his newly-discovered attitude, is accordingly strengthened in it, and becomes disciplined out of the normal routine of pleasures and pains, role-thinking and its limitations, and all the bondage of worldly existence and into a spontaneous, self-expressing routine, a routine of his own making, hardly deserving the name of "routine" at all. We saw in previous chapters that the ultimate enemy to the man of *dharma,* who has succeeded in all else, even in self-control, is the constriction born of his habitual ways of seeing himself as role-bound, as constituted exhaustively of the dispositions of his mind and his body, as a bundle of personal qualities—in short, a kind of morbid self-consciousness which is the enemy of spontaneity. The various paths are meant to combat this constriction of habitual thinking by pushing the seeker out of his usual ruts, by getting him to think of deeper matters, while at the same time safeguarding him against backsliding by making this new kind of thought a severe challenge, the meeting of which constitutes a discipline to end all disciplines. A person so challenged, and intent on meeting the challenge, will have no time to brood upon his inadequacies; he will have to renounce everything else in order to make himself ready for this challenge. (From this point of view, it doesn't so much matter whether the renunciation is physical or not, although some path philosophers seem to lay more emphasis on giving up worldly possessions than others do.) Even though one goes on automatically performing the same activities, to all intents and purposes fulfilling the same role, he is no longer seeing or thinking of himself in that role, as will be evident from his reactions in comparisons with others not reoriented as he is.

Each of the three paths we distinguished functions in its own peculiar way to produce this single-pointedness. By performing only certain ritual activities in a spirit of dedication, one is cut off from the distracting sources of desire. By ecstatically devoting oneself to his deity and thinking of nothing but him, one focuses his energies and thoughts on something which cannot be the source of any limitation, and by seeking symbolically to unite with that god he teaches himself by direct experience the truth of the unlimited nature of his own being. By turning one's attention toward the Self in an act of immediate intuition, one realizes his own spontaneous capacity while yet cultivating the nonattachment to its fruits that is characteristic of the truly free.

Such are the common and basic functions of the various paths, and the underlying community of purpose which practically all Indian philosophers agree to. It is now easier to see why there must be divergences among these same philosophers when it comes to details. For, as the previous paragraph suggests, the different paths have each their peculiar strengths and weaknesses. The first path (performance of required ritual acts), for instance, does not, at least very clearly, seem to turn the thoughts of the seeker beyond himself and toward a more ultimate Self. The second path, that of devotion, is apt to reflect mere emotionalism if not tempered with discipline in action and thought. And the third way of knowledge may lead to the substitution of mere abstractions for living truths, to a misty intellectualism. It is for these reasons that some philosophers in India have advocated the practice of a combined set of paths to achieve the well-rounded result that is desired.

Others, however, are prepared to defend the ability of one path alone to attain the desired results, and in some cases they have marshalled elaborate arguments to defend their views. It is well-known in India that the great eighth-century religious reformer and philosopher Śaṃkarācārya held firmly to the view that the third path alone was the way to freedom; his rival of the eleventh century, Rāmānuja, is believed to have held the view that the path of devotion is the paramount and indispensable means to salvation. The early Mīmāṃsakas concerned themselves with interpreting those scriptural texts which laid down imperatives for action, for they considered the import of the scriptures to be exhausted in its directions for action, sacrifices, and ceremonies; they held that the first path was sufficient for the supreme state without the help of the other two. In Jainism, in Buddhism, and in the *Yogasūtras* of Patañjali we find highly complicated sets of ways and means for attaining freedom, such as the noble eightfold path of the Buddha (right understanding, right mindedness, right speech, right action, right living, right effort, right attentiveness, and right concentration), the "three jewels" of Jainism (right faith, right knowledge, right conduct), and the seven steps of Patañjali's *yoga* which start with right actions and carry through several steps of meditation and concentration to a final state of direct insight (*samādhi*) after which freedom is reached. In these schools of thought it would appear that all the previously distinguished paths are being combined and developed.

The first reason, then, why philosophers differ about the respective merits and weaknesses of a given path is their recognition that each of the classical paths differs from the rest in the manner of emphasis. But this is not a complete explanation for differences in path philosophy. There are, as we have seen, verbal difficulties which confuse one philosopher's view of another's claims. We have seen the ambiguity of "knowledge" and "action" in this connection. An even more thorough case of the same tendency for a word to take on meaning within more than one path is the word *upāsana,* which one frequently runs into in accounts of self-perfecting activity. *Upāsana* can mean ritual worship, it can mean devotional worship, and it can mean the worship of meditation and concentration leading to direct insight into the Self. It is not hard to understand how path philosophers may argue with each other for some time without discovering that they are using the same word in different senses.

Furthermore, there is no general agreement about what constitutes a "path," specifically, about when one actually begins to be on the path instead of satisfying the preliminary requirements of self-knowledge. For instance, according to one of Śaṃkara's pupils, Suresvara, the path of a qualified freedom-seeker apparently consists in nothing more than hearing important truths (*mahāvākya*) of the Vedas or Upanishads (e.g., *tat tvam asi*—"That art Thou"), since Sureśvara holds that to be qualified one must already be one "who has renounced all actions without residue."[2] For many other philosophers, however, renunciation is a part of the path, not the preparation for it. There appear to be no settled rules as to what should count as preparation of the seeker and what should count as path, and as a result, apparent differences between philosophers might in some cases be resolved by a discussion between them about what constitutes an adequate preparation.

But finally, even after the verbal and other difficulties have been resolved, we shall still find important divergences in the beliefs of the various path philosophers in the classical schools. These differences stem from antecedent differences of opinion on ontological and cosmological questions. I cannot hope to demonstrate this here; it can at best be done after one has explored the ontologies and cosmologies of the major philsophical systems. But I can give at least one brief example. The differences among several of the philosophers of Śamkara's time and thereabouts concerning the proper path to follow stemmed at least in part from their divergent views about the nature of reality, which they all called *brahman*. Śaṃkara apparently held that *brahman* is without duality of any kind (*advaita*), whereas, for instance, a near-contemporary of his named Bhāskara held that *brahman* and some if not all of the experienced world are both the same and yet different (*bhedābheda*). Both accepted the principle that in order for one really to perform actions at all there must be real distinctions in the world—otherwise what acts upon what? The evident implication, drawn by both philosophers with unerring logic, was that they could not agree about paths. Śaṃkara could allow only knowledge as a path, since a path of action is meaningless on his view, there being nothing to act upon, while Bhāskara adopts a combined-path position consonant with his views about the nature of the world.

CONCLUSIONS

This brings me to the end of the first part of my study, in which I have tried to explain the spirit and attitudes which lie behind the practical philosophies of India: Hinduism, Buddhism, and Jainism. I have tried to illuminate some of the basic categories in terms of which Indian thinkers have seen life and the improvement of the soul leading ultimately to spontaneity and freedom. In these first three chapters I have intentionally not followed the lead of any source but instead tried to put into terms suitable to Western modes of thinking the main insights implicit in the various ways these matters are formulated in the literature. It has, in addition, seemed worthwhile to try to meet some of the more naive and shallow criticisms which are sometimes brought against Indian thought, if only so that our excursion into the more technical and systematic side of Indian thought, which is firmly based on the practical side, will not suffer through insufficient attention to its ultimate function. The connection between theoretical, i.e., speculative, philosophy and the philosophy of life has become very tenuous in modern British and American thought. One finds a growing and general acceptance of the thesis that philosophy as practiced here has little or nothing to do with the practical problems of life—a feeling which has undobutedly been the spur for the coming of the various philosophies of existentialism on the Continent by way of reaction, and their enthusiastic espousal by many sensitive people. In Indian thought, as in classical and medieval Western thought, the theoretical and the practical function in close harmony—as opposed to the Western position in contemporary times, where there are on the one hand detailed analyses of theoretical problems with no indications of their relevance to practical concerns, and on the other anxious reflections on life's problems without any systematic attention to the investigation of the nature of things. It is because this writer believes that the unity of practical and theoretical philosophy may come to the contemporary Western reader as something of a novelty that he has taken the opportunity in the preceding pages to present an account of the Indian outlook on life which tries to avoid the theological bias within which this outlook is couched in the literature—a bias which tends to produce plain incredulity on the part of a Westerner—without actually departing from discussion of life-problems as contemporary British and American thought tends to do.

The discussion now passes on to the theoretical or speculative side of philosophy, the major interest in this volume. My first task will be to show the links in Indian thinking between what we have discussed in these chapters and the problems which we shall be discussing in later ones. I shall attempt to show that these links can be traced by an examination of the method of investigation and the types of reasoning and argument used, trying to demonstrate that the function of the practical is to engender limiting conditions of relevance for theoretical speculations. That discussion will lead conveniently into the major portion of the book, where I shall try to outline a few of the problems that Indian philosophers have addressed themselves to, showing as I discuss them how the limiting postulates arising from the practical categories engender the types of solution and the interconnections between the problems that actually occur within the literature.

NOTES

1. A description of *nityakarma* observances in some detail is provided in Abbé J. A. Dubois, *Hindu Manners, Customs and Ceremonies,* 3rd ed., pp. 161–170, 235–269. Oxford: Clarendon Press, 1928.

2. Suresvara (commentary on stanza 12), p. 7.

4

HOW SPECULATIVE PHILOSOPHY COMES IN

The reader will not have failed to notice that, as I have moved along through the account of those concepts which serve to elucidate the philosophy of life assumed by the Indians, I have tended to speak as if the arguments that might be offered in favor of thinking of complete freedom as the ultimate value were conclusive. This was necessary in order to get along with the task of exposition, but it is time to make a reckoning. It is easy to talk glibly of complete freedom, of renunciation and non-attachment, but it is when one becomes seriously involved in life's challenges that these concepts become important. And in actual practice it is a very strong-minded person indeed who can turn his whole life over to the kind of ideal that the Indian tradition preaches about, just as it is a very strong-minded person who in our day and age can resist a variety of temptations and dedicate himself merely to being a good man.

I say "strong-minded." Of course, it takes strength of heart too, the courage to stand by one's convictions. But this kind of courage presupposes that one already have convictions, so that commitment of the mind seems to come first. This is, however, arguable, and the split between the advocates of the primacy of reason and those of the primacy of faith is one of the most important in Indian thought. In any case, the enemy of strength, whether of mind or heart, would seem to be fear. A man visited by fears about the crucial matters is rendered incapable of applying himself seriously to the realization of freedom.

There are any number of things about which one may have doubts that effectively undermine self-realizational activity, but there is one sort of doubt that overshadows all others in the profundity of its impact. That is the doubt about whether freedom is possible. Other sorts of doubts appear, by comparison with this one, to be temporary difficulties. For example, if one distrusts one's *guru,* this undermines self-realizational activities because one cannot give unquestioning assent to his directions; but this difficulty is temporary, since one can presumably find another *guru.* If one doubts that he has correctly understood a critical situation and suspects that he has made a bad choice of role, he can be more careful the next time. But if he suspects that events crucial to his realization are quite out of his control, it is hard to see how he will be able to apply himself in a sustained fashion to the challenge of bondage.

But why should anyone fear that events crucial to his freedom are out of his control? To understand this, we must analyze freedom more closely. First, let us try to identify the conditions under which we are willing to apply the word "free." I think these conditions are, broadly speaking, two, and I call them, following some precedent, "freedom-to" and "freedom-from."

To start with, what kinds of things do we call "free"? We call men "free" when they are able to do or not to do certain things; we call the things they are or are not able to do or not to do "free" or "not free" by a natural extension of the term. These things that men are or are not capable of doing are sometimes called "actions," and they are a species of a more general class which I shall call "events." An "event" is something that can occur or not occur. I shall speak of the "occurrence of an event," or the "nonoccurrence of an event." Then I think it will be agreed that a man can be "free" in the sense that he can bring about the occurrence or nonoccurrence of a certain event, and that the occurrence or nonoccurrence can be said to be "free" with respect to that man if it is the case that the man is free with respect to that occurrence or nonoccurrence.

Now, then, what are the conditions under which we apply or refuse to apply the term "free" to men and their actions? First, there is the condition that the occurrence or nonoccurrence in question, in order to be called "free," must have at least one necessary condition or one sufficient condition. This requirement I call the requirement of "freedom-to." If an occurrence does not have a necessary condition then there is no way for anyone to avoid it, for to avoid an occurrence one must see to it that a necessary condition for the occurrence does not occur. And if an occurrence does not have any sufficient condition, there is no way for us to effect it, i.e., to see to it that it occurs, for to be able to see to it that an event occurs presupposes that there is a sufficient condition for that event the occurrence of which will bring about the event in question.

Secondly, there is the condition that, in order to be called "free," an occurrence or nonoccurrence must be such that the agent could have done otherwise, i.e., that a necessary condition or a sufficient condition of that occurrence or nonoccurrence is in the agent's control. I call this requirement the requirement of "freedom-from." It is not merely another way of describing freedom-to; rather, it presupposes freedom-to but exceeds the former requirement. Freedom-to merely says that the event in question must have at least one necessary or one sufficient condition, but says nothing about the relation of those conditions to the agent. Freedom-from says "providing there is freedom-to, then at least one necessary or one sufficient condition of a free event must be in someone's control, i.e., such that he could have done otherwise."

Now clearly if anyone is going to believe in the possibility of becoming free, he is going to have to believe in the possibility of being free-to and free-from with respect to some occurrence or nonoccurrence. Complete freedom (*mokṣa*) may now be explained as the stage where one is free to and free from with respect to every event that occurs in his subsequent history, i.e., every possible occurrence or nonoccurrence that concerns him.

As there are two conditions for complete freedom, namely freedom-to with respect to every event that matters and freedom-from with respect to every event that matters, so there are at least two kinds of fear which undermine the effort to achieve complete freedom.

One kind of fear is skepticism, the fear that in fact the occurrences and nonoccurrences that are involved in the attainment of complete freedom are not regularly connected to necessary and sufficient conditions. Skepticism may be divided into a universal type and a guarded type. One may fear that no events have sufficient or necessary conditions—may fear, that is, that in reality the world is an utter chaos, and that any appearance of regularity in it is due to our thinking it so. This is universal skepticism. There is also the view that, although some events do have necessary or sufficient conditions, at least one event upon the occurrence or nonoccurrence of which the attainment of complete freedom rests is without either necessary condition or sufficient condition, and therefore that, although we may be able to become more free, we cannot become completely free. This is guarded skepticism.

The other kind of fear is fatalism, the fear that in fact the necessary and sufficient conditions of events leading to freedom are not such that they can be within my control, so that I "have a choice," as we say. Fatalism may again be divided into two types, universal and guarded. Universal fatalism is the fear that no necessary or sufficient conditions of any event are open to my control, so that I am completely and irrevocably bound and any appearance to the contrary is merely wishful thinking on my part. Guarded fatalism is the fear that, although some conditions of some events are open to my control, there is at least one event crucial to the attainment of complete freedom which is not open to my control, so that again, although it is in principle possible for me to progress some way along the path to complete freedom, there is a point beyond which I cannot go.

It is the business of speculative philosophy in India to combat skepticism and fatalism of both the universal and the guarded variety. There were, according to tradition, both skeptics and fatalists in ancient India. We have one or two texts of the so-called Cārvāka (Lokāyata) or "materialist" school or schools, notably the *Tattvopaplavasiṃha* of Jayarāśi.[1] This text features an attack on the idea that events are regularly connected, an attack which proceeds by showing that inference based on empirical regularities in nature is unjustifiable. That the skeptics were considered by the vast majority of Indian thinkers to be their common opposition is substantiated by remarks dropped in various summaries of philosophy, such as Mādhava's *Sarvadarśanasaṃgraha*,[2] as well as by the fact that the manuscripts of all except a handful of Cārvāka works have been lost or destroyed. The same is true of the work of the Ājīvikas, a sect of philosophers that flourished around the time of the Buddha and who espoused a rather thorough-going fatalism.[3] The Cārvākas and Ājīvikas were considered universal skeptics and fatalists respectively, and represented extreme positions which had to be avoided in the speculative search for a view of nature which accommodates complete freedom.

It is not the refutation of universal skepticism and fatalism which occupies most of the attention of Indian philosophers of the speculative type, but the refutation of guarded skepticism and fatalism, a refutation which constitutes a much more difficult task. The universal skeptic can be refuted by showing that in arguing that his view is correct he is assuming what he denies, i.e., the validity of some kind of inference. The universal fatalist can be refuted by showing him that in arguing at all he is assuming something nonsensical on his view, namely that it makes a difference to anyone what he says. However, to refute the guarded varieties of skepticism and fatalism requires a much more elaborate treatment, an exposition of a whole metaphysical system, for to convince a guarded skeptic or fatalist that particular events (those lying on paths to complete freedom) are conditioned and yet open to man's control requires one to show that there is nothing about the world, when considered correctly, that implies that such events are without conditions or closed to control. In addition, the guarded skeptic or fatalist has a strong argument on his side to start with, for there is an evident difficulty in saying that one and the same occurrence or nonoccurrence is both conditioned and such that one could have done otherwise, a difficulty we begin to recognize when we ask, "And what caused the cause?"

Before turning to a discussion of the crucial problem of freedom and determinism, however, I wish to broach a topic which most philosophers believe to be logically prior to any substantial solution of a philosophical problem, and which some philosophers in the West consider to be a topic separable from any particular philosophical solution. That is the topic of philosophical method. It is common to suppose, in contemporary Western philosophy, that a decision about what method to pursue in philosophy is, if a philosophical problem at all, at any rate not one which requires a metaphysical position to justify its solution. It is supposed either that we can appeal to common sense to justify our philosophical beginnings (G. E. Moore), or that we can appeal to ordinary usage of words in the English language to discover solutions to philosophical puzzles, or at any rate come to a point where they don't arise (Wittgenstein), or that there is an *a priori* world of abstractions, insight into which is gained by the special techniques of mathematical logic, which contains within it the principles of successful philosophizing (Bertrand Russell). All these views share a common assumption, which might be called the assumption that there can be method without metaphysics, i.e., that methodological decisions can be arrived at prior to an investigation that employs the method in question, that such decisions can be known to be correct independently of any testing of the method in its application to philosophical problems. Moore thinks we just know, non-philosophically, that the object I hold out is a human hand and not something else. The Wittgensteinians think that appreciation of the subtleties of language can be arrived at without appealing to any special theories about the world, and that this unsystematic attention will dissolve most philosophical problems. Russell and company sharply distinguish the justification of what is *a priori* from what is *a posteriori,* claiming that although appeal to the nature of the world is relevant in the justification of the latter, it is not relevant in the justification of the former.

The general assumption among Indian systematic philosophers is different from these, and more like the assumptions about method characteristic of many Pragmatists. They don't recognize a sharp distinction between *a priori* and *a posteriori.* Although they do on occasion appeal to common sense and ordinary language, they do not do so in a spirit of appealing to an uncriticizable authority, and they certainly do not think that philosophical problems can be resolved merely by closer attention to common language or thought. Just what, then, is their attitude toward problems of philosophical method?

MAPPING AGAIN

The remarks that were offered in Chapter 2 about mapping as an analogy to gaining self-knowledge now become applicable in a slightly different connection. We pointed out that every map is made in accordance with a projection, and in the case of mapping the earth onto a flat surface this necessitated some distortion; we pointed out that projections were chosen for a purpose and that the right projection for any purpose is the one which satisfactorily translates into map relationships the judgments which are relevant to that purpose. In Chapter 2 I suggested the applicability of this analogy to the problem of distinguishing appropriate challenges from inappropriate ones. Now I want to suggest that the same analogy can be used to understand how the Indians approach the problem of freedom's possibility.

Thinking in terms of the mapping analogy, I suggest that the question which frames the doubt—"is freedom possible?"—can be reformulated as "is there a projection which translates into map relationships the judgments which we care about, i.e., those judgments whose truth is presupposed by freedom's possibility?" This question is like "is it possible to get to the edge of the universe?" To answer this last question, we might try to find a way of mapping the universe—i.e., a projection—on which one can trace a route from here to the edge of the universe that has no gaps in it, one along which we can travel. That is to say, we might try to find a projection into which we can translate those judgments which are presupposed by our ability to travel to the edge of the universe. Just so Indian philosophers want to find a mapping scheme, a set of categories and relationships, in terms of which they can plot a route from here to complete freedom. The production of such a scheme, if it can be produced, will provide a definite answer to the doubt "is freedom possible?"

What requirements must such a conceptual scheme meet in order to be considered successful? First, it must be adequate, i.e., it must translate all the judgments we care about, all those judgments which are presupposed by freedom's possibility. (A judgment is presupposed by freedom's possibility just if the truth of the judgment is a necessary condition for the truth of "freedom is possible.") Second, it must be accurate, which is to say, it must be a map of *our* universe, not just of some possible universe. It must reflect truths of experience attested by competent observers. Third, it must be consistent. If there are contradictions within the scheme, it is no good to us as a map, for it will in effect give ambiguous directions. We want the scheme, or map, to show us a route to freedom; it is only the belief or faith in such a route that can convince one that freedom is possible. Now a contradiction within the scheme occurs when the scheme translates a given judgment as well as its contradictory, when it allows them both as true: this is tantamount to the map saying to us "do p and don't do p." And such a map leaves us mired in our doubt, for clearly we cannot follow these directions, and therefore a route has not been found, and the scheme has failed. For the same kinds of reasons, the concepts used in the scheme—the guideposts in the map—must be clear, unambiguous within their contexts, and free from any misleading vagueness. Otherwise the route is obscured, and our doubt remains.[4]

The problem, then, is to find a scheme which is adequate, accurate, consistent, and clear and on which a route can be mapped all the way to complete freedom, a path free from gaps and clearly marked. This problem is not quite properly framed by saying that Indian philosophy tries to demonstrate by deductive inference or empirical evidence that the proposition "freedom is possible" is true, since such a demonstration presupposes the adoption of a satisfactory conceptual scheme, and the doubt is precisely whether there *is* any such scheme.

There is no mechanical procedure for discovering a satisfactory conceptual scheme for this purpose, at least as far as anyone can tell. The best one can hope to do is to analyze the nature of the fundamental proposition that the scheme is intended to accommodate—"freedom is possible"—and to work back by imaginative steps toward the position man finds himself in, limited as he is by bondage of the various sorts already discussed. The initial move that might be suggested is to discover by careful thought what judgments are presupposed by freedom's possibility, for these will be the judgments we care about, i.e., the judgments which the scheme is required to translate.

The Indian philosopher's problem can be profitably compared with the kind of problem Kant addressed himself to. Where Kant asks "how are synthetic judgments *a priori* possible?", an Indian philosopher asks "how is complete freedom possible?" Kant's question is not one that an Indian will raise, since he sees no clear distinction between *a priori* and *a posteriori,* but the Indian problem is one Kant eventually finds himself asking toward the conclusion of the *Grundlegung.*[5] But my point here is not to draw your attention to Kant's views but to the similarity between his method and that of the Indian speculative thinkers.

Very generally, the method one must take in addressing a critical problem is to think through the presuppositions of the possibility which is to be explained, and then to discover a mapping technique which satisfies the criteria of adequacy, accuracy, consistency, and clarity with respect to those presuppositions. But how does one go about discovering an appropriate mapping technique? What counts as a good reason for choosing one projection over another? Nothing but the criteria mentioned above. And the surprising thing is that those criteria alone engender what the Indians, and we ourselves, would generally grant to be the criteria of good and bad reasons in philosophy. The next chapter will try to show that this is so.

The comparison with Kant's method in philosophy is fruitful in introducing the coming chapters. The kind of inferences which lead us to accept the categories of a given scheme resembles the kind of reasoning Kant uses in his *Grundlegung* in assessing the implications of the categorical imperative. They are practical inferences. For example, Kant argues that we come to realize that breaking promises is wrong by imagining to ourselves everyone's breaking promises at will. He points out that in such a situation the very function of promising would be nullified, undermined, brought to nought.[6] In a parallel fashion, we can justify the usual canons of reasoning by pointing out that if, for instance, one allows contradictions to slip into one's conceptual scheme, the purpose of the scheme, which is the demonstration of a route from here to complete freedom, will be nullified, undermined, and brought to nought. Likewise, to take another example, if we permitted a situation to arise within the constructed scheme which involved an infinite regress, we should once again have rendered the scheme useless, for the reason that, if the regress is of the harmful type,[a] a man will be unable to enter into the chain of events significantly, since he can, to put it roughly, never get started.

In the next chapter I shall review briefly the major types of good reasons and their correlative fallacies, having suggested how these reasons are in fact related to criteria of adequacy, accuracy, consistency, and clarity with respect to the presuppositions of freedom. It is these criteria which define the range of the proper application of the word "good" in "good reason."

[a] For the distinction between harmful and harmless regresses, see below, pp. 82–83.

NOTES

1. Translated by S. N. Shastri and S. K. Saksena in *Source Book,* pp. 236–246.
2. See Madhava.
3. See Basham.
4. This conception of philosophical method is set forth in detail in Nelson Goodman, *The Structure of Appearance,* esp. Chapters I–III. Cambridge, Mass.: Harvard University Press, 1951.
5. Immanuel Kant, *Foundations of the Metaphysics of Morals,* tr. L. W. Beck, pp. 64 ff. New York: The Liberal Arts Press, 1959.
6. *Ibid.,* p. 40.

5

GOOD REASONS IN PHILOSOPHICAL DISCUSSIONS

I cannot here hope to catalogue every kind of argument that is used in Indian philosophical writings. I shall try to discuss some of those forms of argument which occur frequently enough so that the Indians have given them names or stock phrases to mark them out for memory's sake. When we turn to the third part of the book, and consider the arguments used *in situ* for demonstrating a thesis or attacking an opposing view, we shall have opportunity to discuss the sources of some arguments which do not fall under these stock headings as well as to see in use some of the arguments which we shall discuss in the present section.

This chapter, then, constitutes an introduction to Indian logic. In the West we usually use the word "logic" in philosophy to mean formal logic, the working of formal or deductive reasoning as in the syllogism. It is probable that Indian philosophy never demarcated formal from informal logic, and the terminology used to characterize the theory of argumentation shows this. The general theory of argument in India is called *nyāya.* As a part of the early discussions on the topic of argumentation, there was developed a way of expressing any inference intended for the purpose of demonstrating a thesis for general consumption. This *nyāya* "syllogism," as it is sometimes called nowadays, bears a superficial resemblance to the Aristotelian categorical syllogism, but is actually quite different in nature, as we shall shortly see. Another part of *nyāya* consists in what is known as *tarka. Tarka* is the use of various and assorted forms of reasons to indicate absurdity in the opponent's thesis. It is the negative side of argumentation, and as such was seldom granted the status of a means of correct knowledge (*pramāṇa*) in most Indian systems, while inference (*anumāṇa*), which has a positive use in establishing propositions, is regularly denominated a means of correct knowledge. Different philosophers have held distinct views about the number and nature of the various *pramāṇas,* views I do not intend to review here.[1] Briefly, however, the other most important *pramāṇa*s, besides inference and *tarka,* are perception (*pratyakṣa*) and what is called *āgama* or *śabda,* which consists in knowledge gained from hearing authoritative words, which usually means the *śruti* or sacred scriptures, such as the Vedas and Upanishads.

Along with these types of argument, there developed in early *nyāya* theory a remarkable discussion of the various dodges and tricks used by a clever man to avoid defeat in argument. We shall not spend any time on these, since what they aim at is not the resolution of sincere doubt, but rather the winning of an argument by any means, fair or foul. It is, of course, important for one who engages in philosophical discussion to be able to detect these practices in his own and others' argumentation and to disclose them so that no one will be confused by them.

In this chapter, I shall discuss arguments pertaining to four sources of correct knowledge: perception, inference, *tarka,* and verbal testimony. Besides the four types there are a miscellaneous group of reasons accepted by everyone as telling in argument and which appeal more or less directly to the sanction of the criteria which were elicited in the previous chapters. A few examples of such reasons are given at the end of the present chapter.

PERCEPTION

Under this heading we may think of all those arguments which make appeal to what is directly experienced. "Perception" is perhaps too limited a word to stand duty as translation of *pratyakṣa.* All sources of immediate experience, and not only the awareness born of the functioning of the sense-organs, are included here (although there are those who would limit perception to knowledge born of sensation). For example, some philosophers of the Nyāya-Vaiśesika school speak of unusual (*alaukika*) forms of perception, such as the awareness of the other members of a class which arises from the immediate awareness of a single member of that class as possessing the property which demarcates the class, or again the awareness that the *yogi* has, the experience of the realized, completely free man. Some Buddhists speak of "mental perception" (*mānasapratyakṣa*). Again, memory is a kind of perception, although of a second order, depending as it does upon a previous and more direct awareness, so that although memory is not itself a source of correct knowledge independently, it nevertheless is normally trustworthy, at least according to many Indian philosophers. But there is disagreement among the schools of Indian philosophy as to whether each or any of these nonsensory forms of experience is trustworthy, and indeed as to whether it is proper to class them as *pratyakṣa*.

Nevertheless, all schools of Indian philosophy take perception as a legitimate *pramāṇa* or valid means of knowledge, since there are some events that we directly perceive which are clearly part of the scope of any adequate philosophical system. To put it negatively, if someone produced a map or conceptual scheme in argument for the possibility of freedom, and if this map or scheme had no place in it for the direct experiences of human beings, then it would be proper to criticize the map or scheme on just this ground. Positively put, this means that a philosopher's demonstration that something implied by his map or scheme is in fact regularly experienced by human beings is a point in favor of his system.

The assumption that perception, or at least some perceptions, is or are a valid source of knowledge is presupposed by the possibility of freedom. For it is precisely in our direct experiences that we feel sometimes that our capacity for complete freedom may be restricted or even nonexistent, and it is the self which has these experiences which presumably is hoping to gain complete freedom. Since it is from perception that the doubts and fears about the possibility of freedom arise, it is imperative that a map intended to allay those fears be able to explain any perception which was, is, or could be in the future relevant to the attainment or nonattainment of complete freedom. Concretely, if anyone has any reason to suspect with respect to a direct experience x that x is either uncaused and so inexplicable or else that x is such that one couldn't have avoided having it, then this experience must be shown by the map to be explicable and/or avoidable. Now since any perception is in principle subject to such suspicions, it is always a point in a theory's favor—though not an uncriticizable point—that the theory implies the occurrence of certain sorts of perceptions which in fact are commonly experienced. Assuming that the theory is compatible with the presuppositions of complete freedom's possibility, the demonstration that it accurately predicts and explains actual experiences constitutes a good reason in its favor, while the demonstration that it predicts falsely or fails to explain perceptions constitutes a good reason against the theory. But this test of a theory will clearly not be possible if *no* experiences are accepted as constituting valid knowledge.

Nevertheless, for most philosophers in India some perceptions may be erroneous. Erroneous perception will be discussed in detail in Chapter 10. An important part of any map or scheme involves the explanation of what distinguishes erroneous perception from correct perception. Since perceptions may be erroneous, one must be able to show that the experiences which one appeals to to justify one's theory are not erroneous. For this reason, an appeal to mere *pratyakṣa* is not usually counted as sufficient by itself to verify a theory; one will have to justify his perceptions as valid by appeal to other kinds of good reasons.

INFERENCE

Whereas perception gives us immediate (*aparokṣa*) knowledge, inference gives us only mediate knowledge. It depends upon perceptions of various kinds. Nevertheless, it is a distinct instrument of knowledge in its own right according to most schools of Indian thought, since it establishes judgments about objects and facts which are not directly confronted by the knower.

In considering the Indian account of inference, we must constantly guard against assimilating it to the Western conception of formal or deductive logic. I shall have more to say about this in a moment, but I mention it now so that the reader will not wonder at the "peculiarity" of the formulation that is about to be introduced.

The Structure of an Inference

Let us begin by examining a stock example of an inference. You and I are standing on a hillside overlooking a valley, and on the hillside across the way we see smoke billowing upwards. "There's a fire on that hill," I say to you, "because there's smoke. You know, you've seen fiery things smoking before, e.g., kitchens, and furthermore one never sees smoke where there's no fire, for example in a lake." (This illustration, like most textbook illustrations, is slightly simpleminded, since I would in such a situation hardly have to explain in such detail the reasons for my conclusion; still, in giving a simple example one cannot avoid being somewhat simplistic.)

The argument just quoted has five *terms* and three *members*. Let us state the argument formally:

Hypothesis: That mountain (is) fire-possessing.
Reason: (Because) that mountain (is) smoke-possessing.
Examples: (a) (as in) kitchen
(b) (unlike) lake.

The three members of this inference are the hypothesis (*pratijñā*), the reason (*hetu*), and the example(s) (*dṛṣṭānta*). The five terms are (1) that mountain, (2) fire-possessing, (3) smoke-possessing, (4) kitchen, and (5) lake.

I have underlined the five terms to emphasize something about which one may be easily misled. I have called these five things "terms," and this may lead one to think that I am talking about the words or phrases "that mountain," "fire-possessing," etc. But the Indians conceive inference to be, not about words, but about the things to which the words refer, i.e., to classes of things. Thus each of the five terms underlined are to be considered as classes of things, and can well be pictured as circles—a device I shall avail myself of shortly.

(1) That mountain is a unit class, a class with exactly one member, namely that particular mountain you and I are looking at. Any class which functions in the position that mountain does in this inference, appearing in both the hypothesis and the reason as first element, is called in Sanskrit the *pakṣa*. We shall sometimes abbreviate this term to *p*.

(2) The second term is the class of all those things which possess fire—of all fiery things, as we might say. The class which functions as fire-possessing does in this inference, being the second element in the hypothesis, is called in Sanskrit the *sādhya* or thing to be proved. We shall abbreviate this term as *s*.

(3) The third term is the class of all things which smoke, or possess smoke—all smoking things. Any class which functions as smoke-possessing does in the stock inference, which appears as the second element in the second member, is called the *hetu*, and we shall abbreviate this term as *h*. (Note that the second member and the third term both go under the same name, *hetu*. Do not let this confuse you.)

(4) The fourth term, kitchen, is the class of all kitchens. It is offered as the first of the two examples, as a positive case of something which is

both smoky and fiery. In Sanskrit this term is called the *sapakṣa,* which we shall abbreviate as *sp*.

(5) The fifth term, lake, is the class of all lakes. It is the second of the two examples, and is offered as negative proof, as something which is neither smoky nor fiery, helping to show that where smokiness is, fieriness is too. The Sanskrit for this negative example is *vipakṣa,* abbreviated as *vp*.

As was said, it is possible to symbolize these five terms by means of circles. Then the members can be pictured as follows:

Hypothesis: That mountain (is) fire-possessing
p (is) *s*

Figure 1

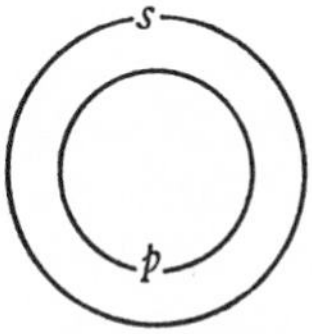

Reason: (because) that mountain (is) smoke-possessing
p (is) *h*

Figure 2

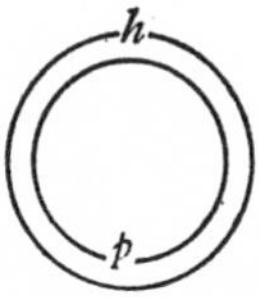

Examples: (a) (as in) kitchen (which overlaps fire-possessing and smoke-possessing)
(as in) *sp* (which overlaps *s* and *h*)

Figure 3

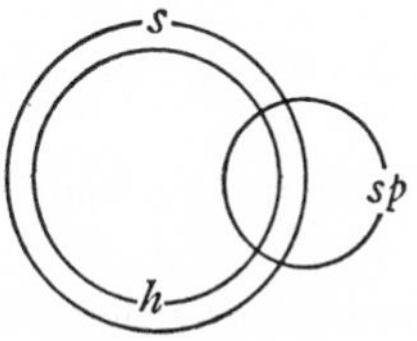

(b) (unlike) lake (which class falls completely outside of fire-possessing and smoke-possessing)
(unlike) *vp* (which excludes *s* and *h*)

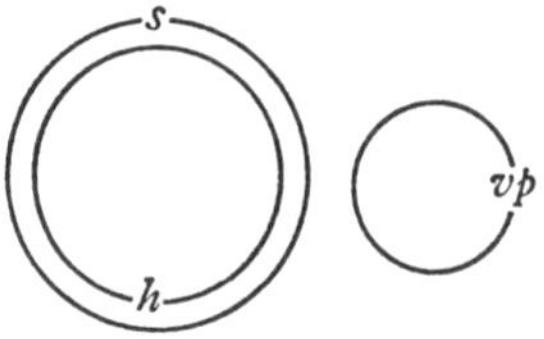

Figure 4

The combination of all these relationships,

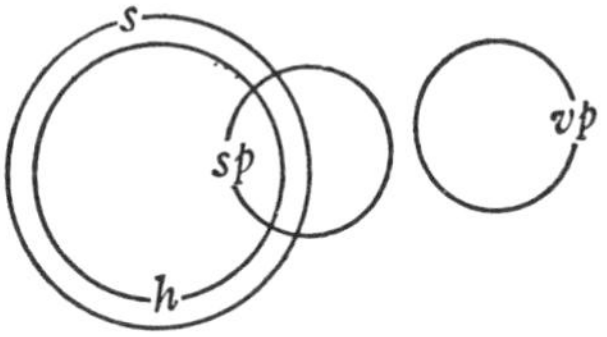

Figure 5

is what an inference asserts, i.e., what one putting forth the inference claims. Obviously, that someone asserts an inference does not mean that what he asserts is the case; there are sound inferences and unsound ones. A *sound* inference is an inference which asserts what is actually the case; an *unsound* inference is one which asserts something which is not the case.

Soundness of an inference is one thing; validity is another. To say that an argument is *valid* is to say that it passes certain tests of validity; but unless these tests exhaust the ways in which an inference may fail to represent what is the case, an argument may be valid but yet unsound, since it remains possible that it fails to picture the world accurately. Every invalid argument is unsound, but an argument may be valid and yet be unsound.

It is important to recognize that the Indian inference is not a formal or deductive type of argument. Indian rules of validity, as we shall see, do not bear merely upon the formal structure of an inference's members, but also upon the truth or falsity of the claims each member is used to make.

A Western categorical syllogism may be a valid inference even though its members be false. E.g., "everyone in this room is over ten feet tall; Jones is in this room; therefore Jones is over ten feet tall" is a valid argument even though no one in this room is over ten feet tall, or for that matter even though Jones is not in this room. Validity means something different in Western syllogistic logic from what it does here.

In examining an Indian inference, then, the first part of the task is to formulate the argument properly; the second is to test its members against certain criteria of validity.

Formulating the Argument

The first task is fairly simple in most cases, although one must be careful. The first thing to do, given an argument in ordinary language, is to identify the terms in class-terminology. Thus, for example, take the old (Western) chestnut "All men are mortal; Socrates is a man; therefore Socrates is mortal." The terms here are <u>Socrates</u> (a unit class), <u>man</u>, and <u>mortal things</u>. The hypothesis is that Socrates is mortal, i.e., that the unit class <u>Socrates</u> is included within the class <u>mortal things</u>. The reason is that Socrates is a man, i.e., that <u>Socrates</u> is included within the class <u>man</u>. The "major premiss," "All men are mortal," does not appear in the inference when properly formulated; if this argument were seriously offered and defended, one would normally go on to offer examples which are intended to provide evidence for the major premiss, but in the form of inference we are considering, that premiss is not enunciated.

Next, take a more complicated argument: "It must have rained upstream, for this river is rising just the way the Ganges does when there's a cloudburst in the Himalayas, and rivers don't rise when the weather in their upper parts has been dry." Here, in order to identify the terms, we do well to consider exactly what is being asserted as our hypothesis and reason. What is being asserted is that it has recently rained upstream, and the reason is that this river is rising. We want to reformulate these two assertions so that their first element is the same class—for p must appear in both the hypothesis and the reason as the first term. Furthermore, temporal distinctions seem to be in point, since the argument links what happened then with what is happening now. Therefore we may formulate the argument as follows:

Hypothesis: <u>this-river-now events</u> (is included within) <u>events closely following upstream-raining events.</u>
Reason: (because) <u>this-river-now events</u> (is included within) <u>rising-river events.</u>

Examples: (a) (as in) Ganges events.
(b) (unlike) events on rivers closely following times when it has been dry upstream.

Here, then, our terms are:

p—this-river-now events
s—events closely following upstream-raining events
h—rising-river events
sp—Ganges events
vp—events on rivers closely following times when it has been dry upstream.

It is not always easy to identify the correct parameters in terms of which to formulate an argument, as this last illustration shows.

No special kind of problem arises in formulating an argument which contains negative terms. For example, "there is no fire on that mountain, because there is no smoke" may be rendered as

Hypothesis: that mountain (is) non-fire-possessing
Reason: (because) that mountain (is) non-smoke-possessing.

A more complicated instance is the following: "There is no jar here, because one is not perceived, although the conditions of perception are fulfilled." The *pakṣa* in this case is the particular place referred to as "here." Thus this goes over into

Hypothesis: this place (is) non-jar-possessing
Reason: (because) this place (is a) place where, although the conditions of perception are fulfilled, jar is not perceived.

The *hetu* here, it will be noted, is quite complex, but despite its complexity the words clearly pick out a class, a class whose members are all those places where the (relevant) conditions of perception are fulfilled and no jar is perceived.

Testing an Inference for Validity

We saw in Chapter 2 that, while it was difficult to explain just how a hypothesis about a role is verified, it was easier to suggest ways in which it is falsified. In a similar fashion, it is more illuminating to discuss how hypotheses (*pratijñās*) are falsified than to try to explain how they are verified. In fact, verification, as I suggested in Chapter 2, means in practice "examined carefully and not found to be falsified," while falsification, although it cannot be exhaustively characterized, can at least be explained more concretely by appeal to various types of error. So it is with "validation" in the sense of "valid" outlined above. To validate an inference is to examine it carefully to see that it satisfies certain rules of validity. These rules may not exhaust all the requirements which would have to be met to guarantee soundness in an inference, but satisfaction of them is a necessary condition for soundness and a sufficient condition for what is here being called "validity."

This is not just my rationalization. Many Indian systems make frequent appeal to the notion of being "unsublated" (*abādhita*). A hypothesis is unsublated when it has not been found to violate one of the general conditions of adequacy, accuracy, consistency, and clarity characteristic of a successful map or scheme. One can sublate a hypothesis by showing that on the basis of it predictions of experiences can be made which are not confirmed, or alternatively by showing that the hypothesis is incompatible with some other hypothesis whose claim to its position within the scheme is better entrenched. The rules of validity which I am about to specify sum up some of the requirements that a proposition must satisfy if it is to appear in a successful map.

Pervasion (*vyāpti*) is the relation of class-inclusion. To say that class A pervades class B is to say that all members of B are members of A but not necessarily vice-versa; some members of A may fall outside of B. To say that class A is pervaded by class B is to say that all members of A are members of B but not necessarily vice-versa. Cases of pervasion are pictured in Figures 1–5. Thus, in Figure 1, which maps a hypothesis, *p* is asserted to be pervaded by *s*, which is to say that it is asserted that *s* pervades *p*.

To assert that *s* pervades *p* is one thing; for it to be the case that *s* in fact does pervade *p* is, of course, quite another. To make a map is not necessarily to make an accurate map. Once an argument has been offered, the next thing is to examine it for validity. For this, we need rules, and what I propose to do below is to summarize the rules that classical Indian philosophers recognized under a few headings. The rules given here are, as I have said, not exhaustive; an argument which satisfies all these rules is, by definition, valid, but it is not necessarily sound.[2]

An argument with five terms and three members, properly arranged, purports to picture an actual situation which has the pattern set forth in Figure 5. Rules of validity specify ways in which arguments may fail, because the facts do not conform to the way an argument pictures them. Put another way, rules of validity are expedient ways to remind one of what to look for in comparing the situation *claimed* by an argument to be the case with what actually *is* the case.

Rule 1: The Rule of Exemplified Terms.[3] This rule requires that all the terms in an argument must have members. Indian logic does not recognize the null class. Thus, for example, any argument which contains reference to the class of round squares would be invalid through violating this rule. A similar example, taken from Indian philosophical literature, is the class of sons of barren women.

The Western logician is likely to suppose that the Indian is here recognizing that self-contradictory concepts cannot enter into correct thinking. But that is not quite the Indian's point. His point is not one about concepts, it is about classes; furthermore, although "round square" and "son of a barren woman" happen to be self-contradictory concepts, the same rule precludes arguments about classes whose correlative concepts are merely unexampled. For instance, the Indians give as examples of improper terms sky-lotus and hare's horn; these are listed alongside of son of a barren woman, and the point of listing is to indicate what the members of the list have in common. What they have in common is that they are all names of classes with no members.

So far as I know, Indian logic does not discriminate between untenable classes such as son of a barren woman, and unexampled classes such as hare's horn. This distinction is, of course, crucial to much of recent Western technical philosophy and logic. It is worthy of note that the distinction is not made by Indian logicians; in fact, there is a general failure on the part of Indian philosophers to distinguish such opposites as *a priori* and *a posteriori,* analytic and synthetic, formal logic and empirical reasoning. No need seems to have been felt for any such distinctions.

One may well ask, however, how he is to be sure that a given concept concerns a class without any members. For example, according to Kumārila, there are no omniscient beings. From Kumārila's standpoint, then, when a Buddhist argues "The Buddha is omniscient. . . ." he is guilty of violating Rule 1. Here we have two disputants who disagree about the propriety of a term, and the issue is not easily settled, since it is not the sort of thing that can be cleared up by inspection. The two opposing claims stem from two different metaphysical theories, and the only way to proceed in settling the dispute here is to explore the presuppositions which lead each theorist to his conclusion, that is, to examine the argument the Buddhist might give for the hypothesis "there are omniscient beings" and the argument Kumārila might give for the opposite hypothesis. Inference always operates in a context, and cannot be properly understood divorced from a context. The context will not only include truths which have been guaranteed by direct experience; it may and usually will include prior metaphysical truths which purport to be the results of prior valid inferences. The "priority" here is not *a priori* in the sense of absolute certainty; rather, it is the priority of what has to be presupposed in order that a given inference be accepted as valid.

The above reflections are pertinent to the tactics of philosophical debate, a topic which prompted a great deal of Indian logic. If one is arguing with someone and wishes to make progress, it is a good tactic not to frame your argument in terms your opponent considers to be unexampled. Rather, what you should do is start further back, say with some reports of direct experience about which the two of you can hardly disagree (e.g., "there is a square object before us") and proceed Socratically until you convince your opponent by valid reasoning of the truth of your position concerning the exemplification of the term in question.

Rule 2: The Rule of the Overlapping Sapakṣa.[4] This rule requires that the class offered as the *sp* must overlap both the *h* and the *s* classes.

To say that two classes overlap is to say that they have a common member, that there is at least one individual which is a member of both classes. Therefore, to say that *sp* overlaps both *h* and *s* is to refer to a situation which can be pictured by Figure 3. For example, in the stock example about fire and smoke the *sp* was kitchen, i.e., the class of kitchens. This is a valid *sp*. There is at least one kitchen which possesses both fire and smoke, though all kitchens do not necessarily do so. That kitchen, whichever it is, falls into *h* and *s*, and so *sp* overlaps those two classes.

Notice, however, that on the definition of "overlaps" just given, an *sp* might well fall completely within *h* and still satisfy the rule, as pictured in Figure 6.

Figure 6

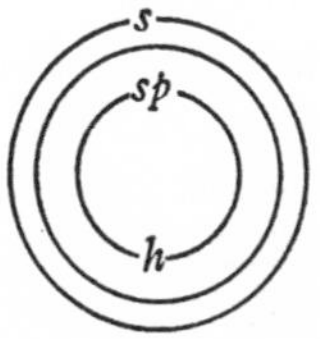

An illustration of this might be "this is a tree, because it's an elm, like the elm in my backyard." Here *s* is the class of trees, *h* is the class of elms, and *sp* is the unit class whose sole member is the elm in my backyard.

Or again, the *sp* might fall within *s* but not completely within *h,* as in Figure 7.

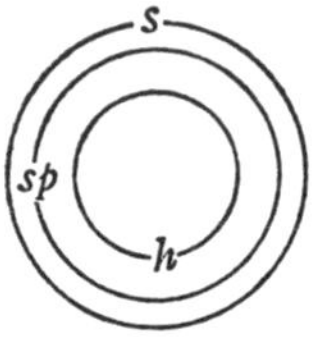

Figure 7

An illustration might be "this is a tree, because it's an elm, like other deciduous trees." Some of the *sp,* deciduous trees, falls within the *h*-class elms, some do not, but all fall within the *s*-class trees.

A proper *sp,* therefore, is a class which contains as member at least one individual which is a member of both *s* and *h.* There is one case satisfying this rule which is, however, objectionable, and that is the case where one offers as his *sp* the *pakṣa* class itself. Thus "this is a tree, because it's an elm, like an elm" is worthless as an argument, as anyone can see, although it satisfies the rule here under discussion. And in general, none of the five terms which figure in an inference may be identical with any of the other four. But the reasons why this is so pertain to the usefulness of the argument rather than to its structure. Therefore, I shall reserve discussion of the requirement of non-identity till later; it will reappear as Principle 2 of the next section.

Rule 3: The Rule of the Excluded Vipakṣa.[5] This rule requires that the class offered as the *vp* must fall completely outside both *h* and *s.* To say that a class falls completely outside of, or is excluded by, another class is to say that they have no members in common.

To further illustrate the second and third rules, I wish to call the reader's attention to an interesting contribution made quite early in the history of Indian logic by the Buddhist logician Dignāga (fifth century A.D.). He called it the *hetucakra* or "wheel of reasons."[6] It is a ninefold classification of arguments showing the proper and improper relationships between the *h, sp,* and *vp.*

Dignāga's classification pertains only to a part of the second and third rules, those parts bearing upon the relationship between the examples and the *hetu*. Its creator was among the first to formulate classifications of logical fallacies; he was followed by others who extended such classifications along the lines I am summarizing in this section.[7]

Dignāga considers the possible ways in which the *sp* and *vp* can be related to the *h* class, and finds nine possibilities:

(1) *h* completely includes *sp*, completely excludes *vp*.

Figure 8

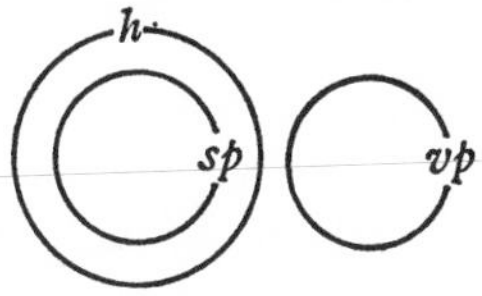

An example would be "that mountain has fire, because it has smoke, as in burning smudge pots and unlike lakes." If we suppose that the *sp* and *vp* are properly related to the *s* class, as they are in our example, then it will be seen that this inference satisfies the requirements of Rules 2 and 3. Rule 2 requires that at least one burning smudge pot be smoky, and this is *a fortiori* the case, since all are. Rule 3 requires that no lakes be smoky, and in fact this is the case. (We may disregard technicalities about smoke from elsewhere settling in right over the water!) Dignāga concludes that this inference is valid as far as the appropriate parts of these two rules are concerned.

(2) *h* completely includes *sp*, includes some but not all *vp*.

Figure 9

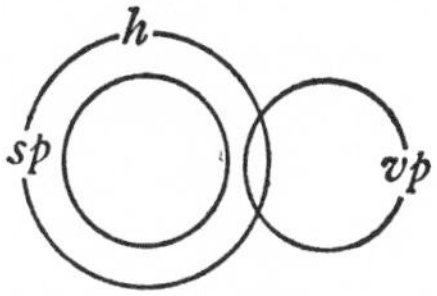

Example: "that mountain has fire, because it has smoke, as in smudge pots and unlike the sky." Here the inference fails the relevant part of Rule 3, since the *vp* does not completely exclude *h*. Some portions of the sky are places where smoke is located, and this violates the requirement of complete exclusion.

(3) *h* completely includes *sp*, completely includes *vp*.

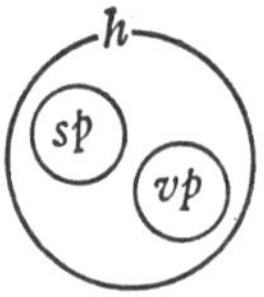

Figure 10

Example: "that mountain has fire, because it has smoke, as in smudge pots and unlike burning wet leaves." Here, of course, a class has been offered as *vp* which ought to have been offered as *sp*. This inference clearly fails Rule 3.

(4) *h* includes some but not all *sp*, completely excludes *vp*.

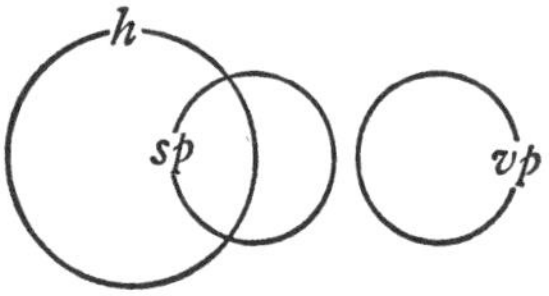

Figure 11

Example: "that mountain has fire, because it has smoke, as in kitchens and unlike lakes." This inference is valid as far as the matters comprehended by Dignāga's wheel are concerned, and for that matter, as it happens, it passes our Rules 2 and 3. Kitchen is an appropriate *sp*, for there is, as has been mentioned, at least one kitchen which is both smoky and fiery; lake is a proper *vp*, since no lakes are either fiery or smoky.

(5) *h* includes some but not all *sp*, includes some but not all *vp*.

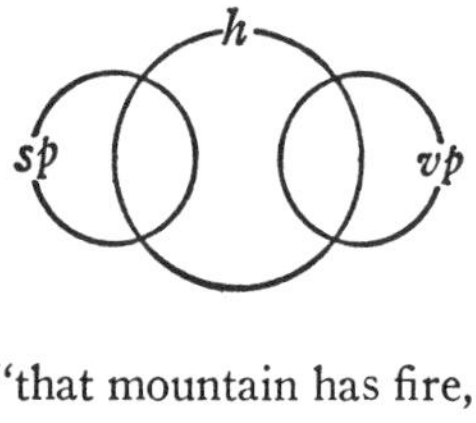

Figure 12

Example: "that mountain has fire, because it has smoke, as in kitchen and unlike the sky." This fails Rule 3, since some portions of sky are smoky.

(6) *h* includes some but not all *sp*, completely includes *vp*.

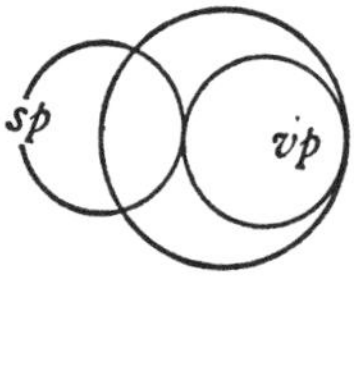

Figure 13

Example: "that mountain has fire, because it has smoke, as in kitchens and unlike burning wet leaves." Like (3), the *vp* should be an *sp*. Invalid.

(7) *h* completely excludes *sp*, completely excludes *vp*.

Figure 14

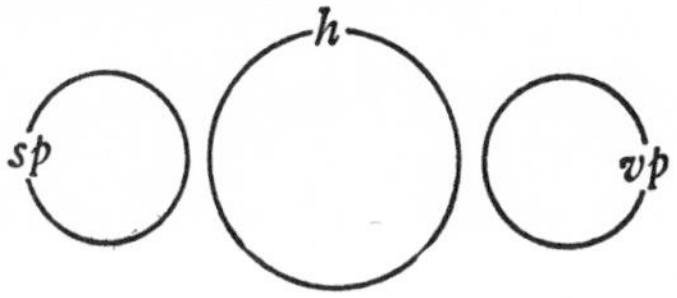

Example: "that mountain has fire, because it has smoke, as in rivers and unlike lakes." This case violates Rule 2 but not Rule 3. The *vp* is properly qualified, but the *sp* fails to do its job, since there are no rivers at all which smoke. Invalid.

(8) *h* completely excludes *sp*, includes some but not all *vp*.

Figure 15

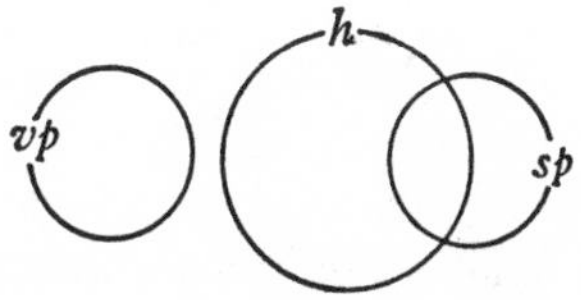

Example: "that mountain has fire, because it has smoke, as in rivers and unlike the sky." This is doubly invalid, since it fails both rules.

(9) *h* completely excludes *sp*, completely includes *vp*.

Figure 16

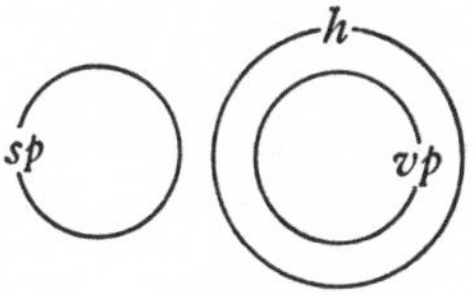

Example: "that mountain has fire, because it has smoke. as in rivers and unlike burning wet leaves." Here what should have been offered as *sp* has been given as *vp*, and vice-versa. Invalid.

Rule 4: The Rule of the hetu-*pervaded* pakṣa. This rule requires that the *pakṣa* fall completely within the *hetu*. There are, it seems clear, two ways in which this rule may be broken.

(1) The *p* may fall entirely outside of the *h*.[8]

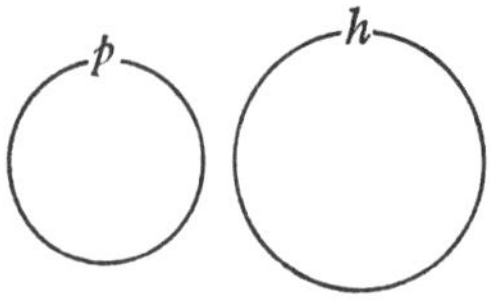

Figure 17

Thus, "this circle is rectangular because it is square" would be an example of this first way of breaking Rule 4. But this kind of situation is comparatively uninteresting and textbookish, since it is unlikely to occur except through linguistic confusion.

(2) The *p* may be a class which overlaps *h* but does not fall completely within it.[9]

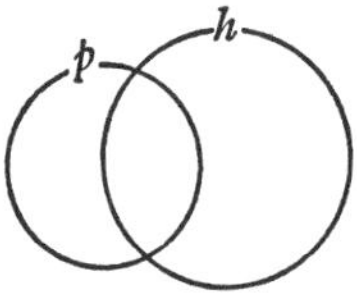

Figure 18

For example, according to Nyāya-Vaiśeṣika, each basic kind of substance is uniquely correlated with a sense-organ and its related sense-quality; thus, for them, earth is the only substance which smells. If someone proposes to a member of this school the following inference: "earth, air, fire, and water are substances, because they smell," the Nyāya-Vaiśeṣika philosopher will reject this inference as invalid, because its *p* overlaps but is not included completely within its *h*. The *pakṣa* here is the class whose members are particles of earth, air, fire, and water, and the *hetu* is the class of all things which smell. But by the Nyāya-Vaiśeṣika presuppositions, some members of this *p* do not fall within *h*, namely elementary particles of air, fire, and water.

Rule 5: The Rule of the sādhya-*pervaded* hetu.[10] This rule requires that the *hetu* fall completely within the *sādhya*.

This is perhaps the most important rule of the five, for at least two reasons. First, the other rules are less likely to be broken by someone who has thought about the matter carefully and who is sincerely seeking the truth. Secondly, in many cases a fallacious inference which breaks one of the first four rules may easily be reformulated unobjectionably once the mistake has been discovered. In the case of the fifth rule, however, once it has been recognized that the rule has been broken, it is not at all easy to reformulate the inference unobjectionably.

To illustrate, let us examine an inference which looks very much like our stock example:

> "This mountain is smoky, because it is on fire, like kitchen and unlike lake."

It is certainly not obvious on casual inspection that this argument is invalid. Furthermore, the examples are quite satisfactory; there is at least one kitchen which is both smoky and fiery, and no lakes are both smoky and fiery. We shall assume a context which assures us that the *p* falls within *h*—e.g., we see a glow over the horizon under circumstances which could only mean that that mountain over the horizon is on fire. Nevertheless, the argument is invalid.

It is invalid because the *hetu,* fiery things, is not completely included within the *sādhya,* smoky things. Although the two classes do overlap, so that it is possible to give a *sapakṣa* such as kitchen, nevertheless it is also possible to give examples of things which are members of *h* but not of *s*. The Indian logicians offer here the example of red-hot iron ball. A red-hot iron ball is fiery but not smoky. One way, then, of discovering a violation of Rule 5 is to try to think of examples of things which are members of *h* but not of *s*.

But one might think for some time and not come up with any such counter-example. How long must he keep thinking? When can he conclude he has thought enough and can accept the inference? There is no answer to this question, unfortunately; one may still be wrong even after thinking a long time. Only when systematic philosophy has completely described the nature of things in all relevant detail can we be sure we have exhausted the possibilities; until then, we have to depend on our imaginations which only too obviously may fail us.

The Indian logicians do, however, talk about another way of identifying violations of Rule 5, a way no more capable of generating a decision procedure but somewhat more general in its nature and therefore perhaps to be appealed to when initial examination has discovered no counter-examples.

This latter way of unmasking Rule 5 fallacies is called "discovering an *upādhi.*" An *upādhi* is literally an obstruction or limitation. In the present context, an *upādhi* is a class which falls within the *sādhya* and *hetu* classes and is easily confused with the *hetu.*

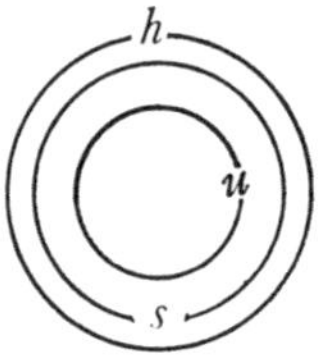

Figure 19

Returning to our example, "this mountain is smoky, because it is on fire," the Indian logicians tell us that this inference may be shown to be invalid by specifying as *upādhi* the class fire-with-wet-fuel-possessing. Specification of this class shows that the inference as it was originally formulated is invalid, since the *hetu,* fire-possessing, is larger than the *upādhi,* and the additional members which represent the difference are individuals which possess fire but do not possess fire-with-wet-fuel.

Specification of an *upādhi* is tantamount to specifying a necessary condition for the presence of the *sādhya,* a condition which is lacking in a part of the *hetu.* The presence of wet fuel is a necessary condition for smoke, but it is left unspecified in the *hetu* which is actually offered. Therefore we cannot accept the inference as it stands, since this necessary condition is not guaranteed to apply and thus we have in particular no guarantee that the *pakṣa* in this particular inference possesses the necessary condition in question.

As I mentioned, it is not easy to reformulate the inference once a violation of Rule 5 has been detected. We cannot just substitute the *upādhi* for the *hetu* without very likely breaking Rule 4. The inference "this mountain is smoky, because it possesses fire with wet fuel" is open to the objection that that mountain doesn't possess fire with wet fuel, or at least that there is no more reason to think that it does than that it doesn't.

The Importance of the Context

In the foregoing we have for the most part made use of examples in which the context was a matter of perception. We could see the smoke on the mountain, we assumed, when considering the inference "the mountain has fire because it has smoke." In the case of "that mountain has smoke because it has fire," we assumed we couldn't see the mountain on fire, but we inferred it from our perception of a rosy glow on the horizon. In "this is a tree, because it's an elm," it is easy to suppose that we just know trees and elms by casual inspection—by the shape of their leaves, etc.

However, the point of analyzing inference is, for the Indian logician, among other things to learn to be able to specify the rules of correct philosophical argument. The point of the investigation of the *pramāṇas*, the means of knowing, was to establish ground rules for successful map-making. Historically (for the earliest philosophers didn't think in terms of map-making) the purpose of analyzing inference was to establish rules of debate among philosophers, so that the best system of thought could be identified without question.

Philosophical debates, and the concerns of map-making, both involve the use of inference in contexts where what is presupposed is by no means evident by direct perception. More frequently, it involves a prior series of inferences whose acceptance is presupposed by the propounder of the argument.

When Indian logicians list the fallacies of inference (*hetvābhāsa*) they frequently include within the topic not only various ways of breaking the five rules already outlined, but also a number of other fallacies which pertain to the usefulness or acceptability of the argument under circumstances engendered by the context.

1. *Unnecessary inferences.* A fallacy regularly identified by logicians is the fault of "proving what has already been accepted" (*siddhasādhanatā*). Here the fault is merely that of wasting time; nevertheless, it blocks the purposes of the practitioners of debate or map-making. Generally, and this is *Principle 1,* inference is only necessary where there is doubt or disbelief. The presence of doubt or disbelief must be learned from context.

2. *Non-identity of terms.* A second fallacy, or rather type of fallacy, pertains to the identity of the terms in an inference. Suppose I offer as argument the inference "this is a bird, because it's a bird." Clearly I am wasting time. This argument doesn't break any of the Rules 1–5, but it is nevertheless objectionable because it helps us not at all.

Principle 2, then, is that none of the terms offered in an inference can be identical with any other. Let us briefly review a few examples.

It will clearly be useless to offer as one's *sp* the *pakṣa* class itself, e.g., "this object is a tree, because it's an elm, like this object. . . ." Nor should the *sp* be identical with either the *hetu* or the *sādhya,* as for example in "that mountain possesses fire, because it possesses smoke, like anything which possesses smoke (or fire)." The reason is that what is to be proved is precisely that anything which possesses fire possesses smoke, and the *sp* is supposed to help prove it, not to assume it as already proved. Nor can the *vp* be identical with any of the other terms, for its very function is to illustrate something which falls outside of all the other classes mentioned in the inference.

The *sp* and the *vp,* then, must not be identical with any of the other terms. In considering the possibility of identity between *s, h* and *p,* matters are slightly more complex, but the same principles prevail.

The complicating circumstance is the possibility that the *word* used for one of these terms may not be properly understood. Consider "all bachelors are single, because they are unmarried males." Here the *p* is the class of bachelors, and the *h* is the same class, since "unmarried male" designates the defining property of bachelorhood. The peculiarity of this example lies in the fact that, although the *p* and *h* classes are identical, there are contexts where such an argument might conceivably be illuminating. The contexts in question are those where the addressee is not aware that "bachelor" means "unmarried male," and what the argument conveys to such a person is that in fact this *is* the way we use (or ought to use) these words. So that in such a context, the argument mentioned is used to convey not so much information about a pervasion not already recognized, but rather information about verbal usage. Thus the hypothesis actually being demonstrated in the context under discussion is "the term 'bachelor' possesses (or ought to possess) the meaning of 'unmarried male.' " Outside of such a context, the argument commits the fallacy of proving what is already accepted, since once the addressee is aware that "bachelor" means (or ought to mean) "unmarried male," he hardly has to have it pointed out to him that all unmarried males are single.

The same point applies in the case of identity between *p* and *s,* or between *s* and *h.*[11] Take, as example of the former case, where *p* is identical with *s,* "all bachelors are unmarried males . . . ," or, as an example of the latter case, where *s* is identical with *h,* "this man is a bachelor, because he is an unmarried male." In both cases what is being conveyed is a truth about linguistic usage, and the appropriate way of formulating the hypothesis being urged would be, rather than the above, "the word 'bachelor' possesses the meaning of 'unmarried male' in ordinary usage." That this *is* the hypothesis is assured by the consideration that, as pointed out above, the only thing one could conceivably be in doubt about in such cases is the meaning of the words; once he has been convinced of the hypothesis about usage, the inference apparently offered becomes useless.

3. *Truncated inferences.* There is a third kind of consideration generated by the context in which an argument is proffered, but about which there is no general agreement among Indian logicians. As we have seen, there are normally five terms in an inference, *p, s, h, sp* and *vp*. True, one can express part of an argument if he is only interested in certain aspects of it but in doing so he presumably does not mean to deny that the other terms can be produced if called for. However, there are cases where it seems that either an *sp* or a *vp* cannot in the nature of the case be produced at all without violating one or another of the foregoing rules and principles.

The cases in question regularly stem from some prior assumption, presumably defensible by some other inference or inferences, about the nature of the world. For example, let us consider the following: "this pot is knowable." Now if we suppose this to be proposed by a Nyāya-Vaiśeṣika philosopher who accepts the tenets of his school, we can put him in an awkward position by asking him to produce a *vp*. For according to Nyāya-Vaiśeṣika, everything which is, is knowable—he doesn't accept the existence of anything which falls outside that class, since it is the universal class. The *vp* must be a class which falls outside *s*, and in this particular case there is, by hypothesis, no such class. Nevertheless, claims the Naiyāyika, the hypothesis is true, and therefore ought to be such that it can in principle be argued for.[12]

Logicians of other schools, however, deny that the inference claiming to demonstrate this hypothesis can be sound. Naturally, the motive for their denial is characteristically their disagreement with the thesis that everything is knowable. Therefore the issue may be said to lie not so much within the purview of logic as within the scope of metaphysics.

On the other hand, there are cases where, so it is claimed, an *sp* cannot be provided. Consider the following: "Living bodies have souls, because they breathe." The Nyāya-Vaiśeṣika philosopher (once again) contends that no *sp* can be provided here because the class of living bodies exhausts the possible individuals which breathe, and a proper *sp* must overlap *h* without being identical with *p*. Nevertheless, he insists, this is a sound inference.[13]

Again, other logicians deny the validity of an inference of this sort. And the inference offered here as example—about living bodies—certainly does seem objectionable on grounds already specified. For the Nyāya-Vaiśeṣika apparently holds that the class of living bodies is identical with the class of things which breathe, and this is a sort of inference which, as was argued, one wishes to reject on the grounds that *h* is identical with *p*. Here, of course, it is not a matter of misunderstanding linguistic usage; we do not ordinarily speak as if breathing were the defining characteristic of living bodies (e.g., trees are, in ordinary parlance, "living bodies," but are not ordinarily taken to breathe). If the Nyāya-Vaiśeṣika has a special theory about how we ought to talk, then he ought to argue that thesis straight-forwardly: the hypothesis should be rather "the term 'living body' ought to be used to mean 'thing which breathes.' " Suppose we become convinced of the wisdom of his way of speaking, and decide to follow him in using the two phrases to refer to one class; then the argument actually offered might be rewritten as "living bodies have souls, because they are living bodies," or as "things which breathe have souls, because they breathe"—and both these inferences fail our second principle of contextual relevance, since *p* and *h* are identical. In sum, this inference turns out upon examination to be an especially misleading way of presenting a Nyāya-Vaiśeṣika thesis which ought to be defended in other ways. This does not in itself show that there are no valid inferences which necessarily lack an *sp,* but it puts the onus on the Nyāya-Vaiśeṣika to prove it.

TARKA

It will be evident upon reading the foregoing section that the acceptance of an inference, or form of inference, ultimately depends upon the metaphysical presuppositions of the philosophers who propose to utilize that inference or form of inference. To be sure, in many cases the acceptability of an inference depends on agreement upon certain facts of experience ("perception"), an agreement which can frequently be obtained; but where such agreement cannot be obtained—and these are the cases of fundamental philosophical importance—other courts of appeal must be resorted to.

When one confronts ultimate differences of opinion on such basic matters, the considerations Indians call *tarka* come into play. Some logicians include these reasons under the rubric of inference also; the decision how to classify *tarka* reasons is not one we have to reach here, however. It is sufficient for us to note merely that *tarka* reasons are brought into the picture precisely when the question shifts from how things are common-sensically supposed to be structured or how we do talk in common speech to the question of how things ought to be mapped or how we ought to talk in an "improved language."

Below, several of the most important kinds of *tarka* reasons are given.

They are presented negatively, as mistakes to be avoided in philosophical construction.

1. *Self-residence* (*ātmāśraya*). The first defect or fallacy we shall consider is that called *ātmāśraya,* which means "having itself as its residence." Everything we care about must have a ground, i.e., something which is sufficient to explain its existence. But clearly nothing is explained, nor is any causation properly speaking taking place, when the cause and the effect are identical, that is to say, when one proposes as the sufficient reason the very same thing which is being explained. In order to control something, that is to say, to be free-to with respect to it, we must be able to identify something other than the thing in question which is that thing's ground—either a necessary or a sufficient condition or both. Self-residence, as well as the other sister fallacies of *tarka,* constitutes a stultifying situation, one which if allowed within a map renders the map useless for the purpose for which it is intended.

Not all apparent cases of self-residence are in fact vicious or fallacious, however. A harmless self-residence occurs when, for instance, two things which in actuality do stand to each other as cause and effect are, for some reason, mistakenly identified with each other by the critic. Vicious self-residence only occurs when no such mistake has been made.

It is not easy to find simple and yet believable examples of self-residence in ordinary English; they tend to sound silly and unlikely unless they occur in context. Nevertheless, here is an unbelievable one, which may suggest to the reader contexts where such a mistake actually was committed. "Why did Ike act as he did?" "Because he's Dwight D. Eisenhower!" Now we must immediately hasten to remark that, like most sentences out of context, this case can be interpreted so as not to involve self-residence. But it comes about as close to this fallacy as one can believably point to, short of waiting for a silly conversation to take place—something the writer of a book cannot do.

By the same token, however, this example may with more kindness be construed as only an apparent, and therefore a nonvicious, variety of self-residence. Thus, if we take the reply to mean that, since Dwight D. Eisenhower was the President, he had the authority to act in the fashion in question, and that he acted because he was aware that he had that authority through the fact of his being President, clearly it does not constitute a vicious fallacy any more, but rather a laconic way of offering an explanation which may in fact be quite enlightening.

The topic of self-residence has special interest because of its kinship with the puzzles of self-reference which are current sources of deep thought among logicians in the West. There is an interesting case of an apparent self-referential fallacy that occurs in Indian logical literature. We saw, in discussing an earlier matter, that everything that is, is knowable, according to some philosophers in India. Now the question that may be posed to such a viewpoint is this: is knowability *itself* knowable? Some Naiyāyikas say yes.[14] But how can knowability be both the explanans and the explanandum at the same time? Surely this constitutes a fallacy of self-residence.

In answer to this, if one wishes to save the theory, one must point out that the knowability which is a characteristic of each knowable individual is a different knowability from that which is common to all knowable individuals, which is to say, common to all existents. Thus for example, we can say "this chair is knowable" and make reference to a class describable as "knowability-of-this-chair." Likewise there is also a "knowability-of-this-table," and so on. But all of these are distinct from "knowability-as-such." Now when it is said "knowability is knowable," what is meant is that each of the particular knowability-classes is included in the class of knowability-as-such.

The solution, it will be noted, resembles in some degree what Western logicians call the theory of types. The difficulty with the resolution, as with the theory of types, is that it seems to trade in self-residence for an infinite regress. If one presses the Naiyāyika to know whether knowability-as-such is knowable, he is caught between two fires: if he says "no," then he gives up his basic thesis that everything that is is knowable, and if he says "yes," then he commits himself to another characteristic, "knowable-ness-ness," about which the same question can be asked. The latter move can be repeated *ad infinitum*. But infinite regress, as we shall shortly see, is only an extension of self-residence.

2. *Reciprocal dependence* (*anyonyāśraya*). Here instead of one term depending upon itself, there are two distinct terms, each one depending upon the other. This is an extension of self-residence, however; if it is vicious, reciprocal dependence is a fault for the same reason that self-residence is. The easiest way to see that this is so is to think of the two terms so related, *a* and *b*, as together constituting one term, *ab*. Then that one term, *ab*, is self-resident. Reciprocal dependence becomes merely a special case of self-residence. Things must be causally and in the order of explanation spread out in a continuous stream. If the stream turns into a whirlpool, our human strivings will go round and round and become futile; freedom and all that makes life worthwhile will become im-

possible of achievement if the way to its attainment leads through the whirlpool.

In Śaṃkarācārya's commentary on the *Brahmasūtras* we find a reference to a stock case of reciprocal dependence of a vicious sort.[15] Śaṃkara says that a certain view which he is attacking at that point in the discussion commits the fallacy of reciprocal dependence, adding that "it is like the well-known example of jejubes in a pot." To expand this: consider the following conversation. "Where's my fruit?" "In your jar." But suppose the first speaker is a new arrival. "Where's my jar?" "Where your fruit is." The first speaker is now rendered helpless—he doesn't know which way to go. Generally, such is the effect of the vicious variety of all four fallacies now under discussion—self-residence, reciprocal dependence, vicious circle and infinite regress—they render man helpless.

On the other hand, a slight alteration of this case will provide us with an example of a non-vicious case of (apparent) reciprocal dependence. "Where's my fruit?" "In your jar." "Where's my jar?" "Where you last saw your fruit." Now we have a harmless case. The tense makes the difference, because in the present case the second speaker is advising the first to recall a previous experience and to locate the plate and the apple by reference to it. Here we are not dealing with a stranger.

3. *Vicious circle* (*cakraka*). Any collection of terms which creates a whirlpool cannot be tolerated. Under the heading of vicious circle come all cases where some finite number of terms greater than two are involved so as to depend one upon the next around in a circle until the last number depends upon the first. In such a case, supposing the series of terms be *a, b, c . . . a,* the totality, i.e., the entity constituted by this series, is self-resident.

A certain school of philosophers in India (the Vaiśeṣikas) have, as all philosophers do eventually, to face the problem of defining, i.e., understanding the nature of, the self. Such a philosopher gives as his definition that the self is the substratum of knowledge—i.e., it is the knower. But when pressed about the nature of knowledge, he tells us that knowledge is anything which has the property of being a case of knowledge. Being pressed about that, he tells us that this property is a universal property. Asked which universal property, he tells us it is one which characterizes a certain specific quality of the self. And asked what a "universal property" is, he says it is that which, because it makes classification possible, is the special condition of knowledge. He is now going around in circles, so it will be urged. Starting out to define the self, he has used the term "self" eventually in his explanation. That is one vicious circle. Another is the one that starts with the question "What is knowledge?" and ends up in the explanation of what a universal property is by appeal to the understanding of what knowledge is. Clearly if the questioner went on pressing, he could force the Vaiśeṣika back and forth from "knowledge" to "universal" endlessly.[16]

If a Vaiśeṣika philosopher should offer as sloppy an explanation as this one, he would deserve the criticism meted out above. But the case is a complicated one, and there is room for misunderstanding. For example, the Vaiśeṣika might point out that there is no vicious circle, for the knowledge that is being explained, which has the special characteristic of knowledge-hood, is not the same knowledge that he ends up with when he refers to "the special condition of knowledge." This latter knowledge is knowledge-in-general, whereas the former knowledges were particular knowledges with specific referents. Thus, he may claim, the apparent sloppiness of the argument is due to the critic's failure to appreciate a crucial distinction.

4. *Infinite regress* (*anavasthā*). Consider a series of events (or things) . . . *cba,* i.e., a series which never begins. One might urge against this situation's occurring in a satisfactory map the same charge that was urged against the previous cases, that it undermines freedom-to. Infinite regress, it is said, is a more complex case of self-residence. It is, if you like, a very large whirlpool, but large or small, whirlpools undermine and render helpless man's attempts to control himself and his world.

However, not all beginningless series are whirlpools. It is only when an entity has no necessary or sufficient conditions that it is out of our control and we are limited in our search for complete freedom. An infinite series constitutes a threat to the program of Indian philosophers just when it is the case that the series is such that no cause can be specified which when brought into existence—or removed from existence—will be regularly followed by the event or thing in question. Thus we must distinguish between vicious and nonvicious regresses.

A vicious infinite regress occurs when an entity *A* turns out to be such that no cause can be specified for its existence except the occurrence of a part of itself, namely an earlier event in the series of which *A* consists. If *A* = . . . *cba,* say, and there is a vicious regress, then *A* at each moment of its existence is resident in itself, since *A* at time *t* consists of, let us say, . . . *ba,* which is resident in . . . *cba* at time *t,* which in turn is resident in . . . *dcba* at time *t,* etc. The fault, notice, is *not* the mere fact of infinity of sequence; everything depends on whether the things in the sequence are constituent parts of the whole.

In *Siddhitraya* by Yamunācārya, we find this argument: "the same Self cannot both perceive itself and be perceived by itself; for this would mean that the Self would have to be split up into two parts, the knowing part and the known part; but in order that the knowing-part-of-the-Self could know what it is, it in turn would have to be split up into two parts, that part which is the knower that itself is the knowing-part-of-the-Self, and that part which is what is known as the knowing-part-of-the-Self. In turn, the knower-of-the-knowing-part-of-the-Self would have to have a knower, and so on to infinity. Therefore, because otherwise knowledge could never take place, the same Self cannot both perceive and be perceived by itself."[17] This argument, if sound, convicts the opponent of a vicious infinite regress.

The stock example of a harmless infinite regress is the case of the seed and the sprout (*bījāñkura*). If someone were to suggest that something else must be the material from which sprouts come beside the seed because if there were nothing else there would be an infinite regress, since the sprout itself is the material from which seeds come, it would be proper to point out that this is not a vicious infinite regress, since there is no breaking down of one entity into its parts. The seed which produces the sprout is a different seed from the one which is produced by the sprout, and so this is merely an indefinitely long, in fact beginningless, causal series, and there is nothing faulty about that as far as the Indians are concerned.

5. *Complexity* (*gaurava*). Besides the four members of the self-residence family listed above, there are various other types of mistakes mentioned by Indian logicians, whose lists conflict with each other. I shall not try to cover any of the others, except the fallacy of over-complexity or "heaviness," which is pretty generally recognized by all schools of thought to constitute a blunder, or rather a kind of blunder with certain varieties—for complexity is a name for a family of fallacies too.

One immediately thinks of "Occam's razor" when one begins to speak of simplicity in philosophy. The Indian notion is somewhat broader than Occam's razor. Simplicity (*lāghava*) has what may be called a "quantitative" and a "qualitative" form, and these are distinct. Whichever form is in point, the consideration of simplicity should not be brought to bear until one has gotten to a position where there is equal reason to believe in either of two competing theories. It is only in such a situation that this requirement of simplicity becomes relevant. When there are two such theories, however, one should choose the one which (1) involves the fewer number of concepts or commits one to the fewer number of entities, and (2) which is easier to comprehend.

The general rationale behind these requirements is clear enough. In the first place, simplicity as understood here is a secondary requirement, to be brought to bear only after the other requirements of good reasoning have been met. Where one does have two valid hypotheses, however, if one chooses the simpler in either of the above senses, one will be less likely to be confused or make a wrong move at some later stage in inquiry. This type of good reason, then, is adduced as a preventive rather than as a cure of bad arguments. The fewer concepts or entities one has to deal with, so the presumption is, the less likely one will be to go wrong; likewise, although ease of comprehension is not the basic requirement of a valid position, still, other things being equal, the theory we understand is the one we ought to choose, since we're less likely to become confused later.

It is worth noting in passing, before leaving this requirement, that the two ways in which I have put the "quantitative" form of the principle of simplicity are not precisely equivalent. In Raghunātha's *Padārthatattvanirūpaṇa,* for instance, the author appeals sometimes to the principle that one should get along with as few entities as he can, and at other times to the principle that one should get along with as few concepts as he can. One may plump for paucity of entities in his theory, or one may plump for paucity in the number of *kinds* of entities to be admitted into his theory—and if he plumps for the latter, he may, though he need not, find himself committed to more entities than otherwise. Thus there is a certain ambiguity even within the "quantitative" variety of simplicity.[18]

VERBAL AUTHORITY (*śabda*)

It is well accepted by everyone, I suppose, that whatever the wisdom of the practice may be, one tends to believe what he is told unless or until he has some reason to suspect the source of his information. Some Indian logicians interpret "verbal authority" in this more or less innocuous way. But that is not the natural way of interpreting the term. It is usually understood as "what is heard from a reliable person," and is sometimes replaced by terms such as *āgama* or *śruti,* meaning "what is heard from sacred authorities."

Most of the philosophers of India rely on some texts or other of hoary vintage and saintly pre-eminence. Many Buddhists rely on the Pāli canon, which contains the words of the Buddha. The Jains have their sacred scriptures. And the Hindu philosophers as a general rule account the Vedas, including those Upanishads whose style and manner testifies to their ancient origin, as authoritative. They will also admit the authoritative character of certain other texts, notably, for example, the Bhagavadgītā.

There can be no doubt about the tremendous weight that the classical philosophers of India have placed on such authoritative scriptures. But when one examines the use made of appeals to the texts, one comes to the conclusion that the argument from authority is not as dogmatic as Westerners are frequently prone to believe. In effect what happens is that philosophers regularly appeal to authorities who say what they wish to say in more elegant language than they can muster. And when it appears that a sacred text runs counter to one's thesis, it is necessary to reconstrue the passage; one is not allowed just to ignore it.

Philosophers differ in the use they make of scripture in their expositions. The eleventh-century philosopher Rāmānuja, for instance, refers continuously to Vedic and Upanishadic texts and appeals to a host of interpretative rules for justification of his readings. A whole school of philosophers called Mīmāṃsakas have traditionally made a special study of the meaning of the sacred texts, and it is in their hands that the science of interpretation reaches its peak. On the other hand, in other branches of Indian thought one seldom finds appeal to scripture, even though these branches are "orthodox," i.e., endorse the validity of the sacred texts.

To study the science of interpretation of scripture at all thoroughly is a task well beyond the scope of this volume. It must be admitted, in addition, that the connection between some of the discussions incorporated in this science and the larger issues involved in gaining freedom and resolving doubts are unclear to this writer. Nevertheless, one cannot pass over the matter without noticing a few things about the appeal to scripture.

For one thing, it is incumbent upon the orthodox to have an explanation for any text within the Vedas. "A Vedic utterance cannot be purposeless"—this seems to be a rule accepted by all.[19] The propositions laid down in scripture have the status of "givens" as do the experiences we have through our senses—they must be explainable, or one's theory is deficient.

But the explanation may not, and frequently does not, stem from the most obvious meaning of the utterance. After all, the very word *upaniṣad* is said to mean "secret teachings," and it is not surprising that the meaning should appear obscure or even double-edged; as is well-known, such apparent obscurity and richness of meaning is characteristic of the most profound pieces of literature in any tradition. Therefore it is permissible, within certain limits, to construe some passages according to secondary rather than primary senses of the terms involved. This is allowed when, for example, the primary interpretation contradicts other passages, or runs counter to the testimony of all the other sources of good reasons. Philosophers differ about the relation of verbal authority to the other sources of knowledge such as perception and inference. A very orthodox philosopher will make inference subserve and bow to the pronouncements of scripture, whereas a less orthodox philosopher will say that scripture and inference cannot in the nature of the case disagree, so that one can use the latter to arrive at the proper interpretation of the former. It is a rare philosopher indeed who can hold to scripture when it contradicts experience, of course; here some explaining is normally adjudged to be in order, as is an appeal to a secondary sense.

Despite the variety of stances a philosopher may take toward the problems of interpretation, we must emphasize that at any rate he must take *some* stance. It is considered a fair gambit to challenge an opponent with a text which appears to contradict his thesis, and the opponent cannot allow this move to pass unanswered. Therefore, any philosopher worth his salt in India must have a good idea of the meaning of the scriptures and of the reasoning which leads him to his interpretation of them. It is frequently said that the scriptures can never be wrong, but men are frequently held to be wrong about what the scriptures mean.

MISCELLANEA

The account we have given of logical classifications does not, of course, begin to exhaust the wealth of material on this subject in the Indian philosophical traditions. One further point that ought perhaps to be mentioned is teachings about definition.

The Naiyāyikas, logicians *par excellence,* came to develop a rather unique method of exposition in the later stages of Indian philosophy—one which, however, is predictable from earlier tendencies. It is said in the *Nyāyabhāṣya* of Vātsyāyana that "the science of reasoning proceeds by three processes—enunciation, definition, and examination."[20] The recognition of definition as an element in reasoning is also found in other schools of thought.

There are some terms which refer to fallacies pertaining uniquely to definitions; I shall mention them even in this brief survey, for they do occur frequently. The three major fallacies of definition, according to the Naiyāyikas, are over-extension (*ativyāpti*), under-extension (*avyāpti*), and mutual exclusion (*asaṃbhava*). Examples can easily be provided for each:

(1) If one should define a cow as an animal with horns, this would be a poor definition, for the definiens would pervade the class of non-cows, i.e., it would over-extend to include other animals such as buffaloes.

(2) On the other hand, if one should define a cow as a black-and-white four-legged animal with a dewlap, this would under-extend, as some cows are all white (or all black).

(3) Finally, if one should define a cow as something with no legs which flies, this would be a case of mutual exclusion—the opposites of the characteristics listed in the definiens apply to the defiiniendum, which is to say that the classes picked out by the two terms mutually exclude one another.

These are clearly close cousins of fallacies of inference that were discussed earlier, the only distinction being that in this case no inference is being proposed. There are, in fact, terms for general use referring to the inapplicability of descriptions in general, whether they occur in inferences, definitions or what-not. A description is *atiprasaṅga* when it applies to too much, *aprasaṅga* when it applies to too little. When the description misses the mark completely, it is frequently referred to as a case of contradiction (*virodha*).

In addition to the sorts of arguments we have described in this chapter, other, less rigidly formulated, reasons are commonly invoked in philosophical discussion. The practical orientation of all Indian philosophizing is attested by the frequency of appeal in the literature to such reasons as the pointlessness or uselessness of an opponent's argument.[21] E.g., an argument may be rejected on the following kinds of grounds: "because it is a mere technicality";[22] "because *mokṣa* would become impossible";[23] "because there would result loss of confidence in everything";[24] "because it is hard to get ascertainment";[25] "because it's beyond the scope of inquiry."[26]

A general charge of inadequacy of explanation can be put forward by saying that a hypothesis is "inconclusively arguable" or "without a means of knowing it."[27] Sometimes it may be said that an opponent's position "cannot stand analysis."[28] Or one can refute the opponent by appeal to parity of reasoning, showing that the argument under discussion is as erroneous as one accepted as fallacious by the opponent.

Finally, there are a variety of rules (*niyama*) which are appealed to by philosophers in justifying their hypotheses, such as, for example, the rule that knowledge of a negation must be preceded by a knowledge of the thing which is negated.[29] These arguments frequently reflect a doctrine of the speaker and the rule may not be accepted by the opponent. Appeal to such a rule frequently results in a general discussion of the defensibility of the rule itself. With this kind of reason we enter upon a discussion of philosophical positions and leave the area of reasons agreed upon as acceptable by all.

CONCLUSIONS

The foregoing summary of good and bad reasons has distorted Indian philosophy in one respect which cannot easily be helped. In reading the literature, one continually runs across delightful and picturesque illustrations as well as references to the well-known fallacies or rules of good argument by means of laconic and frequently humorous allusions to stock examples of them. In what has been said here, I have tried to suggest a little of this, but I'm afraid the general result of this summary has been to suggest that Indian philosophy is arid reading at best. That is not true. The Sanskrit language is compact, but in the hands of a writer with imagination, and when read by a reader conversant with the nuances of the language, it can become as lively as any medium of expression.

This brings me to the end of my necessarily rapid survey of the Indian account of what constitutes good and bad reasoning in philosophy. There is a vast and little-known literature on Indian "logic" and the theory of the *pramāṇas*, and I have only touched on a few elements in it. To sum up, the underlying rationale of the distinction between a good and a bad reason is whether or not the reason offered is compatible with freedom-to and freedom-from. In the case of inference, the relation between the *hetu* and the *sādhya* and *pakṣa* about which the *pratijñā* seeks to establish something must be strong enough to suggest pervasion—constant conjunction—but not so strong as to constitute a tautology or any trivial kind of necessity. The former part of this criterion guarantees the possibility of freedom-to, the latter the possibility of freedom-from. As for the other *pramāṇas,* we have seen how *tarka* subserves the same ends, how perception represents an appeal to empirical events which are relevant to the explanation of hitherto unexplained events which matter, and how the use of verbal testimony as a *pramāṇa* turns out to be subject to the principles governing the proper use of the other valid ways of knowing.

Therefore not only is it true, as we shall see, that all of Indian philosophizing is generated ultimately from the problem of the compossibility of freedom-to and freedom-from, but the methods of reasoning and the kinds of reasons which are appropriate in philosophy are judged by the same criteria as are used to judge when a solution of the generating problem has been found. Those criteria, as we have seen, are *adequacy* to the things or events in the world about which we care, namely those pertinent to freedom-from and freedom-to, *accuracy* in reflecting truths of experience, *consistency* in the scheme through which we hope to come to understand the relations among these things, and *clarity* in our identification of those same things or events, the elements of the ontology which is being sought. Bad reasons in philosophy, therefore, are any reasons or reasonings based on principles which undermine these criteria, which thwart our attempts to identify and clearly and consistently to map the events we care about. Good reasons are those which are based on principles which promote the satisfaction of these criteria.

EXERCISES ON INFERENCE

Here are some exercises to test your comprehension of the material on inference in this chapter. These exercises are drawn from Indian sources. It is also possible to select arguments from any standard logic text and translate them into Indian standard form.

In attempting these exercises, the student should identify the *pakṣa, sādhya* and *hetu,* the *vipakṣa* and *sapakṣa;* rewrite the inference in standard form if necessary; and explain which of the five rules distinguished in the text each example breaks, if any. As was explained, in many cases the success of the argument depends upon the assumptions of the person to whom the argument is addressed; therefore, a brief list of assumptions is offered here, and where necessary further context is provided.

In working the problems below, take it that the following assumptions are made by the respective philosophers:

1. *Jains* believe that everything is both eternal and non-eternal.

2. *Buddhists* affirm that Buddha is omniscient.

3. *Naiyāyikas* hold that everything is cognizable; that sounds are qualities and are impermanent and caused; that space is permanent and uncaused; that jars persist through time.

4. *Mīmāṃsakas* hold that sounds are substances, are permanent and unlimited extension, and deny omniscience.

Exercises

(Drawn from *Buddhist Logic*)

1. The child in the womb of this woman has a dark complexion, because it is her child, just as her other children whom we see.
2. This is a tree, because it is an elm, like any deciduous tree and unlike the oak in my back yard.
3. There is no elm here, because there are no trees, like an icebox and unlike a forest.
4. In this place nobody exhibits symptoms of cold, such as shivering, etc., because there is smoke, like kitchen and unlike lake.
5. (*Naiyāyika to Mīmāṃsaka*): The sounds of speech are impermanent, because they are products, like a jar and unlike space.
6. (*Buddhist to Naiyāyika*): Sounds are momentary, because they exist, like a jar.
7. There is a peacock in this cave, because we hear its cries.
8. (*Mīmāṃsaka to Naiyāyika*): Speech-sounds are eternal, because they are cognizable, like space and unlike jars.
9. (*Mīmāṃsaka to Naiyāyika*): Speech-sounds are not produced by an effort, because they are impermanent, like space and unlike jars.
10. (*Mīmāṃsaka to Naiyāyika*): Speech-sounds are eternal, because they are not limitedly-extended bodies, like space and unlike jars.

(Drawn from *Nyāyāvatāra*)

11. Inference is invalid, because it is a source of knowledge, like perception.
12. Perception is invalid, because it is a source of true knowledge, like a dream.
13. (*Mīmāṃsaka to Buddhist*): An omniscient being does not exist, because he is not apprehended by the senses, like a jar.

14. This person is devoid of passions, because he is mortal, like the man in the street.
15. This person is mortal, because he is full of passions, like the man in the street.
16. (*Mīmāṃsaka to Buddhist*) : This person is not omniscient, because he is full of passions, like the man in the street.
17. Inference is invalid, because it is a source of true knowledge, unlike a dream.
18. (*Jain to Mīmāṃsaka*) : Sound is eternal and non-eternal, because it is an existence, unlike jar.
19. (*Buddhist to Sāṃkhya*) : Kapila is not omniscient, because he is not a propounder of the four noble truths, unlike Buddha.
20. Kapila is not devoid of passions, because he did not give his own flesh to the hungry, unlike Buddha.

NOTES

1. For a summary of these views, see Chatterjee, pp. 55–68.

2. The formulation of these rules is my own; it is not drawn from any single source. Indeed, Indian logicians do not characteristically speak in terms of "rules" in this connection; rather, they list "fallacies" (*hetvābhāsa*). In subsequent footnotes throughout the present section I shall give some of the Sanskrit terms for the fallacies comprehended within my rules. It should be understood, however, that different Indian systems have different names for the same fallacy, one of several reasons why I depart from tradition here and reorganize this material.

3. Fallacies, i.e., ways of breaking this rule, are sometimes called *aprasiddhaviśeṣaṇatā*—literally, "unproved qualification." In other contexts similar fallacies are called *svarūpāsiddha, āśrayāsiddha, pakṣāsiddha.*

4. Violations of this rule and the next two are referred to by a variety of terms, among which I have noted *anaikāntika, sādhāraṇa,* and *savyabhicāra,* all suggesting uncertainty. These rules, as will be seen, cover the ways in which the terms of an inference may be improperly related to one another.

5. See previous note.

6. The source of Dignāga's wheel is in his work *Hetucakranirṇaya* or *Hetucakrahamaru.* Cf. *Indian Historical Quarterly* 9:511–514 (1933). See also *Buddhist Logic* I, pp. 321 ff.

7. It is argued by Stefan Stasiak (cf. Stasiak) that by careful arrangement of the various combinations of relationships among the terms of an inference the Naiyāyika Uddyotakāra created a classification of types of inference numbering 1032 distinct cases.

8. Sometimes breaking this rule is called *sambandhāsiddha.*

9. *Pakṣaikadeśavyāvṛtti.*

10. Violation of this is sometimes called *vyāpyatvāsiddha.*

11. The latter is sometimes called *sādhyāviśiṣṭatva.*

12. Inferences which are by nature lacking *vipakṣa* are called *kevalānvayi* or "only-positive."

13. Inferences which are by nature lacking any *sapakṣa* are called *kevalavyatireki* or "only-negative." Sometimes they are called *anadhyavasīta*.

14. Raghunatha (49.4–51.1), pp. 63–64.

15. *Brahmasutrabhasya* (II.2.17), p. 238.

16. Bagchi, pp. 158–159.

17. *Siddhitraya,* p. 91.

18. Raghunatha, p. 6.

19. E.g., in Prakasananda (p. 47) we are told that a certain interpretation of scripture is to be rejected because it would render certain other Vedic utterances purposeless (*anarthaka*).

20. *Nyayasutra,* pp. 51–52. *Nyayabhasya,* p. 15.

21. Sanskrit terms are, e.g., *prayojanaśūnyatā, vaiyarthya.*

22. *Paribhāṣikam eva.* Cf. Prakasananda, pp. 115 and 120.

23. Prakasananda, p. 120.

24. *Bhamati,* p. 26.

25. *Vadavali* (42), p. 21.

26. *Vadavali* (44), p. 12; (313), p. 86.

27. *Anupapatti* and *mānābhāva,* respectively.

28. *Vikalpāsahatvāt.* Cf. *Vadavali* (4), p. 2.

29. *Pratiyogijñānapūrvakaniyama.*

6

FREEDOM AND CAUSATION

There is fundamental agreement among Indian philosophers of practically all persuasions about the basic problem of systematic philosophy. That problem, in a nutshell, is to discover a conceptual scheme or map in which we can find a route to complete freedom from wherever we are now. The requirements of such a scheme are determined by the nature of freedom-to and freedom-from, with the resulting restrictions on acceptable arguments which were discussed in the previous chapter. The scheme must on the one hand be loose enough to allow for freedom-from, to allow us to enter into events as causal agents, and thus to insure that we are not at the mercy of forces beyond our control; nevertheless, it must not be so loose that the events we care about, those events which enter into the types of sequence through which we may hope to move toward freedom, are irregularly related, unpredictable, and chaotic in their patterns. We must be able to count on the recurrence of certain sequences, but at the same time we must have confidence that our decisions and deliberate actions influence events significantly. We must steer a course between skepticism and fatalism in constructing the scheme.

The doubts and fears that the world will not permit such a course, that either skepticism or fatalism is true, obstruct our ability to improve ourselves. These doubts and fears must be resolved and relieved if we are to address ourselves with conviction to self-knowledge and renunciation. Whether such conviction or faith can be gained progressively by action, devotion, or understanding, as those I shall call "progress philosophers" believe, or only by a sudden leap of insight, as those I shall call "leap philosophers" believe, it must be gained somehow, or the meaning of human existence remains suspect.

If they are to discover a satisfactory scheme, Indian philosophers must look to the features of the tension which gives rise to their musings. They must look, that is, to the tension between freedom-from and freedom-to, to the nature of the relationships between events or things, in particular those relationships we call causal—ones which hold between the types of events or things which make up the sequences which pertain to the ultimate purpose of complete freedom, i.e., the events about which they care. Those relationships cannot be too strong, or we are subject to forces beyond our control; but neither can they be too weak, or we are unable to steer our course. What are the categories of such a scheme? What analogies can one appeal to in order to appreciate the nature of a satisfactory causal relation? These are among the questions which have first priority in Indian philosophy.

The problem of freedom and causation, or better, freedom-to and freedom-from, is the source of all systematic Indian philosophy of which we know, except for what little still remains of skeptic and fatalist views—and even these are pertinent to that problem in that they are what everyone else is concerned to refute.

Western philosophers have not always appreciated this problem that so concerns the Indians. This is partly because the main tradition in Western values, as I pointed out in the opening pages of this book, upgrades rationality at the expense of spontaneity—with the result that, since subjugation of the passions was admitted to require a limitation of human control, freedom-from was not always prized as highly as it should have been. When, therefore, on other grounds we have come to recognize the pricelessness of freedom-from—in social and political matters, for instance—we have found it difficult to relate our need for freedom-from to our commitment to rationality as the superior value. India had to be taught this Western problem of the relation between rationality and freedom-from, and some of its difficulties in finding itself in the modern world stem from the strangeness of the problem, a problem which only came to them with their introduction to Western ways and values.

Another reason why Western philosophers have not always appreciated the Indians' basic problem is that, unlike the Indians, they have pretty well abandoned the notion that man can totally master the forces of nature. To the Indian, to doubt the power of the *yogi* to control not only his body but the bodies of others—indeed, the whole universe—creates suspicion about the possibility of any man's freedom to master, i.e., to anticipate and control, the events which touch him in his limited state as an unperfected person. So accepted a doubt is this last one for the Westerner of contemporary times, however, that he even finds it odd to speak of being at the mercy of his environment, tending to suppose that speaking in such a fashion involves some sort of primitive animistic belief that Nature is another person. The environment, Nature, the causal sequences which take place within the universe, are agreed to be impersonal, neither in our control nor controlling us; those sequences constitute the subject-matter for disinterested observation carried on by natural scientists, but they are held to be completely different from us in kind and unconnected to us in their nature. To be sure, there are corners of science where this assumption has had to be called into question by the very force of the nature of the subject-matter (as in psychology, which studies man himself as an observer but finds it hard to maintain the division between man as observer and man as observed). In addition, Western man has managed to scare himself silly by mastering a good deal more of nature than he really quite supposed possible consonant with his assumptions, so that he now flounders around in fear of his own power, instead of counting this gain in mastery as indicative of progress not only on behalf of observing man, the scientist, but also of free man, the agent.

A widely-prevalent philosophical gambit with respect to freedom and causation in the West stems from this last-mentioned guarded skepticism about man's ability to control nature. Hume and his followers teach that freedom and determinism are compatible because, they say, freedom means freedom from compulsion or constraint, and causal regularity, far from compelling men to act as they do not wish, has nothing whatever to do with compulsion or constraint, being opposed only to indeterminism, i.e., to chaos. The Indians might be able to accept this in its negative implications, but it doesn't go far enough to pose what is to them the crucial problem. The Humean position, from their point of view, merely says that freedom-from is a different thing from freedom-to, that to be unconstrained is one thing and to be able to predict and control future events another. The Indians grant that lack of constraint is distinguishable from ability to control, but insist that man's ultimate goal is the attainment of both, and further that nature, if it is understood to include not only the nature of the physical universe but also the nature of man, is a potential threat both to freedom-from and freedom-to. It is a potential threat to freedom-from by threatening to reduce to none the alternatives among which we may choose; it is a potential threat to freedom-to by threatening to contain within it random events, irregular sequences which can thwart our ability to control ourselves and our environment.

Where the Western empiricist sees two problems, the Indian sees one. For a Humean, there are two realizational problems, one the problem of freeing oneself, up to a point, from constraint, the other the problem of predicting and, up to a point, controlling the "forces" of nature—which aren't actually forces but impersonal sequences of forceless events. He sees no interrelation between these problems, believing the one to be a matter for social adjustment, the other a matter for scientific observation. That is why he adds the "up to a point." The Indian philosopher on the other hand sees only one problem, the problem of mastering everything pertaining to himself, which includes his relations with external nature, with other people in social contexts, and with himself; it is seen as a continuous problem with all its aspects interrelated, not compartmentalized as Western philosophers have frequently been prone to suppose.

It follows, therefore, that when an Indian addresses the problem of freedom and causation he appreciates the distinction between constraint and predictability, between freedom-from and freedom-to, between skepticism and fatalism; he sees the difference, and yet he also sees all too clearly that, though different, these things are interconnected, and that their connections must be explored, mapped, conceptualized, and completely understood or man's capabilities cannot be fully realized. Consequently, he tends to take philosophy so understood as prior in importance even to questions of social adjustment, which accounts for many things about Indian thought that a Westerner finds difficult or absurd.

The tension between freedom-from and freedom-to is the theoretical counterpart to the tension each of us faces when called upon to make choices in conducting our lives. As we saw in Chapter 2, the practical problem of knowing ourselves is the problem of assessing situations properly, mapping them relevantly, and identifying the significant challenges and verified roles from among the alternatives apparently open to us. The general theoretical problem of Indian philosophy is to see the whole universe through a framework which allows for the possibility of self-knowledge and renunciation by guaranteeing both that there is a difference between significant challenges and insignificant ones and that it is possible to distinguish roles which promise to lead to freedom from those which do not. A map which satisfies the postulates we have mentioned resolves the doubts about this view of human striving and its method.

That being the case, the first thing a philosopher in India must do is to understand the tension between freedom-from and freedom-to in detail, so that he may come to grips with it in a way which promises success. This involves, first, the identification of causal chains, of things which regularly are found to occur together or in sequence. Secondly, it requires that those sequences about which we care be distinguished from those about which we do not care, the ones relevant to freedom from those not relevant. That there must be such a distinction has already been established when we discussed, in Chapter 4, the requirement of a criterion of relevance in mapping and pointed out that all human understanding involves an element of selection. Once the relevant chains have been identified, the philosopher's problem is then to show that the relationships between the members of such sequences are neither too strong nor too weak—not so strong as to render our function as agents irrelevant, not so weak as to render us unable to count on the regularity of those relationships continuing in the future. The sequences or chains so related must in addition be shown not to have gaps, for if there is any possibility of gaps in the chain, we remain in doubt about the possibility of attaining complete freedom and this, as we saw, leads in turn to a doubt about all human striving.

In the remainder of this chapter, I shall briefly consider some of the classical accounts of causal sequences about which we care, introducing and identifying some of the philosophers and schools responsible for the initiation of these accounts. In the next chapters, I shall pass on to a consideration of theories about the relation between the members of causal sequences. Later, we shall explore the difficulties encountered by some of the philosophers in following out the implications of their theory of relations into the explication of how we know, that is, into epistemology. The philosophers discussed in these chapters will be those I consider "progress philosophers"; I shall turn to consider the "leap philosophers" in Chapter 11. But perhaps at this point a general introduction to Indian philosophers and schools of philosophy is in order.

A FRESH CLASSIFICATION OF PHILOSOPHICAL SYSTEMS

While the history of Western philosophy is usually carried on by referring to philosophers by name and classifying various of their views as "empiricism," "rationalism," "realism," "nominalism," etc., the common practice in writing of Indian philosophy has been to write about various systems of thought, called *darśanas* (literally, "views") in Sanskrit, without always considering the particular philosophers who espoused the positions of each system. This habit came about partly because of our rather undeveloped knowledge of the history of Indian thought; few texts had been edited, fewer translated, and as a result few scholars who wrote in English knew the individual Indian philosophers in their writings and by name. These limitations are becoming a thing of the past. We can now talk about Indian thinkers by name, and it is probably time for us to dispense with some of the generalizations about certain schools which, while they may have their use in introducing the student to certain aspects of the subject, may also seriously mislead him. In what follows, therefore, I shall whenever possible speak of a particular individual's views and not of the views of a school. Sometimes, however, such a practice is admittedly inadvisable, when the views of several philosophers support each other so concertedly as to make it philosophically irresponsible to try to partition their overall system and so do an injustice to the fruits of their common enterprise. For example, it seems to me advisable to treat old Nyāya-Vaiśeṣika as a system. But it does not seem so in the case of Advaita Vedānta, which is frequently referred to as one system but in fact is composed of a fascinating proliferation of important and individualistic philosophers.

If one picks up a standard introduction to Indian philosophy one will find a classification of Hindu systems into six—Nyāya, Vaiśeṣika, Sāṃkhya, Yoga, Mīmāṃsā and Vedānta. Now there are undoubtedly important historical reasons why this classification came to be accepted and taught by Indian pandits and eventually transmitted to the English-reading public by modern scholars, but here in this volume we are not concerned with such historical reasons so much as we are with distinguishing the presuppositions of Indian thought. Since this is my aim, I have found it fruitful to adopt a fresh classification of systems, one by reference to which I can suggest how the majority of Indian thinkers in the past, and to some extent in the present, stand to each other with respect to the problems raised by the fundamental presuppositions which I have identified.

I have already mentioned the basic divisions of this classification. My first distinction is between what I have called "path philosophy" and "speculative philosophy." The former deals with the problems involved in finding for oneself or one's audience proper path(s) of renunciatory or disciplinary activity leading to complete freedom. The latter deals with the problem of showing that complete freedom is possible. As noted, these two phases of Indian thought bolster each other, since to show by speculative endeavor that there is a route is to suggest truths about possible paths, and to state conclusions about possible paths involves implying things about the nature of a world which makes those paths possible.

As a second division, within the class of speculative philosophy I wish to distinguish "progress philosophy" from "leap philosophy." The distinction is one deriving from what I have argued is the critical problem of Indian thought, namely the problem of how it is possible to have complete freedom-from and complete freedom-to together. The progress philosopher believes that he can specify causal relations between complete freedom (freedom-from-cum-freedom-to) and its necessary and sufficient conditions, which allow men to enter upon a causal series leading to complete freedom. The leap philosopher denies that there are such causal relations; he believes it is possible to attain complete freedom, but that progress along a path of causes and effects is not the correct way of characterizing the route to it. I emphasize that the distinction is a speculative one that concerns causal relations; this distinction is recognized as a crucial one by Indian philosophers themselves, who refer to progress philosophy as *jātivāda* or "causal theory" and leap philosophy as *ajātivāda* or "noncausal theory." However, it is also true that the views of progress philosophers about path philosophy tend to differ from those of the leap philosophers, since the former can believe in the efficacy of *karmayoga* or action-discipline as a way to freedom, actions being a species of events with causes; whereas the latter tend to downgrade *karmayoga,* admitting it only as a preparatory stage leading to the status of an *adhikārin,* since in their view one cannot progress through a causal series to complete freedom. Nevertheless, my distinction is one within speculative philosophy, not path philosophy, and the major concern of the remainder of this book will be with speculation.

Of the classical "six systems" of Indian thought, one, Yoga, is path philosophy and not speculative except in an ancillary fashion. Its sister system, Sāṃkhya, carries the speculative burden of its point of view. The systems called Nyāya and Vaiśeṣika are progress philosophies, differing so little in fundamental assumptions as to be assimilable for most purposes; I shall usually treat them together. Sāṃkhya too is a progress philosophy. The two last systems of the six are called Pūrvamīmāṃsā and Vedānta, and each of these rubrics covers several different things. Pūrvamīmāṃsā philosophy covers the schools of two very important philosophers, Kumārila and Prabhākara. I shall treat these two great Mīmāṃsā philosophers separately, for they take quite distinct stands on many fundamental issues in speculative philosophy.

That brings us to "Vedānta." Literally, the word means "the end of the Veda," presumably suggesting that the philosophers known as "Vedāntins" are peculiarly the custodians of the insights of the Upanishads, which are the more or less speculative appendages to the hymns and ritual directions found in the Vedas. But for our purposes there is no benefit in treating them alike. There are an indefinite number of different types of Vedānta, such as Dvaita ("dualistic"), Advaita ("nondualistic"), Viśiṣṭādvaita (usually translated "qualified nondualistic"), Śuddhādvaita ("pure nondualistic"), Dvaitādvaita ("dualistic-cum-nondualistic"), etc. Even within some of these, notably in the case of Advaita, there are large differences. Most important, some Vedāntins are progress philosophers, some leap philosophers, and some seem to teeter on a fence in this regard without quite deciding either way. For example, Madhva, the leading Dvaitin, seems to be in the last analysis a leap philosopher, for he denies that *mokṣa* can be gained by personal effort, i.e., by progress alone—yet he spends a lot of time examining categories remarkably similar to those employed by progress philosophers. Within Viśiṣṭādvaita, it is probable that Rāmānuja, its founder, was either a progress philosopher or undecided, whereas Vedānta Deśika, a later great name within the school, is an out-and-out leap philosopher. In Advaita, the distinction is even clearer and more developed. Śaṃkarācārya, the Advaitin of the eighth century, seems to teeter between leap and progress philosophy, and his followers divided into three strands: the clear-cut progress philosophers like Vācaspati Miśra; the leap philosophers like Sureśvara and Prakāśānanda; and a large group of those who try to find a way between these extremes, such as Padmapāda, Prakāśātman, and Vidyāraṇya.

The habit of dividing Indian philosophy into six systems is deficient in another respect; it does not cover several types of philosophy which, despite their "heterodox" views on some matters from the Hindu point of view, have nevertheless functioned as important segments of philosophical opinion throughout the history of Indian thought. I am speaking of the philosophies of the Buddhists and the Jains.

I shall treat the Jains as if they were one monolithic system. I am not at all sure that this does proper justice to their views, but I do not know of any clear precedent for distinguishing important speculative differences among Jain philosophers. There is such a precedent in the case of the Buddhists. The tradition is that there are four Buddhist systems, named Vaibhāṣika, Sautrāntika, Yogācāra or Vijñānavāda, and Mādhyamika. The defects in this classification for the student of philosophy are perhaps not as glaring as in the previous case of the Hindu systems, but it certainly could be improved upon. Two points come to mind.

In the first place, the distinction between Vaibhāṣika and Sautrāntika is not an easy one to draw, particularly as we have no Vaibhāṣika texts to speak of. What we know of the Vaibhāṣika tenets we glean wholly from arguments addressed by others against them, with the possible exception of the views found in the *Abhidharmakośa,* and in the case of that justly famous text, Vaibhāṣika and Sautrāntika views are mixed together and can only be unscrambled by assiduous criticism on the part of commentators. I shall accordingly tend to treat these views together.

In the second place, the rubric "Yogācāra" or "Vijñānavāda" is rather unhelpfully vague, since it covers such philosophers as Vasubandhu, the author of the *Vijñaptimātratāsiddhi,* as well as the "Buddhist logicians" Dignāga and Dharmakīrti, whose views appear to diverge in important respects from Vasubandhu's. I shall distinguish, therefore, between Vasubandhu's theory and that of the Buddhist logicians, and will use the terms "Yogācāra" and "Vijñānavāda" to refer to Vasubandhu's philosophy of *vijñapti* and not to the theory of the Buddhist logicians.

The Buddhist theories I have mentioned so far are all progress philosophies. Mādhyamika, however, whose great name is Nāgārjuna, is clearly a leap philosophy. Later, there are philosophers who try to straddle between Mādhyamika and Buddhist logic in the way the third school of Advaita does in Hinduism. This will be explained and illustrated in due course.

The distinct "schools" of philosophy which I shall treat, then, are these: Mādhyamika, Buddhist logic, Yogācāra, (Vaibhāṣika-) Sautrāntika, Prābhākara Mīmāṃsā, Nyāya-Vaiśeṣika, Kumārila's Mīmāṃsā, Jainism, Sāṃkhya, Viśiṣṭādvaita, Bhedābhedavāda (an influential and distinctive fashion of thought usually lumped in with "Vedānta"), progress (Bhāmatī) Advaita, teetering (Vivaraṇa) Advaita, and leap Advaita. The views of Vedānta Deśika and of Madhva will receive separate treatment outside this classification, for they present special problems. The particular order in which I have just listed the schools will be justified in the course of what follows. The reader is referred to Figure 20 for a summary of my scheme in treating the over-all picture of Indian thought. All references to "the left," "the center," and "the right" in what follows pertain to Figure 20.[1]

CAUSAL CHAINS

I now turn to the first problem for an Indian progress philosopher, the identification of causal chains. Remember that the program for speculative philosophers of the progress variety is, as I have outlined it, first to identify the causal chains we care about and to find models whereby to consider their structure, and second to analyze the nature of the causal relation as exhibited among the members of those chains.

1. *The Buddha's chain.* One of the oldest and best-known of the chains of causes proposed by Indian thinkers is the Buddha's "twelvefold chain of causation" or "chain of dependent origination" (*pratītyasamutpāda*). This chain begins with ignorance (*avidyā*), and continues through predispositions, unconscious though formative knowledge, names and forms, the six sense-organs, contacts between the sense-organs and their objects, feeling, desire (or "thirst"), attachment, coming to be, birth, and old age and death.[2] This last item, old age and death, is once again the cause of ignorance, and so the chain constitutes a closed circle.

The main thing to note about this chain is that some of its members are necessary but not sufficient conditions for those that follow. That this must be so follows from the necessity of our being able to break the chain.[3] The places where one can break the chain are the places where one can combat ignorance with truth and desire with nonattachment. But if this chain were a chain of necessary-and-sufficient conditions, it would be impossible to break the chain, for since, e.g., desire would follow necessarily upon the presence of feelings, there would be no way of avoiding desire. Likewise, old age and death, which is to say, sorrow in general, is the necessary condition of the acquisition of ignorance, but not the sufficient condition, for if it were, there would be no way of avoiding ignorance once the chain had started. And the chain has started—for all of us. It is beginningless (*anādi*). There was no time when this chain did not operate.

Skeptics (Cārvāka)	Mādhyamika Buddhism (Nāgārjuna)	Yogācāra Buddhism (Vasubandhu)	Buddhist Logicians (Dharmakīrti)	Prābhākara Mīmāṃsā (Prabhākara)	Nyāya-Vaiśeṣika	Bhāṭṭa Mīmāṃsā (Kumārila)	Jaina	Sāṃkhya (Īśvarakṛṣṇa)	Viśiṣṭādvaita Vedānta (Rāmānuja)	Bhedābhedavāda (Bhartṛprapañca)	Bhāmatī Advaita (Vācaspati Miśra)	Vivarana Advaita (Prakāśātman)	Sureśvara's Advaita	Fatalists (Ājīvikas?)
Anti-freedom	Leap-philosophy (ajātivāda)	Progress Philosophies											Leap-philosophy (ajātivāda)	Anti-freedom
		Asatkāryavāda (effect not pre-existent in cause)				Anekāntavāda (everything both same and different)		Satkāryavāda (effect pre-existent in cause)						
		Sādṛśya (co-ordination)		Sādṛśya and Samavāya	Samavāya (inherence)	Bhedābheda (identity-in-difference)		Pariṇāma (transformation)			Vivarta (manifestation)			
Wholes Unreal				Parts and Wholes Real and Distinct		Wholes Both Equal to and Not Equal to Parts		Whole Equal to Sum of Parts			Parts Unreal			
Nominalism (post rem)				Realism (ante rem)		?		Conceptualism (in re)						
?			Bhedāgraha Apohavāda (similarity is non-grasping of difference)		Abhāvas or Negative Reals		?	No Negative Reals			Abhedāgraha Apohavāda (difference is non-grasping of similarity)	?		
	Asatkhyāti (object of error nonexistent)	Ātmakhyāti (object of error is the self)	Phenomenalism	Akhyāti (no error in simple judgments)	Anyathākhyāti (errors only of misplacement or mistiming)	Viparītakhyāti (error consists in taking things other-wise than they are)		Satkhyāti or Yathārthakhyāti (object of error real or "as is")			Anirvācanīyakhyāti (object of error is False)			

Figure 20
Indian Philosophical Systems

We shall see later that this basic conception of a chain of necessary conditions is capable of various interpretations by later Buddhists, so that one finds several distinct schools springing up and proposing extensions of the original philosophy incorporated within the bare outlines of this chain. The question of the continuity of the series, its nongappiness, as well as its manner of connection or nonconnection with the self and the universe—these are important topics which will be discussed subsequently.

2. *The Jain's chain.* Turning to the philosophy of the Jains, we find, for example, the early thinker Umāsvāti holding that there is a chain of three necessary conditions for bondage, namely (1) wrong attitude (*mithyādarśana*), (2) wrong knowledge (*mithyājñāna*), and (3) wrong conduct (*mithyācāritra*).[4] The opposites of these are, respectively, right (*samyak-*) attitude, knowledge, and conduct. We are told that "of these the succeeding one must still be practiced upon the acquisition of the preceding one. The acquisition of the preceding one, however, is of necessity there on the acquisition of the succeeding one."[5]

But where does the wrong attitude come from in the first place, the error which has to be replaced by right attitude? According to the Jains, the Self, which is intrinsically pure, moves in a world of karmic matter of an astonishing diversity of kinds. The pure Self has a kind of energy (*vīrya*) which brings it into proximity with these karmic particles, and the proximity of the particles "color" its otherwise unsullied energy. The resulting "colored" (*saleśya*) energy is called "activity" (*yoga*), an imperfect expression of the pure, uncolored energy. This *yoga* (which has no relation to the Hindu word meaning "discipline") is limited because of the passionate attachment bred in the *vīrya* by its intermingling with the karmic particles. And the activity breeds the kinds of dispositions and habits which constitute wrong attitude, which in turn leads to wrong knowledge and wrong conduct.

Freedom comes by bringing about two essential steps: *saṃvāra* or prevention of the accretion of karmic matter onto the pure Self, and *nirjarā* or destruction of the karmic matter which clings on to the self from earlier activity. The prevention comes about when the activity stops, and this is brought about, in turn, by controlling the passions, i.e., by adopting the attitude of nonattachment. *Nirjarā,* or destruction of the karmic matter which clings after prevention has been accomplished, is brought about by the great "heat" of the pure Self which has been laid bare by discipline, a pure energy governed by nonattachment but completely spontaneous and unlimited in its power.

3. *The chain of the Nyāyasūtras*. For the author of the *Nyāyasūtras*, traditionally known as Gautama, there is a chain of five elements: pain, birth, activity, defect, and wrong notion. The second *sūtra* tells us "there is cessation of each member of the following series—pain, birth, activity, defect, and wrong notion—the cessation of that which follows bringing about the annihilation of that which precedes it; and this ultimately leads to the Highest Good."[6] Can wrong notion be dispelled, however? That is the doubt which calls forth an elaborate examination, not only of the methods of right knowledge, but also of the nature of the relation which connects wrong notions to the self, and indeed of the nature of that relation's relata. The subject-matter of the Vaiśeṣika system of philosophy consists almost entirely of a discussion of the metaphysical side of this examination.

4. *Īśvarakṛṣṇa's and Rāmānuja's chains*. In the system set forth in the *Sāmkhyakārikās* of Īśvarakṛṣṇa we find an elaborate chain of evolution which is both metaphysical and psychological. According to Īśvarakṛṣṇa, two basic entities, selves (*puruṣa*) and nature (*prakṛti*) co-operate to produce a series of differentiations in the latter, a series which starts with unconscious mental states and becomes progressively more determinate, culminating in the various elements of matter whose combination is supposed to explain the material objects of our ordinary acquaintance.

Rāmānuja proposes an evolutionary scheme much like that of Īśvarakṛṣṇa, except that the double origin in selves and nature is replaced by a single origin in Brahman, the supreme principle.

This summary of a few of the many varieties of chains that can be found in the early philosophical literature of India provides evidence, if any is needed, for my assumption that the problem of causation is paramount in Indian thought. The various ontologies and epistemologies are introduced as a way of showing the continuity of these chains, as well as justifying their character as being chains of necessary but not always sufficient conditions. For all progress philosophers, if the relationship between every member of a chain and the next were that of necessary-and-sufficient condition, there would be no way of entering the chain and thus no way of achieving liberation. On the other hand, if the chain turns out on analysis to be gappy—if there is any failure of the relation of necessary connection between each link in the chain and the next one—then no amount of preparation, effort, or study on our part can guarantee our achievement of the goal of freedom. The doubts and fears that provide the impetus for philosophy then will remain unresolved. The overall problem for the progress philosophers of India, then, is to provide a full understanding of the relationships between the members of that chain which brings about the condition of bondage and whose reverse shows man the route to complete freedom—an understanding which, as we have seen, satisfies the conditions of an adequate, accurate, consistent, and clear map which were outlined in Chapters 4 and 5.

CAUSAL MODELS

The chains we have been discussing are primitive in their conception, dating as they do from the earliest moments of reflection. It is not unnatural, then, to find that the earliest speculations about the nature of the causal relation—the relation which connects the elements in causal chains—should be based on what might be called metaphorical or analogical thinking. Each of the major theories of causation has its basic model or "root metaphor," and we may best begin our study of these theories by sketching these metaphors. What, then, is the model according to which progress philosophers think about causation within the relevant chains?

1. *Satkāryavāda*

Turning first to the models characteristic of those philosophers I have placed on the right-hand side of the diagram in Figure 20, we can consider the view of Īśvarakṛṣṇa, author of *Sāṃkhyakārikās*. His model can be illustrated by the metaphor of milk and curds. Milk, it is maintained, is the cause of curds, which is the effect. But the milk is the same stuff as the curds; it is merely transformed into a solid state, being the same material that was previously in liquid state. The effect is already existent in the cause—in fact, it is the very same stuff as the cause, being altered merely in what we should call its "secondary" qualities.[7]

The view that the effect pre-exists in its cause is called, in Sanskrit, *satkāryavāda*. The particular view of Īśvarakṛṣṇa's Sāṃkhya system, the view that the effect is an actual *transformation* of the cause, is called *pariṇāmavāda* (*-vāda* means something like our "-ism").

The ninth *kārikā* or passage of Īśvarakṛṣṇa's work constitutes a *locus classicus* for arguments defending *satkāryavāda*. This passage reads as follows:

The effect exists [in the cause] because
(1) there is no causing of what is non-existent in the cause,
(2) because [when one wants a particular kind of effect] there is grasping of [its] material cause,
(3) because everything is not possible,
(4) because something which has a capacity causes that only of which it is capable,
(5) because the cause [of that particular kind] exists.[8]

We have here a series of fairly obscure pronouncements, reflecting the primitive character of the Sāṃkhya philosophy as developed by Īśvarakṛṣṇa. The first argument is to the effect that a character which is non-existent in the necessary conditions of something doesn't, indeed can't, get produced at all. You can't get water from a stone, as we say; likewise you can't get oil out of sand, or curds out of water, the Indians add. This is also the meaning of the second argument, which tells us again that we must look for the necessary condition of a given kind of effect in the material out of which that effect is made, and not elsewhere. On the other hand, if we wish to interpret the first two arguments to mean distinct things, we may understand the first argument to mean that from a non-existent entity nothing is caused, that a nothing cannot do anything, and therefore it cannot cause anything either. It is hard to see how this last is relevant, however, since the opponents of *satkāryavāda* do not deny that events have *some* causes.

The third argument in the above passage is a distinct and important one: if things did not have pre-existing necessary conditions, you could get anything from anything, and this runs counter to experience, as well as violating the requirements for freedom-to. The fourth argument more or less repeats the first two. The fifth argument is taken by some commentators on this text to mean that the effect is not different from its cause because it cannot be brought into contact with it or disjoined from it as would be the case if they were distinct.

To get on closer terms with *satkāryavāda,* however, we will do well to consider the objections of the opposite camp, the *asatkāryavādins*, who do not believe that the effect pre-exists in the cause. The first and basic objection that we may suppose them to raise against the account offered in the *Sāṃkhyakārikās* is merely that the account is incomplete. First, is the material cause the *only* necessary condition for the production of the effect? If that is so, the *only* way of avoiding a given effect would be through seeing to it that its material cause never arises. But if all arising of material causes has for its *only* necessary condition the presence of the same material in another form, then we are necessarily chased back to a basic, primordial stuff which is, if you like, unevolved but which itself has no beginning. This is precisely what Īśvarakṛṣṇa holds: he calls his primordial stuff *prakṛti,* and considers that in its original or pure state it is unevolved (*avyakta*). But then why does it ever evolve at all? And, more important, is the process of devolution in our control or not? There must be at least one other necessary condition which is responsible for the evolutionary process starting, the absence of which would be a sufficient condition for devolution of *prakṛti* and the freeing of the soul from its bondage to nature. Otherwise we are at the mercy of *prakṛti* or matter; our bodies are our selves, if this is so, and we are, or rather Sāṃkhya is, reduced to the position of the Cārvākas, who hold that everything is its own cause (*svabhāvavāda*). This is skepticism, and to be avoided at all costs.

So Īśvarakṛṣṇa does not limit his list of necessary conditions for evolution merely to the material cause or *prakṛti*—he also admits a second type of entity, the Selves or *puruṣas*. It is the influence of the Selves upon material nature that constitutes the necessary condition of its evolving. But this influence is to be understood epistemologically, it is the kind of "influence" we have on things when we confuse them in our thinking about them. It is the Self's confusing itself with material stuff which is the necessary condition for bondage, and the discrimination (*viveka*) by the Self of itself from material nature is the sufficient condition for release and freedom.

This is a fresh twist, and turns what started out looking like a metaphysical materialism into an epistemological idealism of sorts. The Selves are completely immaterial—quite distinct from matter—otherwise there would be no way of discriminating a Self from its body and environment. The problem for Sāṃkhya theory is not so much *why* these two quite distinct sorts of things, spirit and matter, must get confused, but *how*. The Sāṃkhya answer is that the confusion is beginningless, which may make metaphysical sense but does not make much epistemological sense, as we ordinarily only confuse those things which have some points of similarity.

The Sāṃkhya theory in effect limits the kind of difference human beings can make to *understanding* rather than effort. Discrimination is the key to salvation; our actions may be at the mercy of the conditions which have produced the evolutionary process and subsequent bondage of the Self, but somehow, it is assumed, our minds are free enough to discriminate, and this discrimination is the sufficient condition for freedom. As the *Sāṃkhyakārikā* picturesquely puts it: "As a dancer desists from dancing, having exhibited herself to the audience, so does Nature desist, having exhibited herself to the Spirit."[9] And later, using a similar metaphor, " 'She has been seen by me,' says one and is indifferent; 'I have been seen,' says the other and desists from evolution; though there be conjunction of these, there is no prompting to further creation."[10]

These and other difficulties with this line of thought must be left for a later exposition. What I do wish to call to the reader's attention, however, is the way in which thinking about the causal relation along the lines of the *satkāryavāda* model, at least in its *pariṇāma* or transformation variety, leads Sāṃkhya toward epistemology, i.e., toward a discussion of the function of ignorance—cosmic in scope, if you like, but nevertheless epistemological in character—as constituting the avoidable necessary condition for the bondage of the Self. The correlative conception is that right knowledge—discrimination or understanding—constitutes a sufficient condition for freedom. Where else can Īśvarakṛṣṇa look to find a model for a type of causal influence which does not breed further influences in the Self, a causal force which brings something about without transmitting its energy to that which is affected? Knowing immediately comes to mind as such a force, and it is hard to think of any others.

Most of the proponents of *satkāryavāda* make little or no attempt to resist this movement to epistemological concepts as the key to the problem. For example, the various propounders of Advaita Vedānta light upon epistemological concepts such as ignorance (*ajñāna, avidyā*), which are made to do double duty as metaphysical concepts too. There are half-way stages to the acceptance of these words, e.g., the use of a term such as *adhyāsa,* which means literally "setting upon" and is adopted by Śaṃkara to refer to the superimposition of one attribute on another in cases of illusion—when one sees a rope and thinks it is a snake, for example—as well as the superimposition of the effect on the cause in a causal relationship. We shall have occasion later to discuss in detail the ways in which these ideas are developed. What is in point now is to indicate how it is that the *satkāryavāda* view of causation, originally espoused by naive realists like Īśvarakṛṣṇa, becomes in the hands of other, later philosophers a way of distinguishing reality from appearance. The Advaitins hold to *satkāryavāda* too, but theirs is a different variety, called *vivartavāda*. Whereas in a transformation theory (*pari-*

ṇāmavāda) like that of Īśvarakṛṣṇa there is a real transformation of a common stuff, in manifestation theory (*vivartavāda*) there is the illusory appearance of one stuff under various guises, all of them unreal by comparison with the underlying substratum.

There are, too, philosophers who try to oppose this movement toward epistemologization, who try to avoid distinguishing sharply between appearance and reality. One such is Rāmānuja, founder of the Viśiṣṭādvaita school. Others include Bhāskara and, before him, Bhartṛprapañca, the best-known of the group of thinkers usually referred to as Bhedābhedavādins, who hold the view that even the ultimate elements can be both the same and yet different. Later this view is taken up again by, for instance, Yādavaprakāśa and Nimbarka.

These last-mentioned philosophers all try to meet the difficulties of the Sāṃkhya transformation-theory by giving up or at any rate modifying the ultimate distinction between *puruṣa* and *prakṛti,* finding a more fundamental source of unity in the conception of *brahman,* a notion which goes back to the Upanishads. They thus appear to avoid the mind-body (or, better, spirit-matter) problem which the Sāṃkhya has on its hands, or at least avoid a fundamental bifurcation in the universe. The difficulty comes home to roost, though, in the shape of several equally irritating dualisms.

Dualism is not, however, the gravest kind of problem that faces a *satkāryavādin.* His major difficulty is roughly that the relation he posits between cause and effect is too strong. His motive for postulating such a relation is, it would seem, sound: he wants to avoid a universe in which things are cut off from each other so completely as to preclude their acting upon each other and producing effects. This constitutes, in addition, motivation for unifying the universe under some cosmic principle—and the appearance of *brahman* as the concept peculiar to most *satkāryavāda* theories is a function of this urge. The universe cannot be unified, however, without running the risk of making the causal relation turn into a logically necessary relationship. When and if that happens, there can be no salvation, since nothing can become other than what it is already. As philosophers become aware of this outcome of the urge to unify, they either return to explore afresh the pluralistic alternatives, or else they change their notion of the method of gaining salvation. If they do the latter, they are what I am calling "leap philosophers." The leap philosopher in India typically removes complete freedom from the universe of ordinary things and events, making that universe irrelevant to it. He reinterprets freedom as either superior knowledge alone, untainted by rational processes, or as devotion alone untainted by any relationship with the conditions prevalent in the universe known to the senses and the intellect.

The grave problem for the process theorist who adopts *satkāryavāda* and unifies the ultimate stuff of the universe under the name of *brahman* is to explain how it is possible for an individual soul to accomplish his own liberation. This comes down to a question of the nature of the causal relation, the relation which is to relate the efforts of a man with those effects which constitute a chain leading to complete freedom. The Bhedābhedavādin believes that relations, or their relata, can have apparently contradictory characteristics. The Advaitin tries to analyze the causal relation afresh by construing it epistemologically. We shall discuss all of these theories at length below.

2. *Asatkāryavāda*

Having followed out the implications of *satkāryavāda* in a general way, we now turn to examine the other side of the ledger, the *asatkāryavāda* view that the effect is not pre-existent in the cause. Where the *satkāryavādin* tends to unify the ultimate stuff in the universe, the *asatkāryavādin* multiplies the number of basic entities which enter as relata into the causal relation. He does this because he wants to multiply the necessary conditions in the chains that matter, in order to allow for the exercise of human effort and knowledge in a way which makes enough of a difference between cause and effect, without making too much of a difference either. The dangers in his theory, it will be apparent, are just the opposite of those inherent in the *satkāryavādin*'s theory—he must avoid fragmenting the universe so thoroughly that his efforts become unavailing because the relation between them and their effects is too *weak,* affording no guarantee that those efforts will succeed. Thus the main varieties of thinking along the *asatkāryavāda* lines stress the multiplicity of conditions which go to make up a causal aggregate (*sāmagrī*).

Within the class of *asatkāryavādins,* two varieties again stand out, with a few philosophers who try to compromise. The two major varieties are the Nyāya-Vaiśeṣika thinkers and the Buddhists. Of the compromisers, we shall have occasion to speak of Prabhākara and his school of Mīmāṃsā.

The favorite examples offered by Naiyāyikas to illustrate the workings of causation are the production of a pot from the combination of its two halves and the production of a piece of cloth from the combination of some threads. The Naiyāyika (as I shall call a member of either the Nyāya or the Vaiśeṣika school) recognizes three kinds of causal factors and some sub-varieties under one kind. First, there is what Īśvarakṛṣṇa called the "material" cause (*upādāna*), which the Naiyāyika calls the "inherence-cause" (*samavāyikāraṇa*). In the stock examples, the pot-halves and the threads are respectively the inherence-causes of the pot and the cloth. Second, there is what is known as the "non-inherence cause" (*asamavāyikāraṇa*). In the case of the pot, the contact between the halves is the non-inherence cause; in the case of the cloth, it is the contact between the threads. Finally, there is the instrumental cause (*nimittakāraṇa* or simply *karaṇa*), which we might, following Aristotle, call the "efficient" cause.[a] It is common among scholars of this system to refer to this cause, however, as the "instrumental cause," and I shall follow this precedent.

There are various kinds of instrumental causes which may operate together. There are the general (*sādhāraṇa*) instrumental causes, such as God's will or "the unseen" (*adṛṣṭa*), which is in the earlier texts certainly a euphemism, meaning in effect a condition which the philosopher cannot otherwise explain, but which develops later into a fairly sophisticated theory of the unconscious energies of the self. Time (*kāla*) and space (*dik*) are two other general instrumental causes for those events which are spatio-temporally located. There are, in addition, specific (*asādhāraṇa*) instrumental causes. For instance, in making a pot, the stick that the potter uses to work together the pot-halves is a specific instrumental cause, as is the conjunction of the stick with the pot-halves. This last, being the last event in the series leading up to the production of the effect, is sometimes referred to as the "operative" cause (*vyāpāra*).

The Buddhists, in contrast, guarantee that the world will not collapse into a congealing unity by the fundamental expedient of assuming that there are no persisting substances at all. Everything, according to the Buddhist, is momentary (*kṣaṇika*). Some Buddhist schools seem inclined to interpret the ultimate stuff of the universe as mental, others to take it as physical, but they all agree that whatever its nature, it is momentary, nonpersisting. The root metaphor of causation for the Buddhists reflects this assumption; it is the metaphor of the "circle of fire" (*ālātacakra*). If one takes a flaming torch and whirls it around in a vertical circle, those watching will get the impression of a persistent object. Just so, say the

[a] One should not suppose that there is any great similarity between Aristotle's analysis of causation and the Naiyāyika's, however.

Buddhists, the momentary occurrences of things in certain patterns gives the effect of persisting objects in the world.

But to explain how bondage came about and how freedom is to be achieved, the Buddhists must be more explicit, and they evolve early an elaborate analysis of "causes and conditions" (*hetupratyaya*) and a complicated psychology to explain these matters. Since nothing persists, there are no "souls" in the sense of the substantialist "self"; there are, however, patterns of momentary occurrences which constitute "personalities" (*pudgala*) and which create habits (more patterns) in certain areas. These habits, through a kind of inertia, regenerate similar habits or patterns, so that personal identity appears to hold over a fair stretch of time. The "personalities" are then analyzed into various components which comprise the causal categories pertinent to the discussion of yogic discipline and training. Thus, the Buddhists maintain, they appreciate the necessity of avoiding a theory which makes the causal relation too strong or too weak. It is not too strong, since nothing persists and so there can be no necessary relationship between cause and effect. It is not too weak, because the habit-forming propensity of occurrences provides regular links between those occurrences.

The *satkāryavādin* steps in at this point with several arguments which force the Buddhist either to capitulate or to stiffen his resistance. The ultimate outcome of stiffened resistance, it turns out, is another variety of leap theory, that espoused by Nāgārjuna and the Mādhyamika school of Mahāyāna Buddhism. The reduction of the Buddhist theory to this conclusion may be thought of as effected in three steps.[11] The first is the position we have outlined, in which the momentary events as well as the circle of fire as a stable (though constructed) entity are taken as part of the world. The second consists in the recognition that the appearance of stability and externality on the part of the circle of fire is illusory, and that the only things that are real are either the momentary flashes of fire which "constitute" the circle or else the mental correlates of these. The third and last step is the Mādhyamika position, which takes advantage of the inability of either the physicalistic or mentalistic interpretations offered in the previous step to prove its own superiority, and concludes that both the flashes and the ideas are illusory, and that there is no "reality" at all in the sense in which the other Buddhists suppose there is; in the Mādhyamika's own words, "everything is void (*śūnya*)." The position of the first step is held by a series of philosophers mostly of the Hīnayāna school culminating in the work of Vasubandhu, author of the *Abhidharmakośa*. Two brothers of the fourth century A.D.,

Asaṅga and Vasubandhu,[12] are responsible for the development of the idealistic branch of the second step, a position I am calling Yogācāra or Vijñānavāda. The realistic branch of the second step is espoused by the Buddhist logicians, notably Dignāga and Dharmakīrti. The Mādhyamika, led by Nāgārjuna, holds the last position.

The Mādhyamika's position is frequently pictured by its opponents as one of skepticism, and it is difficult to know whether this is an accurate picture or not. However, it is the understanding of several scholars[13] that many philosophers of this school, quite possibly including Nāgārjuna himself, did not rest content with the mere negation of the world, but elevated the very voidness which they contended was basic to the stature of a supreme principle. This has much the same effect as the postulation of *brahman* as being beyond causal chains, and Mādhyamika is for that reason best construed, I think, as a leap theory.

3. *Anekāntavāda*

If, as was suggested, the defense of the progress *satkāryavāda* theories like Bhedābhedavāda and Viśiṣṭādvaita depends upon a thorough-going analysis of relations in general, the same is true of the progress *asatkāryavāda* theories such as Nyāya-Vaiśeṣika and the non-Mādhyamika Buddhists. Whereas the problem for the right-wing *satkāryavādins* was to show how there can be a relation between something and itself that isn't too strong, the problem for the left-wing *asatkāryavādins* is to find a relation between two completely distinct things that isn't too weak. There is a pressure forcing the two wings toward a common center, and it is not surprising that we should find a school of thought which attempts to occupy that center.

This school is that of the Jains. The Jains contend that they avoid the pitfalls of both the right and left wings, and that they hold neither of the extreme positions on causation but rather a third, which they call *anekāntavāda* (lit., "the view that ultimates are not single"). The Jain model of causation can be appreciated if we revert to our previous brief discussion of the Jain chain of conditions for bondage and freedom. It will be remembered that the causes of bondage run back eventually to something figuratively referred to as the "coloration" of the pure energy of the Self as a result of the proximity of that Self with karmic particles. The model or metaphor we must focus on, then, is that of the production of qualities, such as color, in substances. Since bondage results from the coming-to-be of qualities in substances, the relation we are concerned to analyze has to do with the relation between a substance at one moment having quality A and the same substance at the next moment lacking quality A and having quality B. Examining this model, it will easily be seen, claims the Jain, that it satisfies both the left-wing and right-wing ways of thinking—or perhaps neither of those two if they are interpreted as mutually exclusive. Considering the relation of the substance at one moment to the substance at the next, the *satkāryavādin* is right, the effect is contained in the cause, but considering the relation of quality A to quality B, the *asatkāryavādin* is right, the effect is not contained in the cause. But furthermore, why must the right-wing and left-wing views be mutually exclusive? Cannot both be right, particularly if there is reason to believe that it will *not* do to *separate* entities into substance and quality though one may distinguish those two aspects of any entity—a different thing from separating them. This last is, in fact, what the Jain holds. Everything is substantial viewed from one aspect, fleeting as viewed from another. And there is a variety of other aspects from which a given entity can be viewed.

The question about Jainism, philosophically speaking, is whether or not it constitutes a genuinely alternative position or merely an *ad hoc* eclecticism, and this once again, depends on how successful an analysis of relations it can provide upon close examination. The Jains are closely allied with the Bhedābhedavādins on the one side and the Nyāya-Vaiśeṣikas on the other, since all three schools attempt to provide a theory of relations wherein two things are in some sense the same and in another distinct. This middle of the road position is also occupied by Kumārila's Bhāṭṭa school of Mīmāṃsā, which shares its sympathies between Nyāya-Vaiśeṣika on one side and Jainism on the other, as well as Sāṃkhya and Rāmānuja's Viśiṣṭādvaita, which sympathize in certain respects with the Bhedābhedavādins and in certain others with Jainism. All these relationships will become clearer in the next three chapters, where we discuss the strengths and weaknesses of the five major theories about relations in general and about the causal relation in particular.

NOTES

1. The chart presented in Figure 20 is set forth and discussed compactly in the writer's article "A Fresh Classification of India's Philosophical Systems," *Journal of Asian Studies* XXI, No. 1, 25–32 (November 1961).

2. *avidyā, saṃskāra, vijñāna, nāmarūpa, ṣadāyatana, sparśa, vedanā, tṛṣṇa, upādāna, bhava, jāti, jarāmarana.* The *locus classicus* for this chain is in the Samyuttanikaya of the Pali canon. Cf. *Source Book,* pp. 278–279.

3. It is possible that Nāgārjuna rejects this interpretation of the chain and makes them all both necessary and sufficient conditions. The interpretation of Nāgārjuna's views is still an open question for scholars, however. Cf. Murti, Robinson.

4. Umasvati, p. 1.

5. *eṣām ca pūrvasya lābhe bhajanīyam uttaram uttaralābhe tu niyataḥ pūrvalābhaḥ*. Quoted in Tatia, p. 148, note 1.

6. *Nyayasutra,* p. 42. *Nyayabhasya,* p. 12.

7. Īśvarakṛṣṇa's *Sāṃkhyakārikās* are surprisingly free of metaphors bearing on causation, but his commentators, such as Gauḍapāda and Vācaspati Miśra, offer a variety of them—that of the milk and the curds being one of the most important. Other metaphors are the sesamum-seed and its oil, the clay and the pot, the yarns and the cloth. See, e.g., *Samkhyakarikabhasya,* pp. 13, 23, 25, etc.; *Tattvakaumudi,* pp. 32 ff., 54 ff.

8. *Sāṃkhyakārikā* 9, my translation. See *Samkhyakarika,* pp. 22 ff.; *Samkhyakarikabhasya,* pp. 13–14; *Tattvakaumudi,* pp. 32–40.

9. *Samkhyakarika,* p. 94.

10. *Samkhyakarika,* p. 101.

11. The three steps were not taken in the order given; this is a logical, not chronological, series.

12. Scholarly controversy still rages about the number and identity of Vasubandhus. See J. Takakusu, "A Study of Paramartha's Life of Vasubandhu and the Date of Vasubandhu," *Journal of the Royal Asiatic Society,* 33–53 (1905) ; N. Peri, "A propos de la date de Vasubandhu," *Bulletin de l'école française de l'Extreme-Orient* 11:339–390 (1911) ; J. Takakusu, "The Date of Vasubandhu, the Great Buddhist Philosopher" in *Indian Studies in Honor of Charles Rockwell Lanman* (Cambridge, Mass.: Harvard University Press, 1929), pp. 79–88; G. Ono, "The Date of Vasubandhu Seen from the History of Buddhistic Philosophy," *ibid.,* pp. 93–94; L. de la Vallée Poussin, "Vasubandhu l'Ancien," *Bulletin de la classe des lettres et des sciences morales et politiques, Academie royale de Belgique* (Bruxelles, 1930), 15–19; E. Frauwallner, "On the Date of the Buddhist Master of the Law Vasubandhu," *Série orientale,* Roma, III (1951) ; P. S. Jaini, "On the Theory of Two Vasubandhus," *Bulletin of the School of Oriental and African Studies* 21:48–53 (1958) ; A. Wayman, *Analysis of the Sravakabhumi Manuscript* (Berkeley, Calif.: University of California Press, 1961), pp. 19–24.

13. See, in particular, Murti. See also Robinson.

7

WEAK DEPENDENCE RELATIONS

So far we have been talking about the causal relation in particular, but it should be clear that parallel sorts of reasoning apply to any relation which we care about. The relations we care about are those which must be adduced to explain the development of the kinds of events we care about, and the kinds of events we care about are precisely the ones that enter into chains of conditions leading to bondage and whose non-occurrences enter into chains of conditions leading to freedom. For the progress philosopher, the problem of speculative thought is to show that such chains contain elements within our control and that the chains have no gaps. To put this a different way, the relation between the members of these chains cannot be *too* strong, for although we can insure the non-gappiness of a chain whose members are related by a relation of necessity, we find that the elements of such a chain are out of our control. Nor can the relation be *too* weak, for the elements in a chain are then back in our control but the non-gappiness of the chain cannot be assured and skepticism remains unanswered.

I shall call a relation which is presumably too strong a "necessary" relation, and one which is presumably too weak a "contingent" relation. Two terms are related by a necessary relation when it is the case that, given the nature of those two terms, the relation could not but hold. More precisely, if A and B are related by necessary relation C, then it must be the case that if A did not hold C to B, it could not be A, and likewise if B did not hold C (or rather the reverse of C) to A, it could not be B. Clearcut cases of necessary relations are found in logical necessities, such as the relation between a son and a parent; if a child did not have a parent, he (or she) would not be a child, and if the parent did not have a child, he (or she) wouldn't be a parent. Two terms are contingently related when it is the case that each of the terms might not bear the relation to the other without ceasing to be what they are. For example, my chair is to the right of my desk but it could be to the left of it and still be my chair, and likewise my desk has not ceased to be mine or a desk by the shift in relative positions.

A necessary causal relation is too strong, since it renders man unable to grow unless he is by nature required to. It precludes spontaneity. It guarantees freedom-to, but at the cost of freedom-from. A contingent causal relation has the opposite defects. It is too weak, since it renders a man unable to grow unless he happens to do so quite by chance. It precludes control. It guarantees freedom-from, but at the cost of freedom-to.

Between necessary relations and contingent ones, however, there is plenty of scope for investigation. The general character of such relations as are not too strong or too weak will be that they are what I shall call dependence relations, relations of one-sided dependence, such that either one or the other but not both of the relata could be other than they are without affecting the remaining one. (I.e., to say that R is a dependence relation is to say that, of its two relata *x* and *y*, one depends on the other but the other does not depend on it.) The search for a satisfactory causal relation may then be described as the search for a causal relation of dependence. Formally speaking, the relation must be asymmetrical.

INHERENCE: THE NYĀYA-VAIŚEṢIKA DEPENDENCE RELATION

The Naiyāyika's inherence (*samavāya*) is intended to be such an asymmetrical dependence relation. Although it is not completely independent of the terms it connects, it is not dictated by the nature of those terms—or so the Naiyāyika claims. According to him, we find inherence connecting the following sets of relata: (1) wholes and the parts of which they are constituted; (2) particular qualities and the particular things which have those qualities; (3) particular motions (upwards, downwards, sideways, etc.) and the particular things which so move;

and (4) general properties and the particular things which they characterize.[a]

The Nyāya-Vaiśeṣika Theory of Whole and Part

The relation between the whole and its parts constitutes a unique feature of the Naiyāyika's theory. According to him, the whole is a distinct entity from the sum of its parts. Therefore, the relation between the whole and its parts is not too strong. But clearly the parts do in some way determine the nature of the whole, so that they are not completely different from that whole; thus the inherence relation is not too weak.

To take a stock example of the Naiyāyika's, inherence relates a pot and the pot-halves which "compose" it. The Naiyāyika, as we have seen, says that the pot-halves cause the pot; the pot-halves are the material cause of the pot. But although the material cause of a given pot A is the pair of pot-halves *a* and *b*, still A is not identical with *a* plus *b*. The mere existence of pot-halves *a* and *b* is not sufficient to produce a pot. If A equalled *a* plus *b*, there would be nothing to stop A from coming into existence before it does. This is the general point of one objection the *asatkāryavādin* has to the *satkāryavāda* view—if the effect pre-exists in the cause, why doesn't it come into existence as soon as the cause does? We saw in the previous chapter how this objection helped to force Īśvarakṛṣṇa to make an essential modification of his view which led in the direction of epistemologization. It is the resulting move toward a distinction between appearance and reality which the Naiyāyika is desperately trying to avoid. He fears that once such a distinction is allowed within the world—or within the map—there is no saving of progress philosophy. His theory of inherence is the cornerstone of his doctrine, for it is inherence which glues together the elements in the chains we care about, a glue which is strong enough to attach those elements but not so strong that they cannot become unglued.

Inherence in Gautama's Chain

The crucial use of inherence in the mapping program comes, however, not so much in relating whole to parts but in analyzing each of the members of Gautama's chain, which is the chain the Naiyāyika cares about most. Gautama's chain consisted of pain, birth, activity, defect, and wrong notion. Although inherence does not connect any of these

[a] In each of the four sets the first kind of entity mentioned (e.g., the whole) is said to "inhere in" the second (e.g., the parts). That which inheres in something is *samaveta;* that in which something inheres is *samavāyin*.

five to each other, it does, according to the Naiyāyika, help connect them all to a common locus, a Self (*ātman*).

There are many Selves according to the Nyāya-Vaiśeṣika account. Pain, defect, and wrong notion are specific characteristics (*guṇa*) of Selves.[1] That is, a particular wrong notion, or a certain sorrow, belongs to—i.e., inheres in—a particular Self. But these characteristics are not related by any necessary relation to the Self. They are not constitutive of a Self, or they could not be avoided except by annihilating the Self, an alternative which leads to leap thinking, and eventually to skepticism, so the Naiyāyika thinks. On the other hand, these characteristics cannot be completely unrelated to the Self; they cannot be independent and merely conjoined occasionally with the Self. If that were the case, as we saw, no explanation would be possible and no resolution to the doubts that gave rise to philosophy could be given. Gaining freedom would be at best a lucky accident.

Activity, the third member of the chain, is "the operating of speech, of mind, and of body,"[2] an operating in which the Self is involved as the underlying substrate or locus. Activity presupposes something which acts, and is related to that something, the Self, by inherence.

Finally, what about birth? At birth, a Self becomes related to some matter, its body. In this case, there is no direct inherence, but indirectly inherence plays its part, and that part is crucial. For an organism, according to the *Nyāyasūtras*, is always the locus of conscious activity as well as of enjoyment, and consciousness and enjoyment are *guṇas* of the Self. Under the influence of its *karma* (in Nyāya called *adṛṣṭa*), a Self comes to be associated with some atoms, and through the force of the *adṛṣṭa* these atoms group in appropriate ways to form a whole we call a body.

The *adṛṣṭa* of a Self inheres in the Self and is an instrumental cause of birth. However, the avoidance of rebirth is precisely what is involved in gaining freedom. The most important function of inherence is to explain how freedom can be gained. It is not gained, claims the Naiyāyika, by annihilating the Self, nor by annihilating the material of the universe, but rather by annihilating a relation between the Self and the qualities and matter which enchain it. Both the Self and matter—ultimate particles of matter—are eternal on the Naiyāyika's view, but a specific inherence relation is not, and freedom is the consequence of the annihilation of the particular inherence relation between a given Self and its specific characteristics as listed in Gautama's chain.

The first annihilation is of wrong notions. Inherence does not connect a Self and material particles directly. Rather, wrong knowledge is a quality of the Self and so is related to it by inherence, and this wrong knowledge is in turn related to matter by a chain of physical events. This chain runs from external occurrences and changes in matter to the activities of the sense-organs which result from them, and from those sensations to the *manàs,* an internal organ which sorts out the sense-impressions and passes them on one by one to the Self. When these events have taken place, knowledge arises, inhering in the Self. This knowledge may be right or wrong. If it is wrong, the result is bondage, following backwards through Gautama's chain. However, since the relation between knowledge and a Self is a dependence relation, the wrong knowledge can be destroyed without destroying the Self. This shows the possibility of complete freedom.

To see the Naiyāyika's theory in more detail, I shall next consider some of the objections to inherence and the account just summarized which are found in Indian philosophical literature. There are at least three major kinds of arguments, stemming from the immediate right (Jainism), the left (Buddhism), and the extremes (Śaṃkara's Advaita and Nāgārjuna's Mādhyamika views). There are other arguments which are also illuminating, but I shall not be able to survey them.[3]

The Jain argument against inherence. What the Jain wishes to force from the Naiyāyika is the admission that the things related by inherence according to the Naiyāyika are actually related by the relationship some call *bhedābheda* or identity-in-difference.[b] If this admission can be obtained, thinks the Jain, the independent entity the Naiyāyika calls inherence can be dispensed with.

The Naiyāyika is not disposed to make such an admission, however, because the Jain will go on to conclude that there are no relations as such in the world at all. The Jain's identity-in-difference is not a dependence relation; it is symmetrical, or at least so it seems on the surface. But as the Naiyāyika sees it, a symmetrical relationship cannot do the job projected by a progress philosopher, for it must be either too strong or too weak. He charges that the Jain can only avoid this difficulty by failing to ask the right questions about his identity-in-difference. The Jain, for

[b] I introduce here a technical convention useful in keeping clear the issues between Nyāya-Vaiśeṣika and Jainism in what follows. A "relation" is an *entity* which connects relata. A "relationship" is not an entity, or at any rate is not necessarily an entity. To say that a relationship exists between two things does not commit us to any entity performing that function. The Naiyāyika believes in relations; the Jain denies relations but finds it convenient to talk about relationships.

his part, denies that his is a symmetrical relationship. But we shall have to examine the Jain's positive theory in its proper place.

The Jain directs his criticism toward the nature of the things related by the inherence relation. The Naiyāyika has said that the relata are, in themselves, distinct—that's why, he adds, we need a third thing, inherence, to connect them. "But surely," the Jain remarks quietly, "every two distinct things are not connected by inherence!" "No," admits the Naiyāyika. "But then," continues the Jain, "what is it about those pairs of distinct things which *are* so connected that makes them fit for such a relation?" The traditional Nyāya-Vaiśeṣika answer to this is that the relata which are connected by inherence are inseparable (*ayutasiddha*).[4] This gives the Jain scope for attack. "What," he continues, "is meant by 'inseparability'?"

The Naiyāyika opines at this point that the ordinary meaning of "inseparable" is "located in the same place at the same time"; two things are said to be inseparable when the one cannot occur without the other occurring along with it, that is to say, when and where it does.[5] "Does that mean," the Jain presses on, "that the relata of an inherence relation have the same locus? But your own view prohibits this. According to you, for instance, the whole has for its locus the parts, and each part has for its locus some other parts—or again, a quality of a thing resides in that thing, while the thing resides in its parts, which on your own view are distinct from the whole.

Clearly the Naiyāyika needs a careful description of "inseparability," one which, presumably, will depend on a fairly sophisticated theory of space and time. In later thought, the Navya-nyāya or new school of Nyāya-Vaiśeṣika did in fact develop a highly complex theory of space and time, which I shall not try to explain here.[6] But suppose there were no such theory, or that such a theory as there is fails: what then? "Then," the Jain concludes, "I must suppose that what you mean by 'inseparable' is merely being non-different. But if that means that the relata are identical, you are in trouble, since identity is a necessary relation, causation becomes *satkāryavāda*, nothing new is ever produced, no change takes place, and freedom cannot become realized." The Jain is just as anxious to avoid this outcome as the Naiyāyika is. "Therefore I conclude that the non-difference of the relata must really be construed as an identity-in-difference. The whole and its parts are the same, and yet different. And if this is so, then there is no need for your inherence relation as a distinct entity; the relata are already related in the way you intend by their very nature." The Jain thinks he has clear sailing once the original admission is made, the admission that inseparability means non-difference.[7] But the Naiyāyika must be given his turn at rebuttal when we turn in the next chapter to the Jain's theory.

The Buddhist Critique of Inherence

The Naiyāyika turns now to meet the threat from the left. We can find a good example of the argument now to be considered in the work of a very argumentative Buddhist, Śāntarakṣita. His aim is not, as is the Jain's, to show that inherence should be dispensed with in favor of some other relationship, but rather to force the Naiyāyika to admit that there can be no persisting relation between *any* two entities—that all entities which we care about are momentary (*kṣaṇika*), non-persistent, fleeting. Śāntarakṣita feels that, despite his evident effort to avoid the traps of *satkāryavāda,* the Naiyāyika will eventually be forced into that trap because of his belief in persisting things. The only way to avoid the trap of reducing all relations to necessary ones and thus of ending in fatalism is, he believes, to hold firmly to the view that all relations between distinct things are relations of complete difference.

The Naiyāyika, for his part, feels that the trap of the extreme left—of positing relations that are too weak—is as dangerous as the other one, and that the Buddhist has fallen into it. Complete difference is no more asymmetrical than complete identity. If complete difference functions as the causal relation, it is too weak to depend on—we are merely spectators at the motion-picture show of existence, exerting no constraint upon events. The possibility of freedom cannot be demonstrated; there cannot even be any complete freedom, since there can be no freedom-to. The Buddhist has a way, so he thinks, of saving himself from the trap of which the Naiyāyika speaks; we shall discuss it later in this chapter. Now, however, our business is with the Buddhist's attack on inherence.

The oldest Nyāya-Vaiśeṣika texts, including the two sets of -Sūtras and several early commentators, put forth the view that not only does inherence persist, but that it is unitary and eternal. According to the old school, there is only one inherence; it is a sort of stuff, a glue we might say, which in some subtle fashion permeates the atmosphere, ready to stick together any two distinct but inseparable things. That is its unitary aspect. In addition, inherence is an eternal object, like a universal. When one pair of inherence-related things breaks up, that doesn't mean that inherence itself is destroyed—only that that particular part of the all-embracing inherence is reduced from actuality to potentiality.[8]

Why did these old theorists hold this apparently creaky view? The main reason for viewing inherence as eternal can be briefly stated, and the necessity of considering it a unity can be seen to follow from the same sort of reasoning. The reason why inherence must be eternal is that it must be around all the time to glue together Selves and their knowledges. If a particular inherence had to come into existence afresh to glue each Self-knowledge pair, one would have to inquire into the causal antecedents of that new inherence. And this is an awkward question from the Naiyāyika's point of view, for the following dilemma arises: either the Self was responsible for producing this particular bit of glue, or it was not. If the Self was responsible for the glue, then why did it allow the production of that bit of glue? And why is there such a problem of getting unglued? Renunciation seems unnecessary; we just stop gluing ourselves to knowledge—i.e., we stop thinking. On the other hand, if the Self was not a causal factor in the production of this particular bit of glue, then how can it hope to remove the glue, since the production of that glue was out of the Self's control? The doctrine that there is an eternal glue, without beginning, solves these difficulties, for it is evidently senseless to ask for the cause of something which is beginningless. However, is this eternal glue itself a unity or a plurality? Clearly, the point of introducing it as an eternal object is spoiled if it is a plurality—therefore it must be single as well as eternal.

The Buddhist imagines that if he can crack this theory he can crack the notion of the persistence of inherence as a distinct entity. Once inherence's eternality is refuted, it will not be hard, so he thinks, to convert the Naiyāyika to the Buddhist view of the world as a flux of momentary flashes of energy. And then there will be no room for doubting man's ability to enter the chain of causation and so to gain freedom.

Śāntarakṣita's first attack runs as follows. "If there's only one inherence, as you say, then there's no reason why, when we see a pot, we shouldn't say 'there's a cloth,' or why, when we see an elephant, we shouldn't think we're looking at a cow. Generally, if there's only one inherence or glue, then any two things that fall together into the glue ought to get glued together."

A Vaiśeṣika philosopher, Praśastamati,[9] springs to the defense. "No!" he cries, "even though there is only one glue, it only glues together those things which are related as locus and located, which are inseparable like the pot and its locus, the pot-halves."

"Really?" says Śāntarakṣita. "What is responsible for this peculiar limitation? It can't be this single, eternal inherence itself which relates each inseparable pair, or else inherence would be many, not one, and this is incompatible with eternality. Therefore it must be something else, say the conjunction between the two inseparable things. But if this be so, then what is the use of inherence? Conjunction is sufficient, and inherence becomes redundant."[c][10]

A second argument, addressed against the eternality of inherence is introduced by Śāntarakṣita. He asks how, if inherence is eternal, anything can ever get destroyed. This is a fundamental objection, because if it is correct, it implies that in the Naiyāyika's world one can never destroy the connection between a Self and its wrong notions. The Naiyāyika's idea is that, although wrong notions may be destroyed, the eternal inherence or glue carries on. The Buddhist first argues that whenever a relatum is destroyed, its relation to everything else is destroyed. The Naiyāyika grants that. Then, concludes the Buddhist, inherence is destructible. No, says the Naiyāyika, because even though *one* relatum is destroyed, the other still persists, glued to *its* locus. Thus, although wrong notion is destroyed, it does not follow that the Self does not persist in its inherence relations to other things, and thus inherence goes on.

At this point Śāntarakṣita unleashes his most powerful attack. He poses the following dilemma: when one relatum A (which we shall suppose has inhered in B) ceases to exist, what is it that *continues* to exist? Is it (a) the inherence which connected A to B, or (b) something else? If it is *that* inherence, then we have the absurdity of a relation without relata—a glue which is designed to connect A to B which persists even when there's no A. On the other hand, if it be something *other* than that inherence which continues to exist, then—the Buddhist triumphantly points out—inherence is clearly not a single entity, but just a collection of bits of glue.[11]

This is a very powerful argument, at least if we can go by the reactions of later Naiyāyikas. For of the two major varieties of thought in the "new school" of Nyāya-Vaiśeṣika, one variety accepts the conclusion of

[c] The Buddhist is relying on the fact that on Praśastamati's theory there is only one conjunction. He believes himself capable of showing the momentariness of anything which is admitted to be noneternal, e.g., conjunction, which is a type of quality that comes and goes as things come into and go out of contact. He knows that the Naiyāyika needs inherence as a distinct thing to connect the quality conjunction with the conjuncts. If the Naiyāyika loses inherence, his whole structure collapses. However, since the usual Naiyāyika theory about conjunction differs from Praśastamati's on the number of *saṃyoga* (see note 9 above), that portion of Śāntarakṣita's argument based upon Praśastamati's peculiar theory about conjunction fails to affect the mainstream of Nyāya-Vaiśeṣika.

the first prong of the dilemma (with reservations, needless to say), while the other school tries to defend the second prong. The philosopher Raghunātha, the leader of the second variety mentioned, capitulates to the second prong: "if inherence were one," he writes, "water would smell."[12] On his view there are indefinite distinct inherences. The other school of Navyanyāya, that of the late summarizer Viśvanātha, appears to accept the view that inherence is single and eternal, thus accepting the first prong of the dilemma—unconcerned, presumably, about the supposed absurdity of a relation without one of its relata.[13]

Raghunātha's view lets him in for nasty difficulties about causation. The main reason for holding the unity and eternality theory of inherence, as we saw, was to avoid having to discuss the cause of inherence. Raghunātha cannot avoid that discussion. Viśvanātha's view avoids the discussion, but at the expense of accepting what certainly seems at first sight absurd. But is it so absurd?

The Infinite Regress Argument Against Inherence

The argument which is generally conceded to be the most telling one against inherence, however, is neither that of the Jains nor of Śāntarakṣita. Śaṃkarācārya—usually thought of as India's greatest philosopher and who, if he was not a leap philosopher, fathered theories which could only lead in that direction—is content to refute the Nyāya-Vaiśeṣika theory of inherence by one argument alone. Nāgārjuna, the arch-dialectician of Mādhyamika Buddhism and the most famous exponent of Śūnyavāda, also depends primarily on the same argument. And it has, of course, a long and honorable history in Western thought, from Aristotle to Bradley. I am speaking, needless to say, of the infinite regress argument against the independent reality of relations.

We may consider the argument as it is formulated by Śaṃkara. He says: "According to you, Naiyāyika, the collocation of two distinct entities is a sufficient condition for their being glued together by inherence. Also, according to you, inherence itself is a distinct entity from the relata which it glues. It follows as a necessary consequence that there must be an infinite regress of a vicious variety. For let us suppose that two entities, *a* and *b,* are glued together by *c,* which is inherence. *a* and *c,* however, are two distinct entities which are collocated, and this, according to your own view, is sufficient to warrant there being a relation of inherence between them. Let us call that inherence *d.* Now *a* and *d* are two distinct entities which are collocated, and this leads us to *e* . . . and so on *ad infinitum.* And the consequence of an infinite regress is that nothing can ever get done. Therefore your view defeats the purpose for which it is intended."[14]

The argument is familiar. The only point we need consider is Śaṃkara's contention that the regress is of the vicious variety. Śaṃkara claims that his regress is vicious, for it involves the extension of self-residence, which we saw distinguished vicious from non-vicious *tarka* fallacies (pp. 79–83). In this case the regress runs from . . . *cba,* which resides in . . . *dcba,* which in turn resides in . . . *edcba,* and so on. This is not the case with the seed and the sprout, for seed *a* resides in sprout *b,* which resides in seed *c,* which resides in sprout *d,* and so on—involving no self-residence and hence no vicious regress.

The Naiyāyika is clearly called upon to answer Śaṃkara's charge, which if allowed to go unresolved threatens to wreck his theory of relations in general and causation in particular. The answer invariably given is succinctly stated by Śrīdhara in his *Nyāyakandalī*: "There is no other relation (to connect) inherence (to its relatum), for it exists by its very own nature, by itself alone (in relation to the relatum), and not by another relation."[15] But the inevitable question is, for the Naiyāyika himself, how should he describe the relation*ship* between inherence and its relatum.[d] And the Naiyāyika now finds himself in an embarrassing position. He has at least four alternatives open to him, none of which seems very pleasant.

(1) He may answer that the relationship is one of identity, that the relatum and its relation are precisely the same individual. However, this apparently won't do. For if, in the example Śaṃkara used, *a* is identical with *c* and *b* is identical with *c,* then surely it ought to follow that *a* is identical with *b,* and everything in the universe becomes identical. That would not only be *satkāryavāda,* it would be sheer monism, welcome possibly to Advaitins but anathema to the Naiyāyika. The only way to defend this first alternative appears to be by denying that identity is transitive, i.e., by denying that if $a = b$ and $b = c$, then $a = c$. Clearly, this is not a happy way out, to say the least.

(2) He may try to say that *a* and *c* are completely different. But Śaṃkara's argument is itself sufficient to turn him back from that road

[d] That is, the objector may grant that in the Naiyāyika's sense of "relation" there is no relation between *a* and *c,* but at the same time insist that their relationship to one another ought to be accounted for. The Naiyāyika's way of speaking allows him to say "there is no relation" when what he *means* is "there is no entity falling into any one of the seven categories of entities that I accept which functions as a connector between *a* and *c*."

unless he should change his general premiss about what is a sufficient condition for two things to inhere (i.e., unless he gives up inseparability as the mark of entities capable of inhering). And if he gives up that premiss, he will fall into one of the traps that Śāntarakṣita and the Jains have set for him.

(3) He may say that *a* and *c* are both identical and different. Considered as that which is related to *b, a* is identical with *c,* but considered as that which is the relation with *b, a* is different from *c,* since in the latter case *c* is a relatum and *a* the relation. This, however, is just what the Naiyāyika is trying to avoid; it is just the use of phrases such as "considered as . . ." or "from the point of view of . . ." which herald the move toward epistemologization—and the Naiyāyika sees only too well, or thinks he does, where *that* move leads.

(4) Of course, he may throw up his hands on the whole matter and become a leap philosopher. He may say "well, you're right; I can't explain how *a* is related to *c,* but it really doesn't matter since none of the things we care about (freedom, cessation of pain, eradication of wrong notions, etc.) are related to things of this world—freedom is a transcendental affair." This is precisely what Śaṃkara and Nāgārjuna want him to do. As a good Naiyāyika, needless to say, he will not, at least before a thorough exploration of the first three paths.

That exploration goes on throughout the history of Navyanyāya, and creates a fascinating subject for investigation. It is in the works of the new school that we hear of "self-linking connectors" (*svarūpasambandha*). As well as this writer can make out, these represent a considered attempt to follow out, despite its unpleasantness, the route marked out by the first alternative above. A self-linking connector seems to be a dependence relation additional to inherence, an "identity" such that it does *not* follow that because one thing bears this relation to a second, the second bears it to the first. This leads us down a long, complicated, and little-understood path, and we must leave it to scholars. But the mere fact of the development of such a counterintuitive theory gives testimony to the unflinching devotion of this school toward a progress-philosophy solution to the doubts which create speculation in Indian philosophy.[16]

I have gone into the Naiyāyika theory of inherence in some detail precisely because of this devotion and because the theory which has resulted constitutes what is undoubtedly the most thorough-going attempt at a "realistic" ontology in Indian thought. It is "realistic" in the sense that it makes a major effort to keep everything on the same "level," to take at face value the analysis of causation and freedom which gave rise to the doubts we have referred to, and to force a solution of the problem which generates those doubts—a solution which does not leave the plane of every-day objects, people, and events and resolves the doubt without revising the common-sense conception of complete freedom as something which is not only worth working for but capable of attainment. But there are, as we have already mentioned, other progress philosophers, notably certain Buddhists and Jains, as well as the philosophers Prabhākara and Kumārila, who are as seriously concerned to maintain a progress theory of the left-hand variety, but who for one reason or another cannot accept the Naiyāyika's inherence theory unqualifiedly as it stands.

The Positions of Prabhākara and Kumārila

The Buddhists cannot accept inherence because it seems to them too strong. The Jains cannot accept it because it seems to them too weak. Prabhākara and Kumārila present an interesting study of positions in between these three basic stances. Prabhākara stands somewhere to the left of Nyāya-Vaiśeṣika, but distinctly to the right of all Buddhists, as he does not accept their flux theory. He accepts inherence as a category, but feels that it is not sufficient to do the job that the Naiyāyika wishes it to do when it comes to considering the relation between the knowing process and the external world.[17] Kumārila stands between Nyāya-Vaiśeṣika and Jainism, i.e., to the right of the Naiyāyikas but short of the full-blooded "non-absolutism" (*anekāntavāda*) of the Jains. His differences, too, from his neighbors stem largely from epistemological concerns.[18] We shall be seeing more of both these thinkers when we turn to the epistemological side of Indian thought in Chapter 10.

SIMILARITY: THE BUDDHIST DEPENDENCE RELATION

I turn next to the attempts of the progress philosophers among the Buddhists to construct or prepare the way for an adequate, accurate, consistent, and clear map of the universe that permits complete freedom's attainment. We have seen how the fear of an unalterable universe led the Buddhists to their doctrine of momentariness (*kṣaṇikavāda*). This doctrine is enunciated early in Buddhist thought—according to tradition in the words of the Buddha himself. The opposing position, upholding the persistence of things, is condemned as heresy regularly in Buddhism from earliest times. The problem for all Buddhist theories, then, is to avoid complete fragmentation, to explain how we can guarantee that freedom is possible in a world where nothing lasts long enough to have anything whatever happen to it.

I have already described the Buddha's twelve-fold chain of causation and pointed out that it is a chain of necessary conditions and that therefore the opposite of each term in the chain is a sufficient condition for the absence of the next one. The problem remaining, then, is how one brings about the production of the opposite of some member of the chain? Is it possible for an individual through his own decision and effort to effectuate the nonoccurrence of a term in the chain? Can one enter the chain?

The two places where it seems most likely one can enter the chain are at the first and eighth terms—ignorance and desire. To produce sufficient conditions for the absence of ignorance or the absence of desire, however, and to be sure that our efforts will succeed, we must be able to avoid a necessary condition for ignorance or desire. If we cannot do so, then freedom is out of our hands; there is no way of entering the chain except by accident. We seem doomed (unless a way can be found) to a spectator's existence, watching helplessly the round of the wheel of life and death, sorrow and rebirth.

Relations in the Abhidharmakośa

The Buddhist's unique problem in searching for a dependence relation is that he starts with the assumption that everything is fleeting, nonpersisting. Since nothing persists, it will be more difficult for the Buddhist than for others to get into his ontology a relation which is stronger than a merely empirical one. A persisting substance, we might admit common-sensically, is able to exert force upon other substances and so affect the outcome of events, but a momentary event doesn't last long enough to affect the outcome of anything else except itself. It is this forcelessness of the elements of reality which seems to render the Buddhist helpless to explain our ability to enter forcefully into chains of events so as to bring about desired results.

But the Buddhist replies that he has no objection to saying that events have power or force, if that merely means that events are by their very nature forceful. In fact, says Vasubandhu, author of *Abhidharmakośa,* everything is a *saṃskāra*—nearly everything anyway—and therefore forceful, exerting activity (for etymologically the root *kṛ* means "to do" or "to make").[19] This doesn't mean that each event has a distinct quality called "its energy," but that the event is itself energy. So no special explanation need be given concerning the forcefulness of events. It is along these lines that the Buddhist at first hopes to avoid the sting of the charge that we have suggested, that his must be a spectator view of the universe, that on his assumptions human beings can never be involved as agents in the course of things.

If human beings *can* be involved in the universe as agents, how is this possible when everything is separate from everything else? In fact, what is a human being? The Buddhist answer to this is unequivocal: there is no Self in the sense of an enduring substance underlying change; what we ordinarily call the "Self" is a group of events. But surely, one might object, not just *any* group; there must be something which holds the stream of events called "me" together and allows me to say that "I" am involved in the course of things. The author of *Abhidharmakośa* admits this: the flux of momentary forces is arranged in patterns (*saṃtāna*). He holds that there is a ubiquitous sort of force called assimilation (*prāpti*) which holds events past, present, and future together in a single series. Furthermore there is another force, nonassimilation (*aprāpti*) which keeps foreign events from getting mixed into series where they are not appropriate.[20]

But this still doesn't explain how one stream can enter into another. Do the streams of energy-moments carry on independently of each other, or do they interact with one another? If the former, in what sense can "I" enter into the course of things, except in the rather unexciting sense that I'm already one—or rather several—events in that course? And if the latter, what saves me from being at the mercy of the other streams with which I interact? For that matter, what saves me from being at the mercy of my past actions, since "I" am now defined as a stream with such-and-such members? How, in other words, can I ever act voluntarily, in the sense that I could have done otherwise?

We are in effect facing the question raised previously: how can the stream of events known as "I" enter into a chain of causation and produce, not another link in the chain, but just the opposite, the nonoccurrence of that link? For that is what it will take to gain freedom. The *Abhidharmakośa* presents us with an elaborate theory of some seventy-five *dharmas,* or elements, outdoing even Nyāya-Vaiśeṣika in its pluralism of causal factors—but the question which remains at the end is the same as that with which we began: how can that which is by law supposed to produce A in fact be made to produce non-A?

Here Vasubandhu makes the natural move under the circumstances. He tells us that there are nonforceful (*asaṃskṛta*) elements, events which do not leave any traces, and that under the influence of them the extinction of the rest of the elements, i.e., their nonoccurrence, takes place, inevitably leading to the condition of an *arhat* or noble being, who then needs only to wait to achieve *nirvāṇa*.[21] There are two things to be said about this.

First, the admission of nonforceful and therefore presumably noncausative events threatens to abrogate the strictness of the Buddhist law of causation, unless another sense of "causative" can be found besides that of "force-exerting" (i.e., trace-producing). And once the strict law of "dependent origination" so prized by all Buddhists is given up, there is not much if any reason for not capitulating to Nyāya-Vaiśeṣika. For a nonforceful element is merely another way of describing a relation or a universal, and once nonforceful elements are admitted, one's theory has most of the problems that visited the Naiyāyika. But perhaps Vasubandhu can get out of this. He could say, "Well, the *asaṃskṛtadharma*s are nonforceful, but still they exert influence insofar as they bring about the extinction of the other elements." But in that case what was the point of describing the other elements as "forceful," since to be forceful is presumably the same thing as to exert influence? We have now to reckon with two kinds of force—i.e., two senses of "causal relation"—(1) the kind which holds between ordinary elements, and (2) the kind which holds between the nonforceful elements and the forceful ones, obstructing their force. We shall want to follow out this distinction in later developments of Buddhist theory.

The second thing to be said about a nonforceful element is: what is *its* cause? How can we produce nonforceful elements that block development of wrong notions, bad habits, and eventually the circle of transmigration itself? Vasubandhu tells us that nonforceful elements do have a cause—and that cause is insight (*prajñā*). When the forceful elements, the ordinary events which constitute the lives of ordinary men, are suffused with this insight, we are told, these ordinary elements begin to fail to cooperate, attachment to them fades, and one is on the path to *nirvāṇa*.[22]

The next question just about asks itself, however: is insight an element or not? According to Vasubandhu it is, being one of the general mental faculties (*cittamahābhūmika*).[23] If so, it too must belong in a chain of causation—and how do we enter *that* chain? We are forced once again to the conclusion that there must be two kinds of causal relations, one connecting forceful elements with other forceful ones, the other connecting forceful elements (like insight) with nonforceful elements.

There is a widely-accepted theory in contemporary Western thought, which goes back at least to Hume, which maintains that freedom and determinism are compatible since freedom means lack of constraint and determinism doesn't have anything to do with constraint.[24] But there is serious reason to believe that Hume's theory doesn't go deep enough or far enough unless causal relations are distinguished into at least two varieties as Vasubandhu does.

This claim will surely provoke opposition and needs to be defended. It will not be out of place to suggest briefly the reason why it is that Hume can rest content, claiming that freedom is compatible with determinism, while Vasubandhu cannot accept this resolution. The difference between Hume's position and that of the *Abhidharmakośa* lies in the difference between their accounts of freedom. Hume thinks of freedom as freedom *from,* i.e., as lack of constraint. He argues that in ordinary parlance we call a man free, or his action a free one, just if he is not being constrained to do something by someone else who is exerting force upon him. This is good enough for Hume, but not for Vasubandhu. Vasubandhu's account of freedom includes not only freedom *from* constraint but also freedom *to* fulfill one's capabilities. On Hume's view of freedom, at least as far as Hume takes it, a man who is at the mercy of his own habits is as free as one who is in control of his habits, since neither can be described as being constrained by external forces. Vasubandhu would find this position shallow, since, he may argue, freedom-from is worth obtaining only in order to gain freedom-to, self-improvement, and eventually complete freedom. He may point out that in a more important sense "constraint" is the opposite, not of freedom-from, but of freedom-to. The problem of determining the necessary conditions of freedom-to is at least as difficult as that of determining the necessary conditions of freedom-from. It is clear that lack of constraint in Hume's sense of "constraint" is not a sufficient condition for freedom-to; it is not clear whether it is even a necessary condition. That is the deeper meaning of the problem of causation in particular, and relations in general, which is being discussed in this chapter. The question might be posed thus: granted that freedom-from is a necessary condition for *complete* freedom—*mokṣa* or *nirvāṇa*—does one gain this complete freedom by accepting the constraint of external forces in order to initiate habits which discipline a personality toward freedom-to, or does one rather gain freedom-to by destroying habits in such a way that their destruction does not itself constitute a constraining force in that sense of constraint which is opposed to freedom-to? It is a paradoxical possibility that, although complete freedom requires freedom-from, the path to complete freedom may involve the sacrifice of freedom-from in order to gain more freedom-to. The "two kinds of causation" which we find Vasubandhu toying with are the metaphysical counterparts of, on the one hand, the kind of causality which is typical of those events which breed habits, produce mental traces, and perpetuate their kind just as events in the physical world seem to do, and, on the other hand, the kind of causality which may be hoped to obstruct the occurrence of certain kinds of events without breeding habits, traces, and chains of events in their turn.

Vasubandhu's problem—and his problem is that of Buddhism and indeed of all Indian progress philosophy—is how to understand this latter kind of causality. It is a problem which Hume never gets to, since he assumes without question, following the libertarianism of his time and tradition, that freedom-from is the only kind of freedom worth troubling about. But once the problem is posed, we can see the pressures leading Buddhism toward what I have been calling "epistemologization." For this latter kind of causality, pertinent to Vasubandhu's "nonforceful elements," is a kind which is never clearly exhibited in the physical world. There every event has its repercussions; there there is nothing new under the sun. To find nonforceful causality we must, it seems, seek within the human being to what is internal for him, his mental states or, possibly, his attitudes, e.g., devotion (*bhakti*). Attitudes seem to exert influence on the world without themselves being events; a man's "posture" (e.g., relaxed, commanding, doubting) colors the "external" events of the world without actually being one of those events.

So Vasubandhu turns inward to find the nonforceful elements, and hits upon the conception of insight (*prajñā*) as being at once a forceful element (as thinking [*mati*]) and yet capable of being transformed into the cause of nonforceful elements. According to legend, this conversion of the outer-directed Vasubandhu, the metaphysician of the *Abhidharmakośa,* to the inner-directed Vasubandhu, the epistemologist of the *Vijñaptimātratāsiddhi,* is supposed to have taken place through the proselytizing activity of his brother Asaṅga. Leaving aside this tradition, we can see in any case the effects of the inward-turning process in passages toward the end of the *Abhidharmakośa,* which are said to mark the transition from the Vaibhāṣika to the Sautrāntika position.

In the *Abhidharmakośa,* instead of two connected chains of causality, one of which is, so to speak, the complement of the other (I am referring to the relation between the chain of necessary conditions A, B, C . . . and the chain of sufficient conditions ~A, ~B, ~C . . .) we have now two different kinds of chains, different because connected by distinct kinds of causal relations. The chain of necessary conditions, the Buddha's twelve-fold chain, is the epitome of the first of these new chains. The second of them starts with insight, which is a condition of some kind for the nonco-operation of the other elements, which in turn is a condition for the complete removal from that stream (known as "I") of all forceful elements, only the nonforceful one remaining.[e] This nonforceful element is a condition for final realization or *parinirvāṇa*.[25] To the author of the *Abhidharmakośa,* worried over the problem of how insight could be both a forceful element and yet breed nonforceful elements, this change of view must have been extremely attractive.

Indeed it is not unreasonable. There is certainly an air of paradox in being told that we can use the same energy which continually breeds binding habits and dissatisfaction to gain freedom from these very things. The paradox is dissipated once we assume that there is not one chain, but two: one physical, one epistemological. In addition, the new view is satisfying for another reason: it suggests that one can attain *nirvāṇa* by training one's understanding only. One does not need to practice extreme acts of physical renunciation, or at least he need only do this if it is absolutely necessary for him in order to gain insight.

In fact, this new orientation is so attractive that one can hardly help generalizing it to include all the mental elements, so that phyical chains are connected in general by different causal relations from mental ones. What matters it, even though our bodies be governed by strictly deterministic laws, if our minds are free from these laws? As long as the mental events are governed by *some* laws we cannot fall into skepticism. The Sautrāntika in the discussion of the latter portions of *Abhidarmakośa* leans toward making *all* mental elements nonforceful, without denying that they can "influence" other elements.

Specifically, the Sautrāntika argues that the stream of consciousness which makes up "me" doesn't *do* anything. Here is a bit of the discussion:

> [Question] But the Sūtra says that a knowledge *knows* its object. What is knowledge doing here?
>
> [Sautrāntika's answer] Nothing at all! Very simply, it comes to be co-ordinately (*sādṛśya*) with the object. Just as an effect, although it does nothing, is said to result from its cause, reflect the cause, because it comes to be co-ordinately with the cause, so a knowledge, although it gets nothing done with respect to its object, is said to know its object because it comes to be co-ordinately with the object.

[e] In all this I am ignoring space (*ākāśa*), which is also a nonforceful element. It is easy to see a part of the rationale for its being so dubbed—while the *arhat* is waiting for final *nirvāṇa,* unaffected by his environment, where does he wait?

This is perhaps the earliest passage in which the word *sādṛśya* (sometimes *sārūpya:* "co-ordination" or "similarity") is used in the very important technical sense that will bulk large in later philosophy in this tradition. Let us see how Vasubandhu, speaking now as Sautrāntika or "epistemologically oriented," explains this co-ordination.

> This co-ordination of knowledge consists in its being an aspect of the object (*tadākāratā*). Because of this co-ordination we say that a knowledge cognizes its object, which is only one of its causes: the sense-organ is also a cause of the knowledge, but we don't say that a knowledge cognizes the sense-organ because the knowledge doesn't grasp an aspect of the sense-organ. . . . This manner of speaking, namely "Knowledge knows," is again justifiable from another point of view. Some later moments of knowledge come to be with respect to an object; an earlier moment is the cause of the later moment. The knowledge is thus the cause of the later knowledge; it is for this reason termed the agent (*kartṛ*) since it is the cause. We attribute to it an activity of knowing as we attribute to a bell the activity of sounding or to a lamp the activity of moving.
>
> 'The lamp moves,' we say: let us see of what the movement of the lamp consists. 'Lamp' is the name attributed by metaphor to an uninterrupted series of moments of fire (i.e., of light) that one considers as a unity. When one of the later moments is born in another place from the preceding moment, we say that the lamp moves: but there exists no 'mover' apart from or distinct from the moments of fire. In the same way we metaphorically call by the name 'knowledge' a series of thoughts: when a moment of thought comes to be relatively to a new object, we say that the knowledge knows that object.[26]

Vasubandhu is here trying to work himself out of a serious variety of the mind-body problem. Consciousness is nonforceful; it doesn't *do* anything. But if so, how can it "influence" other events? The metaphor is imaginative—consciousness "influences" events just as the lamp "influences" the objects its light falls upon. Here we have the first step in the Buddhist's most important contribution to progress philosophy, his theory of co-ordination as the dependence relation that explicates causality properly. Essentially, the Sautrāntika speaker in the quoted passages is appealing to what in the history of modern Western philosophy is called "psycho-physical parallelism." Knowledge doesn't interact with its object, so that it cannot breed bad habits, *karma,* which may bind the personality; instead it is "co-ordinate" with it, it comes to be at the same time as its object and contains or exhibits an "aspect" (*ākāra*) of the object.

But so far this co-ordination is not a *dependence* relation, for the object depends on its correlated knowledge just as much as the knowledge depends on the object. The relation so far has not been shown to be asymmetrical. And as we have seen, progress philosophers have to find a dependence relation, an asymmetrical one, if they are to hold that we progress toward complete freedom by destroying, i.e., producing the complement of, a relation and thereby destroying (or changing) one of its relata but not the other.

What the Sautrāntika has said, therefore, is a start, but it is not enough. Three directions of development offer themselves. One can argue that the object depends on the knowledge, and try to explain in what sense of "dependence" this is so. This is the move of the school of Vasubandhu author of *Vijñaptimātratāsiddhi,* the school I shall call Yogācāra, as I explained above. Or one can argue that the knowledge depends on the object and again one will have to explain in what sense of "depends." This is the move of the so-called "Buddhist logicians," namely Dignāga, Dharmakīrti, and their followers. Finally, one may give up the search for a dependence relation and settle for a symmetrical one, trying to explain away the difficulties so strongly felt by the progress philosopher. This last is the route of the leap philosopher, followed in Buddhism by Nāgārjuna and his Mādhyamika school.

The two types of progress Buddhism described above are sometimes both called Vijñānavāda, and it can now be seen why this is so. Both are at one in what they want to show: that one of the relata of the co-ordination relation can be destroyed without the other being destroyed too. They both agree that the relation in question is an epistemological one, relating the idea to the known. Where they differ is in their decision about which relatum can be destroyed. But even here, their difference is not as decisive as I have so far made it appear, for the Yogācāra, although arguing that the object can be destroyed without the idea of it also being destroyed, makes what remains—the idea—look very much like what the other school calls the object. And the Buddhist logicians, although arguing that the idea can be destroyed without the object also being destroyed, makes what remains—the object—look very much like that which the other school calls the idea. Let us see how this is.

Similarity in Yogācāra

Vasubandhu and his followers argue that of the two, external object and internal idea, the latter is more stable; the former depends upon the latter and, by comparison with it, is "unreal." The reason given is that we know from experience that there are perceptions which do not correspond to any objects, e.g., dreams and hallucinations, while we never experience an object without having ideas. What we are primarily interested in, however, is the relevance of this view of the Yogācāra to the problem of how freedom is possible. How does subjective idealism of Vasubandhu's sort help? To explain this, we may look closely at one of Vasubandhu's short treatises on Yogācāra, the *Triṃśika*.[27]

First of all, what is it that becomes free? This is a puzzling question from the first for the Buddhist, since he has already assumed that there is no persisting self and yet goes on talking about freedom. The general Buddhist reply to this question, however, is to say that what becomes free, although strictly speaking a flux of discrete momentary flashes of energy, nevertheless has a kind of identity through time insofar as it manifests a pattern, like a wave in the ocean.

Vasubandhu adumbrates this general viewpoint somewhat. He distinguishes three kinds of patterns (*saṃtāna*), and although he describes them epistemically, i.e., as kinds of knowledge, it is clear from the way he treats them that they are as ontological as anything can be within Buddhism. These three kinds of patterns are related by the dependence relation of co-ordination or similarity; they are arranged in three tiers.

The bottom tier, on which the other two depend, he calls the *ālaya-vijñāna,* the "abode-consciousness." This pattern of moments is made up of what the Buddhists call *vāsanā*s, mental traces which lead to habits, which in turn lead to particular thoughts and deeds and to particular rebirths in subsequent lives. This "storehouse of consciousness," as it is sometimes called, is like the Self (*ātman*) of the Hindus in many respects, although differing in its constitution. Freedom is the laying bare of this pure consciousness, in which state it is unsullied by the particular manifestations of consciousness which characterize the waking or the dream states.

The other two tiers or patterns depend ultimately on this one, and are caused by the *vāsanā*s that arise in it. The second tier of consciousness is called "mind-consciousness" (*manovijñāna*), and may also be called "internal consciousness," not because its seat is internal but because its object, in a sense, is. This consciousness tells us about ourselves. Vasubandhu says, "it is always accompanied by the four evil desires, namely, ignorance of the self, view of the self (as being real and permanent), self-pride and self-love, and by touch, etc. (volition, feeling, thought, and cognition)."[28]

The third tier or pattern is empirical consciousness, i.e., our consciousness of the "external world." The objects entertained in this form of consciousness are the everyday objects of the senses.

Each tier depends on the one below it. We wouldn't have experience of objects as objects unless we distinguished them from ourselves as knowing subjects; this latter discrimination is effected by the *manovijñāna,* and so its functioning is a necessary condition for empirical consciousness. It follows that if we wish to destroy the habits bred by attachment to external objects by destroying those objects, we must destroy the cause of their externality, which is the *manovijñāna.* But to destroy the *manovijñāna,* the internal consciousness, one must destroy that which gives rise to it, something in the *ālayavijñāna* which activates the *vāsanā*s which, arising in the *ālayavijñāna,* constitute the causes of the erroneous mental impressions about ourselves.

The Yogācāra thinks, therefore, that it is not possible to have empirical knowledge without consciousness of self as other than object, but that it is possible to have consciousness of self without consciousness of object—in *manovijñāna.* The idea of "object" depends upon that of "I," and not vice-versa. But further, the idea of "I" depends on the *vāsanā*s latent in the *ālayavijñāna* and not vice-versa. Thus the *Yogācāra* has offered us a dependence relation between *ideas* as his analysis of cause. Freedom is possible, since to become free from the bad habits experienced in empirical consciousness and in mental consciousness one can now see that he must anaesthetize the *vāsanā*s in the *ālayavijñāna.* Can one do this? Certainly, by avoiding the bad habits and practising the right ones, and eventually by learning the attitude of nonattachment.

The co-ordination between conditioning *vāsanā* and conditioned consciousness at the mental or empirical level guarantees freedom-to, while the dependence of the empirical world of physical things upon the mental world, which in turn depends on the *ālayavijñāna,* guarantees freedom-from. Vasubandhu and his school frequently make appeal to dreams as their model. Just as we understand that in dreams the mental traces produce images which correspond to them in the sense of reflecting, though perhaps deviously, the characteristics of those traces, so the Yogācāra thinks that in waking experience the *vāsanā*s, functioning now under the rubric of "I," generate sense-objects which are conditioned by the characteristics of "I"; since these last are under our control, although not easy to control, we are the masters of our progress toward freedom, and not at the mercy of either the physical objects or the ideas in our mental world of dreams. We shall see this model again in Advaita Vedānta.

The major criticisms of the Yogācāra position come from the Mādhyamikas on the left and from Śaṃkara on the right. Both sets of critics are leap philosophers, and their common purpose is to disabuse the Yogācāra of his feeling that he must make a map which turns around a dependence relation. Vasubandhu wants to make the objective elements in knowledge depend on the subjective elements, but, argue the leap theorists, subject and object interdepend. There is as much reason to say that an external impression of an object depends on an object as there is to say that it depends on a subject. Granted one must have both subject and object to have an instance of empirical knowledge, why does the Yogācāra downgrade the object and glorify the subject?

Śaṃkara adds the following kind of backing to this general criticism. According to the Yogācāra, he argues, the storehouse of consciousness is supposed to contain a *variety* of *vāsanās*. What is responsible for this variety? Since the *vāsanās* in themselves have no objective content—they aren't traces of something or habits with respect to something—on what principle are they individuated?[29] The Yogācāra is tempted at this point to reply that the variety of *vāsanās* is beginningless, but Śaṃkara will quickly point out that what is in question is not the cause of the *vāsanās* collectively but distributively. What, that is to say, is the special cause of the differentiation of each *vāsanā* from the next? Is it not, after all, that each *vāsanā* is characterized by an essential relation to a specific object or class of objects? And if so, the Yogācāra attempt to dispense altogether with objects fails.

Similarity in the Buddhist Logicians

We return now to examine the second of the three directions of development which faced Buddhism when it had taken stock of the Sautrāntika notion of similarity. This second line takes the object as more fundamental than the subject. It was espoused, according to tradition, by Dignāga, Dharmakīrti and their commentators, including such as Dharmottara, Jinendrabuddhi and Vinītadeva.

Where the Yogācāra emphasized the conceptual side of knowledge over the perceptual, making the latter depend on the former, Dignāga's school reverses the order, making concepts depend on percepts. In words which are natural for the purpose of translating the Sanskrit terms in question,[30] the Yogācāra claims that the mental is more *real* than the physical, while the Buddhist logicians claim the reverse. The word "real" here is applied to that one of the two relata of a dependence relation which does not get destroyed when the relation gets destroyed. (This much of the meaning of "real" is, I believe, a common designation throughout process philosophy in India, whether Buddhist, Hindu, or Jain.) Now Dignāga and Dharmakīrti, who believe that the object or "thing-in-itself" is more real than the ideas we have of it, emphasize this theory by using a particularly interesting term to describe the nature of reality. They say that reality has *arthakriyātva,* the character of doing something or, as William James might have put it, of making a difference. We may distinguish this as the *criterion* of reality for this school of thought, as contrasted with the description of its *nature* in terms of dependence.

Reality, then, is a steady stream of point-instants of energy, momentary forceful occurrences which "do something," which are constantly correlated with others in recurrent patterns. In addition to their function as occasions for later events in those patterns, though, they also, through the dependence-relation of similarity, cause a phenomenon known as conceptualization, involving a differentiation of a concept into two polar notions, the "I" and the "that." Concepts are unreal, since they don't do anything. They are erroneous, for they clothe the uncharacterized point-instants of energy with attributes which are distinguished for the satisfaction of the erroneously distinguished "I." All conceptualization, therefore, is erroneous for the Buddhist logician, and conceptualization is the necessary condition for bondage which can be broken to obtain freedom. To gain freedom, we must train ourselves not to think of an "I" distinct from a "that," and to do that, we must train ourselves not to think of "thats" clothed in different attributes. By doing this, we gain freedom; we also gain a direct insight into the things-in-themselves which constitute the stream of reality. Science, therefore, properly understood, constitutes the path toward salvation; and this explains why Dignāga and Dharmakīrti, with such an apparently mystical or anti-intellectual view about freedom, nevertheless contributed more, perhaps, to the development of Indian logic than any others in the history of Indian thought.

The Buddhist logicians develop serious criticisms of their own position, however. I shall mention two, the less disturbing one first. If similarity, the dependence relation in question, links something real to something unreal, the question arises about similarity itself—is it real or unreal? If it is real, then since to be real is to do something, what does this similarity do? The notion of "doing something" then comes under analysis. Clearly, the sense of "doing something" must be—can only be for the Buddhist—the relation between two moments in the flux such that the first is followed by the second, and such that both the first and second moments are "real." But if similarity "does something" then concepts become as real as their causes, and this is clearly not what the Buddhist logicians want to say.

On the other hand, if similarity is unreal, then it doesn't do anything; thinking cannot affect reality. But this seems to do an injustice to whatever it is that *really* is going on when a thought occurs. Granted that it is not true at that moment that a *thought* is occurring—that is, it is not *really* true—still *something* must be occurring in the flux of reality. And, most important, is our thinking capable of altering the reality that the next moment will bring? Because if not, how in the world can we hope to get to freedom? If we can't affect reality, it is hard to see how we can bring about *real* freedom for ourselves; at best, we can only bring about apparent freedom.

As an answer to this line of criticism, the logicians appear to have developed an ingenious theory about similarity, which I shall merely mention here and discuss at more length in a later chapter. This is the peculiar theory of *apoha* or *bhedāgraha,* the theory that when we know something as the same as a second thing, what we really ought to say is that we don't know it as different. The usefulness of this theory in connection with the issues now under discussion is this: since similarity is now to be understood as a negative thing, one can (perhaps) construe it as not doing anything and so not affecting reality, yet allowing us to gain freedom by approximation, so that apparent freedom coincides with real freedom after all!

The more serious criticism is just once again that urged by Nāgārjuna and Śaṃkara against the Yogācāras. Knowledge, they argue, requires both a subject and an object. The Yogācāras err by downgrading the object; Dignāga and Dharmakīrti err by downgrading the subject. If there is any dependence here, it is interdependence—subject and object are both dependent on each other. But if *that* is so, argues Nāgārjuna, there is no substratum or seat of freedom, and others who look for one are wasting their time. The Buddha meant just what he said, argues Nāgārjuna. *Everything* is interdependent with everything else. Therefore, since there is nothing more real than anything else, there is no progress toward freedom. Freedom must be differently understood. I shall try to suggest in Chapter 11 how Nāgārjuna understands it.

NOTES

1. On the peculiarities of the Nyāya-Vaiśeṣika category of "specific quality" (*guṇa*), see K. H. Potter, "Are the Vaiśeṣika *guṇas* Qualities?" *Philosophy East and West* IV, No. 3, 259–264 (1954) and "More on the Vaiśeṣika *guṇas*," *ibid.*, VII, Nos. 1–2, 57–60 (1957).

2. *Nyayabhasya*, p. 42.

3. For such other arguments, see Bhaduri, pp. 241–244; Tatia, pp. 163–164; Santaraksita, pp. 451 ff.

4. *Vaisesika Sutras* (VII.2.13), p. 233, explains why cause and effect are not related by any other relation: "Because of their inseparability, effect and cause cannot be related by contact or disjunction" (*yutasiddhyabhāvāt kāryakāraṇayoḥ saṃyogavibhāgau na vidyate*). See *Indian Philosophical Studies*, p. 111.

5. *Vaisesika Sutras* (VII.2.26) defines inherence as "that because of which we say about the cause and the effect together 'This here'" (*ihedamiti yataḥ kāryakāraṇayoḥ samavāyaḥ*).

6. See Bhaduri, pp. 183–228; Raghunatha (1.1–3.2), pp. 21–25.

7. For this argument in detail, see Mookerjee, pp. 228 ff., 307; Tatia, pp. 163–164 and references given there.

8. See Śaṃkara Miśra's commentary in *Vaisesika Sutras* (VII.2.26), pp. 243–244, for an animated defense of this old theory by a modern exponent.

9. This is the only mention of "Praśastamati" of which I know. The reference might be to "a member of the school of Praśasta(pāda)," except that "Praśastamati" holds the view that there is only one *saṃyoga* (conjunction), while Praśastapada holds that there are many *saṃyogas*. See *Santaraksita*, p. 457; Prasastapada, pp. 302–303.

10. This discussion represents the substance of Śāntarakṣita and Kamalaśīla vs. Praśastamati in Santaraksita (835–853), pp. 455–461.

11. Paraphrase of Santaraksita (855–866), pp. 461–465.

12. Raghunatha (76.1–3), p. 87; Ingalls_1, p. 76, note 165.

13. *Bhasapariccheda* (11), p. 14; *Karikavali*, p. 66.

14. Summary of Śaṃkara on *Brahmasūtras* (II.2.13). See Belvalkar, pp. 57–58 of the Sanskrit, pp. 91–92 of the English translation.

15. *samavāyasya vṛttyantaram nā'sti, tasmād asya svātmanā svarupeṇai 'va vṛttir na vṛttyantareṇa.* Quoted in Bhaduri, p. 35, note 37.

16. The translation of *svarūpasambandha* as "self-linking connector" is partly due to Kuppuswami Sastri, pp. 19 ff. On these peculiar relations he should be consulted, as well as Ingalls_1 (see the index s.v. *viśeṣaṇatā, viśeṣasambandha*), Raghunatha (see the index under "self-linking connector"), Sen, pp. 16–35. On the problems about inherence, see *Indian Philosophical Studies*, pp. 107–115.

17. Prabhākara accepts as categories *both* inherence (*samavāya*) and similarity (*sādṛśya*). His reasoning appears to be that since inherences must be many, as the Buddhists argue, and since absences are not additional entities, as the Naiyāyikas mistakenly think, there must therefore be a distinct category to explain our perception of the likenesses between things. This additional category cannot be *sāmānya* (universals), since "similarity . . . does not form the basis of any comprehensive conception," as Prabhākara says in his *Bṛhatī* (quoted in *Purva Mimamsa*, p. 62).

18. Kumārila refuses to recognize inherence as a category on the same grounds as the Jains, preferring in its place a relationship of identity-in-difference (*bhedābheda* or *tādātmya*). He differs from the Jains, however, in that he distinguishes universals (*sāmānya*) from particular substances, etc. Pārthasārathi Miśra dis-

cusses the whole matter at some length. See Kumarila, pp. 93–94, 203–206; Parthasarathi$_1$, pp. 135–143; Parthasarathi$_2$, pp. 276–292; *Purva Mimamsa*, pp. 65–66.

19. Of the seventy-five sorts of elements (*dharma*) admitted by the system of the *Abhidharmakośa*, seventy-two are *saṃskṛta*, "forceful." Stcherbatsky warns us that "force . . . should not be regarded as a real influence of something extending beyond its own existence in order to penetrate another . . . but as a condition, a fact upon which another fact arises. . . ." Stcherbatsky, p. 18. N. N. Law in *Abhidharmakosa* regularly translates *saṃskṛta* as "constituted." On the other hand, Yaśomitra in his *-Vyākhyā* on the *Abhidharmakośa* says that elementa are called *saṃskṛta* because they produce traces (*saṃskāra*) which take effect later on. Cf. *Abhidharmakosa*, p. 42.

20. *Abhidharmakosa* (II.36–40), pp. 61–73.

21. *Abhidharmakosa* (I.5–6), pp. 15–21.

22. *Abhidharmakosa* (I.2), pp. 6–13; Stcherbatsky, pp. 41–42.

23. *Abhidharmakosa* (II.24), p. 42, mentions *mati* as one of the *cittamahābhūmikas*. Stcherbatsky identifies *prajñā* as developed *mati*. See previous note.

24. David Hume, *An Enquiry Concerning Human Understanding*, Section VI. For a contemporary exposition of this view, see *Readings in Philosophical Analysis*, ed. Feigl and Sellars (New York: Appleton-Century-Crofts, Inc., 1949), pp. 594–615.

25. In Appendix II of Stcherbatsky, p. 78, the reader will find a helpful chart illustrating these chains.

26. My translation of the French translation by Poussin of *Hiuan-tsang* (30), pp. 280–281. This passage is also translated in *Buddhist Logic* II, pp. 346–347.

27. Translated by Wing-Tsit Chan in *Source Book*, pp. 333–337.

28. *Triṃśika* 6; *Source Book* p. 334.

29. Śaṃkara on *Brahmasūtras* (II.2.30). Belvalkar, pp. 74–75 of the Sanskrit, pp. 124–125 of the English.

30. The usual word for "reality" is *sat* or *sattā*.

8

THE JAIN THEORY OF RELATIONS

We have just seen that the Yogācāra view and that of the Buddhist logicians complemented each other in a certain way, a way which brings them under attack from Nāgārjuna for arbitrarily downgrading one side of the knowledge situation while attempting to keep the other. Vasubandhu downgrades the object, Dharmakīrti the subject. Generalizing from this, we might say that anyone who proposes a theory which distinguishes the more real from the less real must explain what makes him think that what he calls less real depends on the more real and not vice-versa. And this will, in general, be a hard demand to meet, for in one sense or another, everything in the world we know is bound up with and dependent on every other thing.

It is on this last point that the Jain takes his stand. The fault of the theories to the left, he claims, is that they have allowed analysis to carry them away. Everything is interdependent, to be sure; yet it is still possible to distinguish the more real from the less real, as long as one does not go on to suppose that one can *separate* the aspects of things so distinguished. Everything in the world has various aspects (*nayas*). Every thing can therefore be viewed from various angles, each one emphasizing a different aspect, i.e., making it from that point of view the aspect on which others depend.

Everything, therefore, is in certain respects dependent on something else and in certain respects has other things dependent on it. Thus for example in the knowledge situation which perplexes the Yogācāras and Buddhist logicians, the Jain will say that it is true both that the subject depends on the object and that the object depends on the subject; both these statements are true, but from different standpoints.

Furthermore, any entity is at the same time one and many. It is one from the point of view of practical convention, but it is many from each of the various viewpoints which emphasize one or another of the various aspects. This feature of the Jain theory is the one which gives it its name, *anekāntavāda*, suggesting an ultimate variety of aspects.

How does this theory help us in understanding how it is possible that freedom can be gained? The Jain's idea is this: the other theories under review suppose that the material responsible for bondage must be dependent upon something unbound in order that the former can be destroyed without destroying the latter. In this they are right. But it does not follow that in addition the unbound must be a Self, or a mind, or a thing-in-itself, or any one kind of item for that matter.

Specifically, in the world of the unbound there are *two* kinds of stuff—*jīvas* or living things and *ajīva* or inert matter. As we have noted, the Jain thinks of the *jīvas* as swimming around in a suspension of particles of *ajīva*. When some of these particles attach themselves to a *jīva,* the *jīva* is said to be bound—but so, from another point of view, are the particles of *ajīva*. Now the particles are not related by a dependence relation to the *jīva; ajīva* and *jīva* are quite different in nature. But the *ajīva* which constitutes bondage depends on the nonbinding *ajīva* as its substratum, just as the *jīva* which is bound depends on the unbound *jīva* as its substratum. Freedom is possible just because it is possible for the binding *ajīva* to be destroyed without destroying the nonbinding *ajīva*, and (more importantly) because it is possible for the bound *jīva* to be destroyed without destroying the unbound *jīva*. Both the *jīva* and the *ajīva* become free; there are two parts to the program of freedom, and that is why the Jain is so insistent on distinguishing *saṃvāra* or prevention from *nirjarā* or annihilation. *Saṃvāra* is the freeing of the unbound *jīva* from the bondage of the bound *jīva*. *Nirjarā* is the freeing of the unbound *ajīva* from the bound *ajīva,* at least that portion of the *ajīva* which was previously mixed up with a particular *jīva*.

The Jain theory, it would seem, if it is successful should resolve those criticisms of other progress philosophy views which stemmed from a felt bias in favor of one or the other side of the bondage situation, say the knower or known. But not all of the criticisms of other theories are of this type, and with respect to those that are not, Jainism may be felt to compound the felony by merely duplicating the already troublesome notion of a dependence relation. And for the leap theories Jainism is so foreign as to be almost unintelligible; we shall see that Śaṃkara professes to fail to understand it. From the criticisms of Jainism that appear in the literature, I shall select three sorts, that of the Naiyāyika, that of the Buddhist and finally that of Śaṃkara insofar as it *is* a criticism.

The Naiyāyika's Criticism

Either the *jīva* and the *ajīva* can be related or they cannot, the Naiyāyika points out. The Jain seems to want to say one thing at one time, the other at another—but he cannot have it both ways. When the karmic particles filter through the *jīva,* we were told, some attached themselves to the *jīva*—or the *jīva* attached itself to them, if you prefer. Now is this or is this not a relation between *jīva* and *ajīva*? If not, how can any disciplined activity on the part of the *jīva* affect the *ajīva,* since they are completely unrelated? And yet, according to the Jain, *nirjarā* or cleansing of the *ajīva* is an essential part of freedom for the *jīva!* On the other hand, if there *is* a relation between *jīva* and *ajīva,* is it a dependence relation? If so, which relatum is the one on which the other depends? And finally, how does it help to solve the kinds of problems which Buddhists and Naiyāyikas wrestle with in trying to work out the analysis of dependence, if the Jain merely duplicates, or actually trebles, these relationships?

The Buddhist's Criticism

For the Buddhist reaction to the Jain's theory we turn again to Śāntarakṣita, who is concerned to show the Jain that on his own principles he has no right to believe in the existence of *jīva*s at all. His argument can be stated in terms of the formal reasoning that was described in Chapter 5, as his pupil Kamalaśīla explains.[1]

> "You, the Jains, have said that even if nothing else has any property from all points of view, at least there is a hard and fast difference between living being (*jīva*) and nonliving being (*ajīva*). The living being is distinguished by a particular property of sentience, which is lacking in non-living being."
>
> "Yes," says the Jain. "What then?"
>
> "You also think that a *jīva* is neither one nor many absolutely—it is one considered collectively, and many considered distributively."
>
> "That's my position," says the Jain.
>
> "Well, now, you can't hold both these views. Your position actually

must come to ours in the end—our position being that there is no such entity as the *jīva* but only the several distributive elements which make up a person's 'history.' "

"State your argument, then."

"I gather you don't accept our position, which must mean that you think that the substrate of the property of sentience is the *collective* aspect of the *jīva* and not the distributive aspect. For if you thought that the various successive elements in a self's history were identical with the self (using 'self' for '*jīva*' for the moment), then I'd have no quarrel with you, since you would have admitted that there is no single sentient substance which persists throughout a person's 'history.' "

"You're right," says the Jain, "I don't accept your position. But what harm is there in saying that sentience is a property of the *jīva* in its collective aspect?"

"Just this. I'll state the argument formally:

Pratijñā: A *jīva* cannot change.

Hetu: Because it cannot be differentiated from one state to the next.

Dṛṣṭānta: Like space (*ākāśa*).

Therefore on your own view a *jīva* cannot change and consequently the attainment of freedom becomes impossible."

"Now just a minute!" cries the Jain. "Your *hetu* is unproved (*asiddha*).[2] A *jīva*, even when considered collectively, is not absolutely undifferentiated like space. I only meant that relatively speaking it is one—relatively to the states spread out through time, which are many. If you like, you may say just that there is nondifference (*abheda*) between the collective self and the distributed states of its history."

"Still," says Śāntarakṣita, "this nondifference must be absolute—there can't also be difference too. And so the *jīva* turns out to be identical with the series of states, which is what *I* hold!"

And then, rather unwisely, Śāntarakṣita adds: "Besides:

Pratijñā: The successive states of the *jīva* cannot appear and disappear.

Hetu: Because the successive states of the *jīva* are nondifferent from the collective *jīva* (as admitted by you just now).

Dṛṣṭānta: Whatever is nondifferent from the collective *jīva* cannot appear and disappear), like the collective *jīva* itself."

The Jain is silenced by this last argument as far as Śāntarakṣita is concerned. Of course, we can give him a strong come-back by pointing out that the argument either violates Principle 1 (see p. 75) or else breaks Rule 4 (see pp. 71–72) depending on the meaning of the ambiguous *pratijñā*. If the *pakṣa* in the argument is supposed to be the collective totality of the *jīva*'s history, then the argument simply proves what the Jain accepts, that the *jīva* is eternal. So the Buddhist must intend the *pakṣa* to be the various states in that history considered distributively. In that case, however, the *hetu*-term "nondifferent from the collective *jīva*" is unrelated to the *pakṣa,* since the states considered one by one, distributively, *are* different from the collective *jīva*. In Western logic the argument thus understood would be said to commit the fallacy of division.

In the end, though the logical pyrotechnics make a good exercise for both parties, the arguments of Śāntarakṣita come to just about the same thing as those of the Naiyāyika. This is not surprising, since they both lie to the left of the Jains and share many of the same concerns.

Śaṃkara's Criticism

Śaṃkara's argument takes issue with the implications of the Jain's contention that there is nothing in the world which unqualifiedly has or does not have a given quality. Śaṃkara reminds us that the point of philosophy in India is to resolve doubts and thus to make it possible for the teacher to inspire the pupil to discipline himself. How can a philosophy which keeps talking about things as being so from one point of view but not so from another ever resolve doubts? In fact, isn't a doubt precisely what comes in the form "well, from one point of view this seems true, but from this other, it doesn't?" The Jain, rather than addressing himself to the resolution of doubts, seems to glorify them! Is it any solace to be told by the Jains that the only thing that is certain in this world is that everything is uncertain!

Śaṃkara's attitude suggests that he can't really take the Jain seriously —that he doesn't really understand the point of the theory. It may be worth hearing him in his own words.

> And how too can those who may claim to follow [the teaching of the Jain] find an impulse to act up to the teaching laid down by him, when just what he has taught is itself of a nondeterminate form? For, it is only when the fruit is definitely ascertained to be its unfailing consequence that all the world can, without confusion or hesitation, proceed to practice what may have been laid down as the means to that end; and not otherwise. Hence it follows that one laying down a doctrine-and-code nondeterminate in sense would, like a maniac or like one intoxicated, have his statement deemed unworthy of acceptance.[3]

NOTES

1. The dialogue that follows is a very free rendering of the gist of Santaraksita (311–320), pp. 204–208.
2. Specifically, what is unproved is the relation of the *hetu* to the *pakṣa;* Rule 4 is broken (see pp. 71–72).
3. Belvalkar, p. 128 of the English.

9

STRONG DEPENDENCE RELATIONS

PARINĀMA OR TRANSFORMATION AS THE DEPENDENCE RELATION

We have now discussed in detail two of the three major divisions of causal theories among the progress philosophers. There remain the *satkāryavādins*, who believe that the effect pre-exists in the cause. The distinction may be put thus: the theorists of the left, the *asatkāryavādins*, hold that since the ultimate nature of reality is plural, causation occurs by a combining of causal factors to produce a single effect. The *satkāryavādins*, on the other hand, believe that since on their assumptions the ultimate nature of reality is single, causation occurs by an evolution of plurality out of the ultimate one-ness. The *anekāntavādins*, the Jains, whom we have just finished discussing, believe that the ultimate reality is both one and many, so that causation is the production of one and many from one and many.

Sāṃkhya Reviewed

In the light of what has now been developed, we may take a moment to re-examine Sāṃkhya, which was treated previously (pp. 106–109). Although Īśvarakṛṣṇa is adamant in his espousal of *satkāryavāda,* his views about the nature of ultimate reality are puzzling. He clearly announces that there are many *puruṣa*s or Selves, which suggests a view more like the philosophies we have already examined than like the ones we are coming to; but he also says there is only one *prakṛti,* at least when it is in its unmanifest condition. Sāṃkhya resembles Jainism in an important respect, since it draws a strong distinction between living and nonliving matter, but it differs from Jainism in that the living matter is incapable of transformation and is, strictly speaking, never *bound* in the way that the Jain's *jīva* is. The appearance of bondage is a confusion, as the Sāṃkhya sees it, a result of the nondiscrimination between the world and the Self. But since the Self does not change, the nondiscrimination must occur in the world of *prakṛti,* and in order to make this plausible, the Sāṃkhya has to produce a theory about the world.

This is where the *pariṇāma* or transformation relation comes in. The Sāṃkhya postulates that the world is an emanation from unevolved *prakṛti.* The world as we know it evolves from *prakṛti,* and the various parts of this world are identical with *prakṛti* but yet different from it: they are identical in substance, but different since they are only parts. This evolved world includes, beside the material objects we cognize, our organs of cognition themselves, including our body, our sense-organs, and even our mind—in fact, the whole apparatus that produces in us what we call "consciousness." The *puruṣa* is merely the passive witness (*sākṣin*) of all this. Mental activity is a kind of material change; it doesn't affect the *puruṣa* in any way. Nevertheless, it is this very mental activity which becomes confused with the witness, and this nondiscrimination is what has to be destroyed. The chain of sufficient conditions for freedom, the chain we care about, runs from discrimination of *puruṣa* from *prakṛti* on up to the destruction of bondage, bondage being the evolved *prakṛti,* the empirical world as we know it. The reverse of this chain, the chain of necessary conditions for bondage, runs from the unmanifested *prakṛti* unconditioned by nondiscrimination to its manifest condition as "my" mind and the apparent embodiment of "my" *puruṣa.* The dependence relation between unmanifested *prakṛti* and a part of its manifest form guarantees that the chain is without gaps, that destruction of nondiscrimination will surely be followed by liberation.

We may notice here that there is heavy pressure on Sāṃkhya to combine into one its two basic metaphysical entities—*puruṣa* and *prakṛti*—since the Sāṃkhya philosopher cannot intelligibly say how they come together into relation with one another. By splitting *puruṣa* from *prakṛti,* Īśvarakṛṣṇa appears to render bondage impossible, for in order for something to be bound it must be limited by something else, which involves a relation of limitation between the bound and that which binds. According to one of Sāṃkhya's stock examples, causation is a relation exemplified in the connection between the sesamum-seed and the oil it contains. The seed is identical with, and yet different from, the oil. The analogy is with the unmanifested *prakṛti:* it contains within it the whole world of evolutes. But what triggers the evolution? In the case of the seed, something has to come along and open the shell. In the case of *prakṛti,* by analogy, something has to operate upon the *upādhis* (obstructions to evolution corresponding to the shell) in order that *prakṛti* may evolve into "names and forms," as the Indian puts it. This raises serious problems. (1) Of what nature are these *upādhis* that can stop *prakṛti* from manifesting itself? Why does Īśvarakṛṣṇa fail to number them among the causal factors? This is the perennial challenge of the *asatkāryavādin.* (2) Passing that, however, and supposing there are *upādhis*, what is it which removes an *upādhi*? And whatever it is, isn't it necessary that to remove the *upādhi* it must come into relation with *prakṛti* in its unmanifest state at least, just as in order to remove the shell an agent must come in contact with the seed? Now if Īśvarakṛṣṇa is going to introduce *puruṣa* as the agent which removes the *upādhi,* how can he deny that the *puruṣa* becomes related to *prakṛti*? And if *puruṣa* comes into relation with *prakṛti* in the production of karmic matter (that which binds), then the nature of the relation between *puruṣa* and *prakṛti* becomes of critical importance. If that relation is one of absolute identity, then to destroy that relation is to destroy both *puruṣa* and *prakṛti*—and this is not release, it is cosmic suicide.

Sāṃkhya tries to meet these problems to a certain extent, but seems to have to give way ultimately to the second criticism. Its answer to the first problem—what are the *upādhis* which stop *prakṛti* from manifesting itself—is interesting and reminiscent of Dharmakīrti's theory of *apoha.* The *upādhis*, say Sāṃkhya commentators, are negative; the *absences* of the proper time and the proper place for manifestation to occur are two such *upādhis*. The *puruṣa* does not bring anything positive to *prakṛti* to trigger the process because to remove an absence the mere presence of the opposite is sufficient; no positive additional action need be brought in. Of course, this presupposes that the absence of something is not itself a thing, and that raises a whole distinct set of problems about negative entities, to which we shall come in due course.

On the second problem, however, Īśvarakṛṣṇa can only offer analogies which are somehow unconvincing. The *puruṣa,* he says, is that for the edification of which *prakṛti* evolves. If there were no evolution, there would be no challenges for the *puruṣa;* if there were no challenges, there would be no liberation, since we should already be free. "As a dancer desists from dancing, having exhibited herself to the audience, so does *prakṛti* desist, having exhibited herself to the *puruṣa.*"[1] *Prakṛti*'s function is to please the *puruṣas*. It gains nothing from its display, "like a servant that helps, in manifold ways, the master that does not requite her. . . ."[2] But the reader will probably find this already excessively anthropomorphic, despite the attractiveness of the similes.

The Position of Rāmānuja

If he does not find Sāṃkhya too anthropomorphic, however, the reader may find considerable attraction in the next theory we shall discuss, that of the Viśiṣṭādvaitin Rāmānuja and his followers insofar as they remain progress philosophers.[3] For Rāmānuja's theory is not different from Īśvarakṛṣṇa's in its view of the nature of the dependence relation; its major difference is that it reduces the dualism of *puruṣa* and *prakṛti* found in Sāṃkhya to a unity, the resulting conception constituting a God which may be referred to either in personal terms or in impersonal ones. In impersonal terms, Rāmānuja identifies this basic being as *brahman,* the holy principle or power celebrated in the Upanishads. In personal terms, this *brahman* is Viṣṇu (for Rāmānuja) or Śiva (for others), these being the two major personal deities of popular Hindu religion. The result of this identification is a very powerful correlation of theism and philosophy.

The teleological element which might appear unsatisfactory in the dualism of Īśvarakṛṣṇa is found eminently satisfying by Rāmānuja when it is incorporated in theistic garb. However, it is our business here to inquire into Rāmānuja's theory of relations, and it is not clear that his view on this point is any different from that of Sāṃkhya. The *pariṇāma* relation is merely relocated and, in point of fact, reduplicated. Where Īśvarakṛṣṇa denied any relation between *puruṣa* and *prakṛti,* Rāmānuja finds the relation in the common character of Selves and matter as aspects of *brahman. Brahman* is related to both Selves and matter, in Rāmānuja's own analogy, as soul to its body. *Brahman* does not evolve the Selves and the unmanifest *prakṛti;* they constitute *brahman,* are identical with it collectively, though different distributively. The Selves and the material world constitute the body of *brahman* for Rāmānuja, and it is easy to see, given this analogy, how it is that the Selves and the world are teleologically oriented toward the realization of *brahman,* just as the organs of the body are teleologically oriented toward the bodily fulfilment of the soul's needs.

It is presumably this organic notion of the relation between *brahman* and its body that explains how Rāmānuja can deny that his is an identity-in-difference view of the sort the next philosophers to be considered hold. What he is denying is that *brahman* is affected by changes in the world. For, having explained the relation between *brahman* and its body (consisting of Selves and unmanifested *prakṛti*) there is still the problem of how the *prakṛti* is moved to evolve itself into the world as we know it. This is the same problem that Īśvarakṛṣṇa had to face, and it is rendered no less prickly by the fact that the Selves and *prakṛti* are now caught up in a higher synthesis of *brahman*. Rāmānuja appeals to *pariṇāma* to solve it, just as Sāṃkhya does.

Then why does *prakṛti* evolve at all? The unsatisfactory analogies of Sāṃkhya are replaced in Rāmānuja's system by theological appeals; *prakṛti* manifests itself at God's will and for God's purposes—or rather, in Rāmānuja, for no purpose at all, for according to him God creates in the spontaneous spirit of play (*līlā*).

What are the implications of this theory for our major questions about the chain of necessary or sufficient conditions? It is possible that Rāmānuja gets nongappiness in his chain at too much expense when he appeals to a supra-personal power for explanation. For if the chain of necessary conditions which we care about runs from God's sport to the bondage of a Self, we are forced to conclude from our prior reasoning about necessary and sufficient conditions that one must depend in the last analysis on God's grace in getting liberation. This is precisely what Rāmānuja concludes, and it only remains to be noted that the two major schools of thought among his followers are supposed to have split over whether or not any effort at all on the part of a Self is necessary in seeking freedom. In medieval Hinduism one hears of a distinction between monkey-salvation and cat-salvation. The difference is this: the monkey-child saves himself from harm by hanging on to its mother as she escapes from her chains; the kitten, on the other hand, is picked up in its mother's mouth. The young monkey makes an effort just in hanging on, without which it will be lost; the kitten makes no effort, and may be saved despite itself. Among Rāmānuja's followers, those of the Teṅgalai school are supposed to have believed in cat-salvation and those of the Vaḍagalai school in monkey-salvation. In any case, however, in the *bhakti* philosophy of Rāmānuja there develops a new "path" to freedom which is not a path at all in the sense we have used, since it involves no discipline in our sense; this is the path of *prapatti,* or grace through resignation to the will of God.[4]

Bhedābheda *in Bhartṛprapañca*

For those who are suspicious of the doctrine of grace and the philosophical system which leads to it, there are other alternatives developed within the group of theories which base themselves on transformation as the crucial dependence relation. When philosophers in India refer to *bhedābhedavāda* they regularly have in mind a kind of theory which we have not yet described, one which was undoubtedly held by several important philosophers in their day but by philosophers whose work has, unfortunately, largely been lost. We do have part of a commentary by one Bhāskara, and we have fragments dealing with the theory of an earlier philosopher still, Bhartṛprapañca. We also have quite a bit of material written by later philosophers whose identification with Bhedābhedavāda may be disputed, men such as Yādavaprakāśa and Nimbārka. In dealing with the theory I shall stay close to Bhartṛprapañca, following Hiriyanna's admirable reconstruction.[5]

Bhartṛprapañca combines the monistic hypothesis of Rāmānuja with the "pure witness" hypothesis of the Sāṃkhya. According to Bhartṛprapañca the nature of the world is three-in-one, three aspects (*rāśi*) identical with but different from the one Brahman. Brahman is not, however, conceived as a personal deity as in Rāmānuja; rather, God for Bhartṛprapañca is identified as one of the three aspects of Brahman. These three aspects are: (1) God (*paramātmārāśi*), i.e., Brahman as inner controller (*antaryāmin*); (2) the witness (*sākṣin*) together with the bound selves making up the *jīvarāśi* or soul-aspect; (3) the world (*mūrtāmūrtarāśi*), which contains the unmanifest and its manifest forms divided into categories, categories different from those of Sāṃkhya, which Bhartṛprapañca draws from the Upanishadic texts.

A relation, generically called "identity-in-difference" (*bhedābheda*), which connects a collective totality with its distributive elements, is adduced several times in explaining the relations among these several aspects. The relation between Brahman and the *jīvarāśi* or soul-aspect is identity-in-difference of a particular sort called "ignorance" (*avidyā*). The relation between Brahman and the world is also identity-in-difference. So is the relation between the witness and the bound *jīva*s or selves. And so is the relation between the unmanifest and its manifestations in the world. For Bhartṛprapañca there is even a fifth use of identity-in-difference in the relation between a superior and an inferior variety of Brahman.[6]

The most prickly problem for all the right-hand theories is to explain how the Self becomes bound at all. Sāṃkhya, we saw, had to resort to unsatisfactory and anthropomorphic analogies; Rāmānuja solved the problem only by appeal to a supernatural force. Bhartṛprapañca avoids the theistic move of the latter and tries to avoid the unsatisfactory analogies of the former by complicating the account somewhat. In Bhartṛprapañca appeal is made to an important philosophical notion, one that we have met already in connection with Buddhism. This is the notion of *vāsanā,* literally "fragrance," used regularly in Indian thought to refer to the unconscious traces or habits which bind a self. The very word "*vāsanā*" gives Bhartṛprapañca a metaphor to illustrate what binds the pure witness. Though not material, it is bound by unconscious habits which belong originally in the material world, just as the fragrance of a flower which belongs originally to the flower is distilled into oil.[7] This beginningless attachment to habits makes the witness subject to the circle of birth and rebirth. That there are finite souls at all is a consequence of the ignorance which limits Brahman, dividing it into a plurality of limited selves (*jīvas*). The limited self is a consequence of two transformations of Brahman, one the transformation of Brahman limited by ignorance into "pure" *jīva,* the other the transformation of the "pure" *jīva* under the influence of attachment to habits into bound *jīva.* It follows that the road to liberation has two steps, first the cessation of the habits (which frees one from the circle of rebirth), second the cessation of ignorance, which gains one complete freedom. But even this complete freedom is only a union with the lower form of Brahman for Bhartṛprapañca, that form which is in its very nature a unity-in-difference. The path adopted by the Bhedābhedavādin is *jñānakarmasamuccaya,* a combination of action and knowledge: first one must practice an attitude of nonattachment to break the ties of unconscious habits, and then one can meditate in order to break the bonds of ignorance.

Although Bhartṛprapañca thus complicates the account by developing the Sāṃkhya ontology within a monistic framework, his critics are quick to see a fatal difficulty in which he is involved. Since the transformation of Brahman into selves is a *real* transformation (cause and effect are equally real), and since the attachment of the selves to habits is a real attachment, one must conclude that Brahman is itself infected with the very evils of bondage which infect its constituent factors, since they pre-exist in Brahman. Really to crush all those evils which constitute bondage, one must crush a part at least of Brahman itself. The difficulty stems, as we have seen before, from the fact that the transformation relation is too strong (or so the critic argues); to break such a relationship, one must destroy both of its terms.

Bhedābhedavāda of Bhartṛprapañca's sort therefore avoids the teleological difficulties that beset Sāṃkhya and Rāmānuja, but only to fall prey to the problem of evil. It will have been noted as well that the three theories we have discussed in this chapter represent a progression when, abstracting from other considerations, we consider the number of times identity-in-difference is used. Sāṃkhya uses it once, and cannot connect the Self to its bondage plausibly. Rāmānuja uses it twice—to connect God with the Self, and to connect the Self to the material world. But the Self becomes completely subordinate to Brahman in his system, and it becomes unclear how a Self by its own efforts can break the chains which bind it. Finally, the Bhedābhedavādins invoke the relation at least four times but cannot escape the dilemma—either freedom goes out of our control, or else there is no satisfactory explanation for the relation of Self and bondage which guarantees the nongappiness of the chain in which we are interested. To avoid this dilemma, it would seem, means either to relapse into the indeterminate position of the Jains or to revert to the inherence relation of Nyāya-Vaiśeṣika.

Unless, that is, another kind of dependence relation can be found which does not have the awkward consequences of transformation, which does not visit the relatum on which a second relatum depends with the defects of that second relatum. The trouble with transformation as a dependence relation can be seen by recalling the original metaphor: to transform a seed into oil, or milk into curds, one must destroy a part or essential property of the seed or of the milk. In the case of the seed, one must break it into parts to get at the oil; in the case of the milk, one must destroy its liquidity and sweetness to get curds. Transformation is only a half-hearted dependence relation. But perhaps a better sort can be found. The Advaitin thinks he has it in his *vivarta* or "manifestation" relation.

VIVARTA OR MANIFESTATION AS THE DEPENDENCE RELATION

Advaita Vedānta has been held by scholars over the centuries to have been a most important school of thought in India, but it has been a strange quirk of philosophical scholarship that so large has the figure of one of its early proponents, Śaṃkarācārya, loomed that rather scant attention was paid for a long time to the other members of the tradition.

Recent scholarship has, however, made advances toward filling this lacuna, so that we are now in a position to treat the system as a series of branches with important peculiarities of their own.

Before considering the branches, though, I ought to explain what is common to the whole Advaita Vedānta in its account of relations. We have seen, and it was apparent to some of the philosophers of the eighth century who were attempting to interpret the Upanishads, that the transformation model would not serve to resolve the problems of causation of which we have spoken. Nor would the theory of the Jains do for them, since it involved such an indeterminacy of speaking as to be no resolution at all of the doubts which philosophy is taken to be responsible for quieting. Nor, for various reasons, are the theories farther to the left, such as Nyāya-Vaiśeṣika, satisfactory to the followers of the Upanishads.

Where the Bhedābhedavādins found the world and the Selves to be a transformation (*pariṇāma*) of Brahman, the Advaitin finds the world and the Selves to be an appearance (*vivarta*) of Brahman. An analogy such as that of the rope and the snake may be used to indicate the exact character of *vivarta:* A man has an experience of a snake coiled to strike, caused by his coming upon a coiled rope in the dusk. The Advaitins all agree that this provides a handy analogy to our experience of the world, caused by our coming upon Brahman under the influence of our ignorance. Where the sub-schools of Advaita disagree is about the specific places in the chain that this relation applies, and about the ways and means of resolving difficulties which arise from the consequences of using this relation in those areas.

We have seen in our examination of *pariṇāmavāda* that, among other things, there is a tendency among the philosophers of this persuasion to consider freedom as something which is not in the last analysis attainable through human effort alone. In the Sāṃkhya, it is discrimination, which the *puruṣa* learns to make between itself in its pure state and the gross and subtle material of *prakṛti,* that breaks the bond. It is not clear in Sāṃkhya how this bond got made in the first place, and therefore how it can be broken by mere knowledge, but it has been indicated more than once that the very nature of the Sāṃkhya theory leads it to a kind of intellectualism. Rāmānuja, to be sure, avoids this by leaning towards devotion and grace as the means to salvation, but the point is the same: no longer are we talking, as we were when discussing Nyāya-Vaiśeṣika, Buddhism, and Jainism, of overt effort or action-discipline—which was taken by them to break bonds conceived in an almost literally material way. In Rāmānuja, the Self practises devotion, but Rāmānuja's problem is precisely how devotion by itself can break a bond between a material entity (*karma*) and a spiritual one (the Self), and he appeals finally to God as the source of the bond-breaking activity, without actually explaining how God manages this feat. In Bhedābhedavāda proper, we find the notion of *jñānakarmasamuccaya,* that is to say, of a progression toward liberation; effort can get one only so far—to be precise, only up to the breaking of the bondage which ties the unconscious habits to the self—even after that, ignorance remains as a block between the Self and freedom, and this is to be overcome by knowledge and not by effort.

The use of a relation whose best illustration is an epistemological one, the illustration of the rope and the snake, can be seen now as a natural result of the tendency we have just noticed. The more we try to explain how the Self by its own effort can break a material bond between itself and the world, and the more frequently we fail in the attempt, the more tempting it seems to construe *karma* not as a material bond at all but as an epistemological or spiritual one—a bond to be broken not by overt activity but by realizing something one had not realized before, a realization which changes the nature of things radically. To make this plausible, one is forced to construe the material world as somehow not merely a material entity independent of our thinking or feeling, for if it were completely independent, it would be recalcitrant to efforts other than overt, active use of our bodies. In short, one who abandons an explanation of bondage in material terms (of the sort to be found in Nyāya-Vaiśeṣika, Jainism, and early Buddhism) seems also to have to abandon epistemological realism. Thus it is not surprising that a large amount of the attention of Advaitins, like their counterparts on the opposite side of our chart (the Yogācāras of the left-hand side), is devoted to epistemological rather than metaphysical analysis. The epistemology of Advaita will be treated at some length in the next chapter. In this chapter, however, I am concerned with the implications of the Advaitin's theory of relations.

The Theory of Maṇḍana Miśra

A philosopher of great influence in his own day and for centuries after his death, Maṇḍana has been peculiarly neglected by Western scholars until the last few years. But it seems to have been Maṇḍana who first clearly formulated the consequences of the use of *vivarta* to resolve the problems we are concerned with.

Maṇḍana represents an interesting offshoot of a type of thinking stemming from Bhartṛhari and others, whose practitioners are referred to sometimes as the "grammarians." These thinkers conceived of Brahman or the world-principle as somehow being essentially speech or word; they practiced a mysterious cult of the sacred syllable *aum,* authority for which can be found in the Upanishads (among other places). This sacred and essential word *aum* is related, for Maṇḍana and his predecessors, to the objects of the world by the *vivarta* relation—those objects are the appearances of and dependent upon their names and ultimately nondifferent from these names and from the ultimate Name itself. Whatever one can make of this theory, Maṇḍana thought that it fits the needs of the present problem admirably, if we but identify the word *aum* with Brahman and treat a conscious self as partaking of this very nature, as the Upanishads teach ("That [Brahman] art thou [self], Śvetaketu," says Uddālaka, his father, in the *mahāvākya* or great saying of the Chāndogya Upanishad).[8]

Maṇḍana therefore introduces the *vivarta* relation to explain the connection between Brahman and the world.[9] About the precise kind of relation between Brahman and self his view is not so clear. On this and several other questions there is disagreement among the sub-schools of Advaita, and it will be helpful to summarize Maṇḍana's reasoning on these points for future reference.

1. What is it that is bound—the self (*jīva*) or Brahman? Surely, says Maṇḍana, it must be the *jīva,* for the Upanishads clearly speak of Brahman as undisturbed by bondage.

2. Then when the Upanishads say "That art thou, Śvetaketu," do they mean to suggest that there is only one *jīva*? Certainly not, says Maṇḍana, since if there were only one *jīva* no one could be freed without everyone else's being freed at the same time, and this is contradicted by other passages in the Upanishads (e.g., Bṛhadāraṇyaka Upanishad I.4.10) which tell of certain sages being freed in the past without their contemporaries, or for that matter their heirs, being freed. There are many *jīva*s, says Maṇḍana, just as we ordinarily suppose. Whatever the Upanishads mean, it is not that there is only one *jīva.*

3. To whom does ignorance belong? Ignorance is the source of bondage, but does it belong to Brahman or the *jīva*s? Who becomes ignorant—Brahman or selves? Clearly, thinks Maṇḍana, it is the selves that become ignorant, and not Brahman: Brahman is by its very nature pure consciousness (*cit*) and cannot be ignorant. Furthermore, if Brahman could become bound by ignorance, freedom would have to be something that Brahman gains, and not something the selves gain. But

what does this imply about disciplinary activity? Must we then wait for Brahman to become free, and if so, what is the point of renunciation?

4. Then how many ignorances are there? One imagines that for Maṇḍana there must be as many ignorances as there are selves which are ignorant, although Maṇḍana's precise view on this point is not well understood.[10]

These four problems about Advaita theory, and two more to be introduced in a moment, occupy a central place in the later development of the system. Any Advaita theorist must juggle several disparate conceptions successfully. There is Brahman; there is the world we experience; there is oneself, and other selves. And there must be relations among these various things.

On the first of the four points we have listed there is no disagreement among Advaitins. It is the self, or selves, which is or are bound. But on the other three topics there is conspicuous lack of unanimity. We shall have occasion to return to the views of other Advaitins below.

If there is to be any sense in which Brahman is the cause of the world, Brahman must be linked with that world by the *vivarta* relation. The Advaitin thinks of the relation as a type of ignorance. Maṇḍana calls this type of ignorance the projective (*vikṣepa*) type, a causal ignorance which produces, like a magician, the illusion that there is an empirical world of things, qualities, and so forth. But what is it that is bound by its connection with this empirical illusion? Not Brahman, for Brahman is pure and unsullied, unaffected by the magic-show. Thus there must be selves, says Maṇḍana, many selves producing through their ignorances a world or worlds. From what do these selves spring? What is *their* cause? Again, it must be Brahman. But the causal ignorance that begets selves cannot be the same ignorance that begets the world, since the projective ignorance cannot come into existence until there are selves, and we are asking about the cause of the selves. Therefore there must be a second causal ignorance, and Maṇḍana distinguishes it by calling it the concealing (*āvaraṇa*) ignorance. Brahman conceals Itself from itself and thus there come to be several selves; the selves then project an illusion (or several illusions), and thus the appearance of an empirical world is explained.

Maṇḍana's distinction between the two types of ignorance, concealing and projecting, leads him to a fascinating theory which concerns the proper distinction between a *jīvanmukta* or completely free self and an unrealized self who is fast asleep. According to Maṇḍana, the two types of ignorance can operate independently, i.e., either one can operate without the other. When the concealing type operates without the projective one, we get the state, very important in the Upanishads and therefore for all Vedāntins, of deep sleep (*suṣupti*).[11] When the projective type operates without the concealing sort, on the other hand, one has achieved a state which can properly be described as freedom, but in which one is still aware of the illusory world. In this state, Maṇḍana claims, although one is technically speaking "free," one must still continue practicing meditation in order to remove the remaining "shiver" (*kampa*) of the projective ignorance as well.[12]

Meditation, Maṇḍana supposes, although a positive action and therefore a result of the projective illusion, removes the concealing ignorance and, as a result, the projective type as well, just as the *kaṭaka*-nut (*strychnos potatorum,* commonly called "soap-nut"), though a bit of solid matter, when placed in water removes the other solid matter in the water and removes itself in the process![13] This intriguing analogy has an interesting and noteworthy implication: it allows Maṇḍana to say that overt renunciation (*sannyāsa*) is not necessary for liberation—all that is necessary is meditation. One can gain freedom even as a householder, and need not renounce all worldly possessions and seek the forest.[14]

For Maṇḍana, then, the relation between the Highest Self (or Brahman) and a bound individual self is one of concealment, but a relation which can be destroyed by the cleansing activity of meditation. Furthermore, as we have seen, this concealing relation pluralizes also—there are many selves, and the freeing of one does not mean the freeing of all, as we know from experience. What sort of a model can we appeal to from our everyday experience which will clarify this complicated relationship?

The point of introducing *vivarta* in place of *pariṇāma* was to avoid visiting the stable relatum in a dependence relation with the defects of the unstable one. The Advaitin, like the Yogācāras and Buddhist logicians, finds it natural at this point to begin talking about the "real" and the "unreal." In a dependence relation, the stable relatum is real, the unstable relatum unreal. What kind of model will be helpful in understanding how the real can manifest itself as unreal without being affected thereby?

The most frequent appeal in Advaita literature is probably to the model of the snake and the rope, i.e., to illusions. As I walk in the dusk I see a snake, which on closer examination turns out to be a rope. It surely was a rope all the time, but manifested itself as a snake. The snaky characteristics did not, however, affect the rope even during the illusion. Thus Brahman, the real, is unaffected by its manifestations as empirical world and individual ego, even during the manifestation.

The model is direct and intriguing, but brings up some problems. One is this: what becomes free, Brahman or the self? I.e., is the rope in the model analogous to Brahman or to the individual self? We need an analogy which explains a three-way relation—among Brahman, self, and world. How can we use the epistemological model of illusion, which presupposes the existence of a knower and a known, to throw light on the relation among Brahman, a knower, and the known? A more sophisticated analogy seems to be called for. Two other models are sometimes appealed to in later Advaita literature, models I shall call "limitationism" and "reflectionism," and which will be discussed later, where we shall see that they present difficulties of their own.

At any rate, all Advaitins agree that the world must be placed on a lower level of reality than Brahman, the ultimately real. What, one might ask, is the status of this lower level? Is it a complete negation, a nothing? If so, the Advaitin would be committing the howler of positing a relation which lacks a term, i.e., of reifying Nothing. A relation between Brahman and nothing is no relation at all but a verbal confusion. Therefore the Advaitin must endow empirical unreality with more being than nothing, and less being than Brahman. The technical term for this status, which seems to have been the contribution of Maṇḍana, is *anirvācanīya*, literally "that about which we cannot speak"—or at least about which we cannot speak correctly, since our language appears to endow the referents of our words either with complete reality or with complete unreality.[15]

In addition to the four problems listed above, then, there are others about which later Advaitins are also much concerned. For example:

5. If each self projects its own world through its own projective ignorance, numerically (at least) distinct from any other self's ignorance, does this mean that there is no common world that we all experience? Or is there perhaps a super-self (God) which co-ordinates the various worlds of the various selves? Again there are three possibilities—no common world, a common world but no God, and a common world with a God. All possibilities are explored within Advaita literature.

6. The nature of the relation among Brahman, selves, and world seems to require a more complex model than the simple one of the rope and the snake. We shall examine alternative models below.

Śaṃkara's Contributions to Advaita

With these six problems in mind, I next turn to Maṇḍana's much more famous near-contemporary, the man who is frequently referred to as Hinduism's greatest single figure, Saṃkarācārya.

It is sometimes contended that the greatness of a piece of writing, be it philosophical or literary, is proportionate to the number of different meaningful interpretations which can be found to be consistent with the text. Assuming that a great philosopher is one who writes great works, we can conclude that the greatest philosophical geniuses are those whose statements are not so specific as to preclude several meaningful interpretations. Śaṃkara's greatness is a case in point. He differs from Maṇḍana largely in not committing himself where Maṇḍana does, and thereby becomes the source of further speculation, while Maṇḍana's theory is something of a dead-end. I shall take a moment or two to call attention to the points on which Śaṃkara seems not to come to any firm conclusion in comparison with Maṇḍana's relative decisiveness.

Maṇḍana clearly holds that there are many selves and that a self is distinct from Brahman at least in the sense that a part is distinct from the whole. Śaṃkara does not offer any definite conclusions about whether there are many selves or only one self. Secondly, Maṇḍana clearly states that the ignorance which binds us and prevents us from being completely free binds only the individual selves and not Brahman. On this topic Śaṃkara's position is unclear; recent scholarship has suggested that he pointedly avoided the question "whose is ignorance?"[16] Thirdly, Maṇḍana distinguishes two types of ignorance, the concealing kind and the projective kind; the distinction, if it is recognized by Śaṃkara, is not used or clearly enunciated in his works. Fourthly, Maṇḍana is driven to postulate a category of *anirvācanīyatva*,[a] which leads to the suspicion that he is committed to a many-valued logic. Śaṃkara uses the expression "*anirvācanīya*" little and even there not in this connection;[17] he refuses to speculate about the logical status of the empirical world, whether it is a negative entity, a positive one, both, or neither. Fifthly, we may notice Śaṃkara's willingness to use a vast variety of analogies to illustrate the *vivarta* relationship, while Maṇḍana's list is rather short by comparison. Śaṃkara, for example, uses the rope-snake model frequently, but also uses illustrations such as the crystal which becomes red when it is near a red object, the foam and the waves, the magic-show

[a] The suffix-*tva* in Sanskrit makes an abstract noun from concrete nouns and adjectives, like English "-ness" or "-hood."

and the magician, water in a mirage, space and the space enclosed in a jar, the magnet which attracts without doing anything—even favorites of the *pariṇāmavādins*' such as the milk and the curds.[18] These various illustrations lead in various different directions, and the last suggests what seems in general to be true, that Śaṃkara uses the word "*vivarta*" hardly at all and doesn't seem to mind talking in terms of *pariṇāma*—although in the last analysis he will perhaps have no causal theory at all.[19]

Śaṃkara, like the Buddha, apparently was more interested in teaching his pupils to overcome ignorance than in discovering the proper account of the relation between Brahman, the self or selves, and the world. He philosophized not so much by propounding a satisfactory theory of relations of his own as by criticizing the theories, in his view inadequate, of other schools. The acuteness of those criticisms bears witness to the fact that he was probably the intellectual equal of, say, a Maṇḍana, and suggests that his failure to give a clear account of the problems summarized in the preceding paragraph is not a result of failing to see them but rather of a deliberate decision to avoid them. Thus he is not only the instigator of positive discussion about the relation of *vivarta* in subsequent Vedānta, but is also responsible for a group of dialecticians who conceive of the refutation of alternative views as the only function of philosophical analysis. For example, a philosopher like Śrīharṣa, adopting the novel techniques of neo-Naiyāyika logic, relentlessly criticizes others without offering any positive theory of his own in his *Khaṇḍanakhaṇḍakhādya*. Although it is not clear that Śaṃkara thought that philosophy could not make positive pronouncements on speculative topics, he certainly leads the way to this conception of philosophy by not pronouncing definitely on many such issues. In the terminology I have been using, these latter-day Advaitins are leap theorists by default, since they offer no theory about causation. Śaṃkara by his silence seems to have been given credit for the progress philosophy which followed him as well as those critical leap philosophers who profess their allegiance to Advaita.[b]

However, a comparison of Śaṃkara with Maṇḍana provides only a partial understanding of Śaṃkara's contribution to Advaita theory. We

[b] However, there is some reason to think that the dialecticians owe their method more to Maṇḍana than to Śaṃkara. Śaṃkara's use of argument is apologetic, though forceful; Maṇḍana, on the other hand, appears to revel in it. Citsukha, whose importance in later Advaita has been underestimated, commented on Maṇḍana's *Brahmasiddhi* and, it may be conjectured, learned a great deal from that source.

have yet to discuss the most famous concept associated with Śaṃkara's name, the concept of *māyā*.[c]

One of the meanings of the Sanskrit word *māyā* is "magic," and Śaṃkara himself frequently seems to use it that way.[20] Specifically, Śaṃkara thinks of it, in one aspect, as God's power to project the magic-show which is this world of empirical objects.[21] This projective power is also sometimes attributed to the self, "the shining one."[22] What it is not attributed to, however, is Brahman—or at least not clearly in Śaṃkara. For Śaṃkara God is not synonymous with Brahman, but is, as in Bhartṛprapañca's thought, the *antaryāmin* or inner controller of everything through His *māyā*.

Śaṃkara treats epistemological topics much more fully than ontological ones, and as a result *māyā* is most often thought of by him on the analogy of false *knowledge* (*ajñāna*, *mithyājñāna*). Śaṃkara tends to distinguish three levels of knowledge on the basis of the analogy of the rope and the snake. The highest level, called *paramārthika,* is the level on which, if we could, we should conceive Brahman in its pure aspect, and from this highest point of view Brahman is completely unqualified by any properties or relations—so that *māyā* is not his. Thus Śaṃkara avoids the identity-in-difference difficulties consequent upon visiting Brahman with worldly properties, such as the property of being the source of bondage. The second level, *vyavahārika,* is the level of *māyā*—it is produced by *māyā,* but it also is *māyā* intrinsically. This level is the empirical one from which human beings view the world, and the world so viewed is itself of the nature of *māyā*. A third level, *pratibhāṣika,* is the level of dream-appearances, hallucinations, and illusion: it stands to the empirical level in the same relation that the two lower levels stand to the highest. (This may remind us of Plato's divided line, which is also largely an epistemological conception.)

Was Śaṃkara a progress or a leap philosopher? Did he believe in a causal chain of necessary conditions the complement of which could be effected by man to attain freedom? Since the empirical world is a result of our limited (*vyavahārika*) outlook, it seems that from the highest point of view any chain of empirical conditions leading to bondage, or in reverse to release, must also be a product of *māyā* and thus, in the last analysis, lacking in complete reality. Śaṃkara sometimes advocates what the Hindus call *ajātivāda,* leap philosophy, the view that nothing is ever caused. Since Brahman, properly considered, is completely un-

c It's not *his,* really; it goes back to the Upanishads and Maṇḍana uses it.

affected by anything (like the *puruṣa* of the Sāṃkhya), it cannot create. And since nothing is ever really produced, nothing ever really gets destroyed. When the snake-illusion disappears, nothing has really been destroyed, since nothing was really ever produced. On the other hand, Śaṃkara sometimes speaks as if he were quite willing to commit himself to Brahman as a cause. In the *Brahmasūtrabhāṣya*, for example, he states that the origin, subsistence, and dissolution of the world are caused by Brahman—and where other, later Advaitins will hedge about calling Brahman a "cause" in any but the *vivarta* sense, Śaṃkara's admission is free from any such qualification here.[23]

It would seem that either Śaṃkara failed to see the contradictions in the different portions of his writings, or else he didn't care. There is, however, an alternative way of construing Śaṃkara's contribution, one which has been suggested by at least one contemporary writer[24] and which is certainly plausible. So far we have, if anything, been suggesting that Śaṃkara demurs on or fails to see metaphysical problems because he tends to see problems as essentially epistemological. But there is another possibility, and that is that he doesn't see problems as either metaphysical or epistemological, but rather as essentially problems of "value," i.e., of the relative importance of what one believes. On this reading, Śaṃkara's penchant for talking about relations of causation between Brahman and the world of selves while at the same time denying that causation is in the last analysis intelligible may be explained by pointing out that what Śaṃkara is interested in is not the *truth* of alternative accounts of ultimate causation but rather the relative *importance* of the seeker's believing in one of them. No theory of causation or relations is true, he may be thought to be saying, but the reason why it is important not to believe what those other fellows—Buddhists, Naiyāyikas, and the rest—believe is because such beliefs block liberation. The belief about causation which doesn't block liberation is just the belief that everything—world and selves—depends on Brahman. It doesn't matter what logical faults one may find in this belief—believe it anyway! It is better for you if you do. Such an interpretation makes Śaṃkara out to emphasize nonrational intuition or faith and the negative dialectical criticism of all rationally defended beliefs, while ignoring the logical defects in his own theory.[25]

Later Advaita

I now propose to return to some of the problems we have raised about Advaita ontology and its bearing upon relations. For the remainder of this chapter, I shall consider various solutions to these problems. Following my general plan, I shall not necessarily discuss views in chronological order, and therefore those who are acquainted with Advaita in its historical development may find some strange juxtapositions.

Maṇḍana, the reader will remember, was positive that the primary ignorance—which he thought of as the concealing kind—had its abode in the selves. We considered his arguments in favor of that theory and against the alternative that ignorance resides in Brahman, and need not repeat them here. But there are also arguments against his view, arguments he himself suggests. In his *Brahmasiddhi*, Maṇḍana writes:

> But whose is the distorting ignorance? Surely not Brahman's, for he, being the True Self, is devoid of ignorance. Not the selves' either, for they aren't there yet to be ignorant, and thus there is the fault of reciprocal dependence, since the distinction between selves rests on ignorance and ignorance rests on the selves.[26]

He goes on to suggest ways of avoiding these criticisms. The most important is the one we should expect from our previous consideration of the fallacy of reciprocal dependence (pp. 80–81). Maṇḍana says that there is a beginningless series of dependences, on the seed-and-sprout analogy, between the selves and ignorance, so that the situation does not constitute a vicious case. But he apparently doesn't expect to convince many people along those lines. Then, if that fails to satisfy, one must admit, says Maṇḍana, that ignorance, being magical, is inexplicable and we shouldn't press the issue.[27] And he doesn't.

But Advaitins working out the implications of their position can hardly avoid pressing the issue. The difference between those Advaitins who believe that the primal ignorance resides in Brahman (*brahmāśrita*) and those who believe that it resides in the individual self or selves (*jīvāśrita*) constitutes an important cleavage within the school, and terminology for recording the divergence developed among later writers. The residing-in-Brahman group is frequently referred to as the "Vivaraṇa school" after the title of a commentary written by one of them, Prakāśātman; the residing-in-self(ves) group is usually referred to as the "Bhāmatī school," after the name of a commentary written by one of them, Vācaspati Miśra.

What is significant is that neither of these schools is named after works written by their logical originators, Maṇḍana in the latter case, and Śaṃkara's pupil Padmapāda in the former. The reason is not hard to guess: Maṇḍana and Padmapāda were not specific about certain crucial parts of the respective systems; they tended to give up on puzzles, as we just saw Maṇḍana doing—for whatever reasons. To see the implications of the two schools of thought one does best to consult the two works after which they are named, along with the major divergent strains within each school.

The Bhāmatī School: Vācaspati's Theory. I shall deal first with those who accept Maṇḍana's preference for the view that ignorance resides in the self or selves. But the very way I have been forced to put this raises a most important issue: how many selves are there? Vācaspati is quite clear on this, as was Maṇḍana: there are as many selves as we ordinarily think. If there were only one self, he points out following Maṇḍana, when one gets liberated, everyone else would get liberated too. He assumes, not that it is logically impossible that everyone should be liberated at a stroke, but that it is opposed to experience and verbal testimony—everyone knows perfectly well that Śaṃkara, for example, was liberated while his pupils were still ignorant, and the Upanishads speak about Vāmadeva and Śuka being free while others weren't.[28] But he assumes in saying this, we must point out, that there is a common world in which Śaṃkara and his pupils both experience their relative freedoms and bondages. How does this common world come about? If this assumption cannot be substantiated, is it not more reasonable, in keeping with the thesis that one's ignorance is one's own, to conclude that there is only one self and that all the "others" are part of the illusory world that the self projects through its *māyā?*

If he wishes to avoid such metaphysical solipsism Vācaspati must justify the existence of a common world. This is not quite the same problem as the epistemological one about the "existence of the external world" that the British empiricists had on their minds. The question here is not about the priority of the mental over the physical or vice-versa. Advaitins all tend to think of ignorance as at one and the same time "mental" and "physical"—i.e., it is called "ignorance," which suggests a cognitive function, but is also held to be "inert" (*jaḍa*). The question is rather about the priority of something other than the self in the establishment of a common world. If we are to indulge in comparisons, the problem for Vācaspati, who is not a solipsist, is more like Leibniz's: each self is caught up in a beginningless series—or an inexplicable relationship—with a primal ignorance (*mulāvidyā*) of his own, and he also projects, by a secondary ignorance (*tulāvidyā*) equally his own, the empirical world in which his body moves and his senses operate. Does this make him a "windowless monad?" Yes, unless some appeal is made to a principle other than the self to co-ordinate or otherwise provide the occasion for simultaneity and similarity of experiences. But Vācaspati himself turns out to be somewhat inadequate on this topic.[29]

There are, in principle, four alternative views that an ignorance-resides-in-self(ves) theorist may espouse. He may say, as Vācaspati does, that there are many selves and a different primal ignorance for each of them. He may say that there are many selves but only one primal ignorance. He might even say that there is only one self but many primal ignorances.[d] And finally, he may hold that there is only one self and one primal ignorance.

It is fairly clear what the broad outlines of Vācaspati's theory are, but much more doubtful what the details of his theory involve. To get an idea of the sorts of things that Indian philosophers have said and what Vācaspati may have believed, I turn to a difficult but suggestive passage which occurs in the *Saṃkṣepaśārīraka* of Sarvajñātman, a philosopher whose own views figure prominently in this discussion and who keenly combats the rival positions of which he was aware. He lists no less than seven different theories in addition to his own, several of which are of the Bhāmatī type.[e] Unfortunately, Sarvajñātman does not designate by name the holders of these views, and his commentators[30] are only able to spot Maṇḍana's views among them. Actually, we know little about the Bhāmatī school outside of the works of Maṇḍana, Vācaspati, and one or two commentaries on the latter's *Bhāmatī*,[31] and we are missing one very important work by Vācaspati, his commentary on Maṇḍana's *Brahmasiddhi*.[32]

Maṇḍana, we saw, held that there are many selves and many ignorances, but he failed to comment upon the question of a common world. Three of the views set forth in *Saṃkṣepaśārīraka* suggest ways of completing Maṇḍana's theory. I shall consider them briefly.

The proponent of the first argument that I want to consider—we may call him "A"—is made to say:

> There are many ignorances and also unnumbered selves. These selves are the abodes of both true knowledges and ignorant ones. For those who seek freedom there is cessation of pain in one age or another.

[d] As far as I know, no one holds this view; it is, in addition, not easy to see why anyone should want to. It involves an unnecessary complication. In the discussion which follows, I shall assume it is not a feasible alternative.

[e] His own theory is not, however, being a residence-in-Brahman theory. See below.

So far so good. But now how about the common world?

> *Māyā*, by entering into a relationship with God, turns the wheel of transmigration.

But this seems just to *add* an ignorance—God's. And it brings an unwelcome consequence, as Nṛsiṃhāśrama (a commentator) brings out, for if we are bound by God's ignorance as well as our own, then how can we ever get salvation unless God does? And worse yet, how can there be one liberation without all getting liberation, since everyone must wait on God's liberation? All this, retorts A, is irreverent prattle and admits of a perfectly natural explanation:

> Hearing a few words of scripture, (the seekers) become mindful of the contradictory nature of divinity.[33]

God, it seems, is beyond logic. We are led to a consideration of the complexities of divinity, and shall turn to them shortly. First, however, we want to see if justice can be done to the problem at hand in any other fashion.

Whereas A's account referred us to God to explain the community of experience between the various selves, the next one, B's, will refer us to what the Hindus call the "internal cause" or "organ" (*antaḥkāraṇa*). Authorities differ about its makeup,[f] but for us the psychology doesn't matter. What B says is this:

> Even as [in common experience] the mind by its own functioning produces the obscuring darkness in an otherwise pure object, just so the internal organ, which is exceedingly subtle but external and always present, must produce the darknesses in that pure consciousness which is the essential nature of Brahman.[34]

The idea is this: each individual ignorance produces an individual self, as Maṇḍana holds. But external to these ignorances lies the very subtle internal cause, and it is only when each ignorance comes into relation with the internal cause that a self comes into being. Conversely, it is by separating one's ignorance from the internal cause that one becomes free.

This, however, seems only to push the problem back a step. Where does this internal cause come from? Brahman? God? The individual

[f] The *antaḥkāraṇa* is frequently taken to consist at least of the *buddhi*, the *manas* and the *ahaṃkāra*. It is a conception, important in Sāṃkhya, which Advaita has assimilated into its own framework. It is usually called the "internal organ" in English, but since in Advaita it is not really an "organ" I shall translate it here as "internal cause"—a literal rendering.

selves? And besides, what sort of an entity is it which is an "internal" cause and yet is "external"? Clearly, the situation is being complicated, but it is not at all clear that the complications are worth the effort.

One might suppose that once the notion that there is a plurality of primal ignorances is abandoned in favor of the theory that there is only one ignorance residing in the many selves, the problem about the common world would resolve itself easily. Unfortunately, it's not that easy. The question then is: how can we understand a single entity producing a plurality—i.e., on what model? How does the single primal ignorance come to produce a multitude of souls? On this point there are two, possibly three, major suggestions which occupy an important niche in Advaitic lore.

One model, known as "limitationism" (*avacchedavāda*), derives from the fact that there are entities that we ordinarily assume not to break into parts even when they are limited by other entities. For example, the general property of blueness remains general even though at this moment it is instantiated in the cover of the book at my elbow; the particular spatio-temporal location of it is merely accidental and does not affect the essence, blueness. Again, considering space as an entity which pervades the universe, we ordinarily assume that space remains unaffected when it gets limited within the confines of, say, a certain jar. The space in the jar is essentially space itself, and the limitations of the occurrences of certain material patterns are merely accidental, as we can see by smashing the jar and observing that the space remains.

A second model, known as "reflectionism" (*pratibimbavāda*), takes its lead from the experience of seeing, say, my face reflected in a mirror; when this happens it is not that my face has broken into two parts—if so, I would be in pain. Nevertheless, the mirror-image is not something distinct from my face, as we can see by the fact that the image disappears when my face is removed from its vicinity. Technically, in this model, my face may be called the prototype (*bimba*) and the mirror-image the reflection (*pratibimba*).

There may even be a third model, according to which consciousness strikes off splinters of itself to form apparent individual consciousnesses (selves). This is sometimes referred to as "appearance-theory" (*ābhāsavāda*), but as there is some question as to whether it is a *model* like the others or rather a *theory* in its own right, it is frequently not mentioned as an alternative.[35]

The tradition is that the Bhāmatī school propounds limitationism and the Vivaraṇa school reflectionism; the appearance-theory is usually associated with Sureśvara and his followers, whom I interpret as leap-theorists. But in fact we find Vācaspati in the *Bhāmatī* itself using both the language of limitation and of reflection indiscriminately. And some philosophers apparently used both models together. For example, "C," another gentleman in Sarvajñātman's unidentified group, says:

> Ignorance, like a universal which among material things produces the erroneous impression that it has parts, is like a mirror which reflects the selves where Brahman is the prototype.[36]

Here both models are used together. Each model has its peculiar difficulties, and it is a fair question whether an explanation such as C's doesn't face both sorts of difficulty together. In any case, some modern scholars have tried to associate this view with Vācaspati's name. Since their explanation is valuable in its own right, I pause for a moment to sketch it for the reader.

One thorny problem for Vācaspati is what to do with God. Śaṃkara clearly makes room for God. Maṇḍana seems more or less atheistic. Vācaspati is in the position of trying to effect a compromise. He wishes to preserve Maṇḍana's view of ignorance residing in many selves, but he also wishes to find a function for God in order to interpret the passages in the Brahmasūtras and in Śaṃkara's commentary on which Vācaspati's *Bhāmatī* is itself a sub-commentary. A translator of the *Bhāmatī*, S. Suryanarayana Sastri, with help from his mentor S. Kuppuswami Sastri, suggests the following view as Vācaspati's.

Ignorance has two aspects: it belongs to someone, and it is controlled by someone. In most cases, these functions coincide, so that we ordinarily mean by saying that something is "mine" both that it belongs to me and that it is in my control. Not so with ignorance. When we say "I am ignorant" we do not mean that the ignorance is in my control but rather merely that it belongs to me in the sense that it affects me. The selves are the locus of ignorance in the sense that it affects them, but ignorance is under the control, not of the selves, but of God. God, using the ignorance of each one of us, creates the common world, just as one might, by an elaborate set-up of mirrors and private rooms, produce a series of "common worlds" for percipients in the private rooms by holding up an object in front of the "master mirror."[37]

The only trouble with this interpretation of Vācaspati, fascinating though it be in itself, is that it fails utterly to explain why the *Bhāmatī* became linked with limitationism rather than reflectionism.[38] But that is a problem for scholars. It rather looks, in any case, as if Vācaspati was unclear about some issues and in such a way that we don't know which issues he left unresolved.

Metaphysical Solipsism. Continuing to suppose that ignorance resides in selves, we have seen that there are at least two pressing questions on the agenda: how many ignorances are there?, and how many selves are there? We have discussed two possibilities—that there are many selves and either one or many ignorances. Now we must consider the possibility that there is only one self. It is certainly not Maṇḍana's view.[39] I shall denominate it as "metaphysical solipsism," the view that the existence of the world depends on the functioning of one self only. It should be distinguished from "epistemological solipsism," which is the view that I cannot *know* that any other selves exist. Note too that one does not, in order to be a metaphysical solipsist in my sense, have to suppose that *his* is the one self on which the existence of the world depends—the question of ownership, as we saw in discussing Vācaspati and the mirrors, is a tricky one. The Indians call metaphysical solipsism "the belief that seeing precedes creating" (*dṛṣṭisṛṣṭivāda*) and contrast it with "the belief that creating precedes seeing" (*sṛṣṭidṛṣṭivāda*). "Seeing" here does not mean a mental as opposed to a physical creation, but a private rather than a public creation.

The metaphysical solipsist can easily explain our experience of a common world: it is the only world there can be. But of course his view has the awkward consequence that there is only one liberation—that of the one self—and therefore that *jīvānmukti* or liberation-while-living on the part of other selves is only a sham liberation.

Metaphysical solipsism in Advaita is particularly associated with the name of Prakāśānanda, the author of *Vedāntasiddhāntamuktāvalī*. However, the fact is that Prakāśānanda is rather clearly a leap theorist. He takes *ajātivāda* very seriously indeed and refuses to speculate about the relation between Brahman and the self. Therefore, it may be pointed out, the scholarly controversy about whether Prakāśānanda's solipsism is the logical outcome of the Bhāmatī or of the Vivaraṇa type of Advaita is a controversy which should not arise at all, since Prakāśānanda is, if anything, a follower of Sureśvara's type of Advaita, which is of the leap sort.[40] We shall have more to say about Prakāśānanda in Chapter 11.

The Vivaraṇa School: Padmapāda's System. Suppose we are dissatisfied with the implications of Maṇḍana's system: can we do any better on the view that the primal ignorance resides in Brahman itself? As Maṇḍana pointed out, the primary objection to this alternative is that, since Brahman is perfect, is the pure Witness, It can't very well become ignorant Itself. How, then, can it be said that ignorance belongs to Brahman?

Once again, we may conveniently survey the field by considering in turn those philosophers who (1) believe there are many selves and one ignorance, (2) believe there are many selves and many ignorances, and (3) believe there is only one self and, therefore, one ignorance.

Before doing so, however, we should pay our respects to the philosopher who is really the father of the Vivaraṇa school, Śaṃkara's other pupil besides Sureśvara, Padmapāda. In his *Pañcapādikā*, a commentary on the first bit of his teacher's great commentary on the Brahmasūtras, Padmapāda introduces the characteristic features of the Vivaraṇa school's interpretation of Advaita. Ignorance resides in Brahman,[41] and there is a tendency to emphasize reflectionism over limitationism.[42] His position on the number of selves and the number of ignorances remains somewhat obscure, however. When Padmapāda uses the term "self" (*jīva*) he regularly uses it in the singular, which might suggest that he was a metaphysical solipsist; unhappily, though, his use of the Sanskrit language is such that these instances aren't conclusive.[43] The question we are interested in answering is whether Padmapāda believes that in addition to the One Self, Brahman the Witness, and the illusory egos of our experience, there is also a self which projects the egos and which enjoys the bliss of release. If we could be sure he admits at least one such self, we might ask in turn whether there is more than one. But Padmapāda's way of putting things doesn't even let us get to this latter question, for every time he suspects the reader of forgetting that the truth of Advaita is that we are essentially of the nature of Brahman, he reminds us that the self (*jīva*) is identical with the Self (*ātman*). What is dubious is whether he is speaking in the abstract or in the concrete—does he mean that the *nature* of selves is essentially pure, or does he mean that the only self there is is the One Self?

His use of the reflection model is particularly instructive in this connection. In an important passage, he compares the situation to our seeing two moons in the lake when the water is rippling slightly. "By means of the example of the double-moon," he writes, "the illusion of difference between the self(ves) and God, and among the selves, is shown to be not of the nature of the Self."[44] The Sanskrit doesn't distinguish in the first occurrence of "self" in this passage between singular and plural—an unhappy drawback of an otherwise magnificent language. To clarify the situation, it seems, we shall have to consult Padmapāda's commentators and see how the model of reflectionism is spelled out in more detail.

True to Śaṃkara's lead, Padmapāda talks quite a bit about God, e.g., as in the above-quoted passage, or as the creator of the internal cause(s), for instance. But when the question arises as to who exactly God is Padmapāda turns decidedly evasive. On the basis of the quotation just offered, he has to say that somehow God and the self(ves) are one, but it is not clear whether this means "in the final analysis" or from our point of view too. In a later passage, discussing the topic, he first offers a "no comment" attitude ("there's no point in discussing the various views about the objects denoted by 'I' "),[45] and then seems to treat that as not really doing justice to Śaṃkara, suggesting that one ought to use one's reason and consult the scriptures to find out the truth—which is that the self is essentially the Self![46] It would seem that we had better consult the commentators for a clearer view about God also.

Nevertheless, we can at this point get a good picture of the differences between Padmapāda and Sureśvara, the two students of the master Śaṃkarācārya. While Sureśvara, as we shall see, tends toward leap thinking by taking *ajātivāda* very seriously, Padmapāda tries to stay within the framework of progress philosophy, with some hesitation at times, as his treatment of God shows. In fact, he seems to try to walk an extremely tight rope to avoid Sureśvara's incipient mysticism and Maṇḍana's robust use of reason. And it is this tight-rope walking that seems to have inspired much of the most important philosophical activity within Advaita; whereas there are extremely few famous members of the Bhāmatī school besides its founder Vācaspati, there are any number of important names to consider when we turn to the Vivaraṇa branch of Advaita. And so, now, we shall.

The Vivaraṇa *Itself: Prakāśātman's System*. Prakāśātman, the author of the *Vivaraṇa*, which is a commentary on Padmapāda's *Pañcapādikā*, uses elements of practically every one of the views we have considered so far, and develops an elaborate ontology. Brahman, he avers, has two natures, one essential (*svarūpalakṣaṇa*), the other accidental (*taṭastha-lakṣaṇa*).[47] The former we may call the pure Witness (*sākṣin*), while the latter is God (*īśvara*). The pure Witness is, of course, unblemished by any relation with ignorance, but God is a lower manifestation of the Witness through the *vivarta*-type of relation, i.e., through the Witness' being qualified "as it were" by primal ignorance.[48] Now God is both the material and the efficient cause of the world: he is efficient in his conscious and active powers as *śakti* ("power"), and he is the stuff of the world through his nature as primal ignorance. God, then, creates the world out of the primal ignorance, or rather—since there's nobody around yet to experience a world—he creates the subtle source of the world, the internal cause (*antaḥkāraṇa*).

But so far there are no selves to experience this subtle stuff. Prakāśātman explains, then, that the pure Witness is reflected as a diversity of images which are the selves, just as the moon becomes reflected in a diversity of "moons" in the water, or as my face becomes many in a room full of mirrors. The water, or the mirror, is in fact the internal cause itself. However, and this is an important point, although the reflecting medium is insentient, being made of ignorance, the selves reflected in it are conscious; they cannot be called "pure" witnesses, since they are not free, but *essentially* they are of the same stuff as the pure Witness, Brahman itself. That is how, though they are apparently "born" of the reflection in the subtle medium, they themselves do not become inert like the medium. Just so, we know, the selves are conscious *of* the medium and, due to their limited nature, project through a secondary ignorance the illusion of an empirical world. The empirical world, in turn, is explained by the Vivaraṇa school much as Sāṃkhya, e.g., Īśvarakṛṣṇa, explained it: in fact, Sāṃkhya enters into Advaita just at this point, and consequently tends to lose its identity outside of the Advaitic tradition in more recent philosophy.[49]

The Vivaraṇa view solves several of the problems raised by Maṇḍana's and Vācaspati's interpretations, but only to raise more problems of its own. It succeeds in explaining how there can be a common world, how the "internal cause" can be "external" (the two descriptions have different references), where the internal cause comes from, and who God is. But it runs into trouble particularly on the topic of how freedom is obtained. We saw that Maṇḍana's major point against the ignorance-resides-in-Brahman view was that Brahman must in that case be that which becomes free. This difficulty haunts the Vivaraṇa system. Prakāśātman is forced to hold that ignorance resides in Brahman but that the right knowledge which removes ignorance resides in the particular selves.[50] The right knowledge which removes ignorance cannot be the pure and uncontaminated omniscience of the Witness, since the Witness never loses its omniscience and so cannot rediscover it.

It is for reasons such as this one that the Vivaranist develops the challenging thesis that the selves, as reflections, are *identical* with the supreme Self and just as "real" as Brahman.[51] By somehow equating the selves with Brahman, he can hold that Brahman is after all the residence of both true and false knowledge about itself. This is where the model of reflectionism proves so handy. The Vivaranist argues that even in our experience we know that in truth the image of my face in the mirror is nothing different from my face itself; it is just as real. We sometimes get fooled, however, when we see a mirror-image and don't see its prototype. Temporarily we think the face is located where the image is, but as soon as we realize that the face is somewhere else, we are no longer deluded. Not that, of course, we stop seeing the image—that goes on as long as the face and the mirror remain where they are. But when we realize that the image *is* an image we no longer think of it as something different from its prototype. Just so, says the Vivaranist, in truth the self is nothing different from the Self, but because of ignorance we see ourselves but not their prototype, the Self. Freedom comes when we realize that the self is just a reflection of the Self—not that of course we stop seeing ourselves as before; that goes on as long as the Self and the internal cause remain as they are; but the self is free as soon as it understands the truth.

There are difficulties with this model, of course. One is that if the individual self is like the image of my face, it is insentient—and how then can it think itself to be different from the Self or discover that it is identical? This is admittedly a defect in the model, as Padmapāda has himself shown in the *Pañcapādikā*.[52] The self is not *just* like my face—the former is conscious by nature, being identical with the Witness; the latter is insentient by nature, being an evolute from the internal cause.

Another disturbing difficulty arises with respect to what happens when one self becomes free. Since gaining freedom is now identified with understanding one's identity with the Self, and not as suddenly transcending ordinary consciousness, the Vivaranist can say that other selves continue to exist even after one becomes free. In this he echoes Upanishadic passages in which we are told of the previous liberation of such saints as Vāmadeva and Śuka. This would hardly be possible otherwise, one would think. But granted that freedom does not put an end to experience, what happens when the *karma* which hangs on, and is to be worked off (*prārabdhakarma*), comes to an end, and the free self *does* stop experiencing? How does this affect the machinery? If there is only one ignorance and one internal cause, how can one self be free of all his *karma* and another not? Sarvajñātman pushes this attack strongly:

> If in the self-luminous Brahman qualified by delusion there could be the introduction of an *upādhi*, the mental organ [*antaḥkāraṇa*], just like the throwing of fire by means of a firebrand, the delusion would not remain fixed in a certain spot. The thrown fire, through the fire brand, pervading the place [where it lands] causes the whole to flame

> up; just so in our case the darkness [of ignorance] begins by pervading the appearance [i.e., the self] but then goes on to pervade the whole of Brahman.[53]

Sarvajñātman concludes that the internal cause cannot produce bondage for one self without producing it for all, and conversely there can be no liberation for one self at a time. He, in fact, concludes that there is only one self.

The System of Sarvajñātman's Saṃkṣepaśārīraka. Sarvajñātman is supposed to have been a pupil of Sureśvara, whose views we have yet to consider, but whom we have mentioned as the logical heir to Śaṃkara's leap-philosophy propensities. Sarvajñātman represents an interesting intermediate position between the frank acceptance of relations by Padmapāda and Prakāśātman and Sureśvara's refusal to discuss relations.

Sarvajñātman believes that ignorance resides in Brahman. He believes there is only one ignorance, and only one individual self. But his solipsism is hedged around with a good deal of ontological apparatus—unlike that, say, of Prakāśānanda, whose picture of the world is extremely simple (it consists of Brahman, period).

Sarvajñātman recognizes at least five distinct categories worthy of discussion—the pure Witness, God, the primal ignorance, the self, and the world. The Witness is unrelated to anything—on this point Sarvajñātman assumes a stand of *ajātivāda* as uncompromising as Sureśvara's. But below the unrelated Absolute one can say a good deal about relations.

In the center of Sarvajñātman's picture of the cosmos looms the one primal ignorance, called both *avidyā* and *māyā*,[54] having both the concealing and projective powers. God and the self are closely related to these two powers of ignorance. God is the controller of the projective power of ignorance;[55] omniscient, He is not dependent upon this power, but because of His association with it, He is not on the highest plane of reality with the Witness. The self is controlled by the concealing power of this same ignorance or magic, being deluded by it.[56] God creates this illusion by reflecting Himself in the internal cause (*antaḥkāraṇa*) as the external world. A peculiarity of Sarvajñātman's account is that the world is actually external though there is only one self to experience it. The model of reflectionism is used by Sarvajñātman to illustrate the relation between God and the self—God is the prototype, the self the reflection, and the world, i.e., the internal cause, is the mirror.[57] (It will have been noted that in Prakāśātman's theory, the Witness was the prototype, not God.)

Freedom for the self is obtained by destroying the concealing type of ignorance,[58] but knowledge alone is sufficient to effect the destruction, and when ignorance is destroyed, "nothing special happens"[59]—as in the *Vivaraṇa*, freedom consists in understanding one's identity with the Witness, not in blotting out all appearances.

But how is the concealing ignorance to be destroyed? Other theories can say that one seeks out a *guru* and is enlightened with his aid, but in the world of the *Saṃkṣepaśārīraka*, since there's only one self, "me," there is no *guru* to consult! True, answers Sarvajñātman, the *guru* is a creature of your imagination, in the same sense in which the rest of the world is, but his teachings are none the less efficacious. Sarvajñātman offers several analogies from Hindu lore to illustrate how erroneous knowledge can enlighten one; he also points out that one can be killed by an imaginary snake—out of sheer fright, presumably![60] So it is that one should be taught by an imaginary *guru*.

One or two criticisms are neatly met in this clever defense of Advaita. For instance, it is said that God is omniscient, but according to the *Saṃkṣepaśārīraka* he is limited by ignorance. How can this be the proper way of understanding God? The answer is that "omniscience" means "lacking the concealing type of ignorance." God can be omniscient, in this sense, and still limited by His connection with the *projective* aspect of *māyā*.[61] Vidyāraṇya in his *Pañcadaśī* takes over this explanation and improves upon it slightly by linking God with the *guṇa sattva*, while the self is linked with the *guṇa tamas*.[62]

A less happy defense is occasioned by a familiar and particularly thorny problem. There is only one self, according to Sarvajñātman, and yet, as we know, scripture tells us that Vāmadeva and Śuka were freed while others remained bound. How can that be explained on solipsistic terms? Sarvajñātman wriggles under this difficulty. In one place he says that if the scripture were taken literally the whole Advaita doctrine would be undermined,[63] so that the passages in question must be understood as true only from the lower standpoint, as intended to direct our understanding in the proper direction.[64] Elsewhere he ascribes this appearance of some being saved while others are not to temporal abnormalities of the kind noticed in our dreams, where events really far apart in time are juxtaposed and simultaneous occurrences are separated.[65]

Other Advaitins. The picture one forms of post-Śaṃkara Advaita is three-pronged. On the one hand there are the Bhāmatī theorists, following Maṇḍana and Vācaspati, who use the model of limitation and locate ignorance in the self or selves. Amalānanda and Appaya Dīkṣita have written commentaries in this tradition. In the middle are the Vivaraṇa theorists, following Padmapāda and Prakāśātman, who use the model of reflection and locate ignorance in Brahman. On the other hand is the no-relations, leap-philosophy of Sureśvara. All Advaitins have a leap-philosophy side; it appears at some point in everyone's explanation, although some labor harder to keep it as hidden as possible. The tendency toward metaphysical solipsism is, one suspects, in part this tendency to leap-philosophy working itself out in systematic fashion.

There are many other famous names in Advaitic literature besides those we have mentioned, but the theories of all of them can be appreciated by linking them to the three main prongs spoken of above. For example, developing from Sarvajñātman's hedged solipsism, a branch of the Vivaraṇa school which tends to touch on leap-thinking, one can identify the franker solipsism of Ānandabodha and Citsukha, both of whom combine a belief in one self only with a lively inclination toward negative dialectics designed to refute all ontological speculation except the minimal amount required in a "solipsistic ontology."

Another effect of the gradual Sureśvarizing of Advaita is the substitution of Sureśvara's language in place of either the models of limitationism or reflectionism. For example, we find this in Vidyāraṇya's *Pañcadaśī,* which, though often quoted as an expression of Prakāśātman's system, is equally well understood as an expression of Sarvajñātman's line of thought. Vidyāraṇya speaks constantly of the selves as "appearances of consciousness" (*cidābhāsa*), by which he seems to mean particular rays of the pure light given off by the Witness. The expression "appearances of consciousness" is a favorite of Sureśvara.

Perhaps the most impressive development of Advaitic thought is in the direction of compromise and adjustment among all three of the "prongs." We find this expressed in the most easily available English translations of works of post-Śaṃkara Advaita, such as the *Vedāntaparibhāṣā* of Dharmarājādhvarīndra and the *Vedāntasāra* of Sadānanda. The most thorough-going synthesizer was, however, quite possibly the author of an enormous compendium of Advaita, *Advaitasiddhi,* the consummate philosopher named Madhusūdana Sarasvatī. A fourth important source of compromise is Appaya Dīkṣita's *Siddhāntaleśasaṃgraha.* In all these works we find two significant tendencies. First, these writers tend to steer clear of the kind of intramural controversies we have been discussing just now—so that they are content merely to list, for example, the different sorts of models with a noncommittal "some say this" and make no attempt at resolution. And second, they show a penchant for explaining their reluctance to resolve these difficulties through appeal to the unimportance of speculation and the relatively greater importance of teaching, which, though ultimately false, nevertheless guides the pupil in the right direction. One may see here an attempt on the part of Advaita to absolve itself of responsibility toward the kind of doubt I have been suggesting gives rise to systematic philosophy. Philosophy becomes, for these Advaitins as for other leap philosophers, not the concern of clarifying doubts in order to clear the way for renunciation, but guidance toward that very renunciation itself. As Advaita develops, there is a growing awareness that the only proper function of the philosopher's tools is the production of greater maturity—greater readiness for freedom—by the use of negative dialectic and subtle readings of the scriptures. Positive theories or systems become *passé*. With this development, Advaita begins to take on the look that it has come to have today, that of an eschewal of systematic philosophy rather than an espousal of it.

CONCLUSIONS

I have tried to survey in some detail the five major theories of relations found among the philosophies of India, to indicate their strengths and their difficulties, and to give the reader some idea of the way in which the interrelationships among these five major types of theory provide a kind of scheme by reference to which one can see the most important points of similarity and contrast among the various systems of philosophy we have mentioned. To review this scheme rapidly: in the middle stand the Jains, who hold a view of double dependence relations. On the extreme wings stand the leap theorists, Nāgārjuna on the left, Sureśvara on the right, denying the existence of any dependence relations whatsoever. In between come the other speculative systems—Nyāya-Vaiśeṣika and the Buddhists to the left, Sāṃkhya and the Vedāntists to the right.

What are the major points of comparison and contrast among these schools? First, with respect to the problem of the One and the Many, the schools on the left believe that the many are more real than the one, while those on the right believe that unity is more basic than diversity. As a result, where the left-hand theorists require an explanation for unity, the right-hand theorists require an explanation for diversity. Therefore, the causal relation is a many-one relation for the left-hand group, a one-many relation for the right-hand group. For the Jains, both kinds of relations operate together.

A second point of differentiation concerns the various systems' willingness to draw a reality-appearance distinction. This is not merely an epistemological distinction, as it turns out. The Nyāya-Vaiśeṣikas on the left do not draw any distinction between reality and appearance, but the Sautrāntikas waver, and in Yogācāra and Buddhist logic the distinction is clearly made. Likewise, to the right Sāṃkhya, Rāmānuja and Bhedābhedavāda do not emphasize such a distinction; Maṇḍana and the Bhāmatī school of Advaita waver, and in Śaṃkara and the Vivaraṇa school there is a clear distinction drawn between the real and the unreal. The comparison between the extremes is even more impressive when we remember that just as Śaṃkara and his followers draw a three-fold distinction between the real, the empirical and the illusory realms, so do those Buddhist logicians of later times who are trying to straddle the line between the views of Dignāga and those of Nāgārjuna.

These major points of comparison and contrast can be utilized by the thoughtful reader to generate fairly accurate predictions about what sorts of views the various systems are likely to hold on other philosophical problems. For example, on universals one expects, quite correctly, that the right-hand theorists will take the particular as dependent upon the universal and that the left-hand theorists will take the universal to depend upon the particular.

And following upon the second point of difference mentioned above, concerning the reality-appearance distinction, one may make certain guesses about the theories of these schools of thought about the nature of knowledge. In the next chapter, I shall explore the topic of erroneous knowledge (and in the course of that negation as well), suggesting that the nature of the view of each of the systematic thinkers on negation and error is dominated by his views about the causal or dependence relation.

NOTES

1. *Samkhyakarika* (59), p. 94.
2. S. S. S. Shastri's alternative translation of *Samkhyakarika* (60), p. 95.
3. In Chapter 11 we will see that the emphasis on devotion (*bhakti*) as the primary path is often symptomatic of a tendency to leap thinking. This emphasis is clear in Rāmānuja and becomes more pronounced in his followers. Despite this, and despite the fact that many of the outstanding scholars read Rāmānuja himself as a leap theorist, I still feel that Rāmānuja represents a logical continuation of Sāṃkhya intellectualism, as witness that side of Viśiṣṭādvaita found in Yāmuna and Ātreya Rāmānuja, for example. In any case, his contributions to progress philosophy, like Śaṃkara's, are so profound that they cannot be overlooked. Śaṃkara presents a similar problem in classification.
4. See, however, K. C. Varadachari, "Some Reflections and Notes on South Indian Mysticism," submitted to the All-India Oriental Conference at Annamalainagara, December 1955, and read at the Religion and Philosophy Section, pp. 315 ff.

Varadachari thinks that the usual identification of cat-salvation with *prapatti* and the distinction between *prapatti* and *bhakti* is the result of "some kind of loose thinking."

5. The present discussion is based on M. Hiriyanna, "Fragments of Bhartr-Prapanca," *Proceedings of the All-India Oriental Conference* 3:439–450 (1924), and Hiriyanna's summary of Bhartṛprapañca's views in *Indian Philosophical Studies*, pp. 79–94 (from *Indian Antiquary*, pp. 77–86 (1924).

6. But not for Bhāskara. See *Philosophy of Bhedabheda*, pp. 34–39.

7. *Indian Philosophical Studies*, p. 85.

8. *Source Book*, pp. 69–70.

9. The term *vivarta* seems to come into Advaita from the grammarians through Maṇḍana. Śaṃkara does not use it in the sense we are discussing. See *Vivarta*, especially pp. 13 ff., 24, 34.

10. Mandana, pp. 11–12. For this account of the material in the *Brahmasiddhi*, as for much else in this section on Advaita, I am indebted to Mr. A. J. Alston's unpublished manuscript of an introduction to his translation of the *Naiṣkarmyasiddhi* of Sureśvara, as well as to private discussions with him. He is not responsible for any failings in my treatment, however.

11. Mandana, p. 22.

12. Mandana, pp. 130–132.

13. Mandana, p. 12.

14. Mandana, p. 36.

15. Mandana, p. 9. Ingalls thinks the use of this concept leads Advaita to a "multivalued logic." Cf. Ingalls$_2$, p. 72, note 3.

16. Cf. Hacker and Ingalls$_2$.

17. See previous note.

18. For the rope-snake example, see, e.g., *Upadesasahasri*, p. 219. For the red crystal, *Upadesasahasri*, p. 102. For foam and waves, *Upadesasahasri*, p. 12 and Belvalkar, pp. 28–29 of the English. Magic-show, *Upadesasahasri*, p. 200. Mirage, Belvalkar, p. 30 of the English. Space in a jar, Belvalkar, pp. 29–30 of the English. Magnet, *Upadesasahasri*, p. 214. Milk and curds, Belvalkar, pp. 52–53 of the English. This represents a hurried sampling; no doubt there are many other illustrations that could be gleaned by consulting all Śaṃkara's writings.

19. Singh, pp. 355 ff. *Vivarta*, p. 208.

20. E.g., in his commentary on Gauḍapāda's *Māṇḍūkyakārikābhāṣya* (I.7) in *Upanishadbhasya*, p. 431.

21. *Gitabhasya* (IV.6), p. 121; (VII.14), p. 213; (VII.25), p. 218.

22. Śaṃkara on Gauḍapāda on *Māṇḍūkyakārikās* (II.12, 19) in *Upanishadbhasya*, pp. 445, 447. Gaudapada, pp. 22, 29.

23. *Brahmasutrabhasya* (I.1.2), pp. 7–9.

24. Cf. Singh.

25. There are still other ways of reading Śaṃkara. Father De Smet, for example, a Catholic, reads him as a "theologian," seeing in him that peculiar combination of faith and reason characteristic of, e.g., St. Thomas. Cf. De Smet.

26. Mandana, p. 10. My translation.

27. Mandana, p. 10.

28. Hasurkar, pp. 187–188.

29. As suggested by Hasurkar, p. 200.

30. Nṛsiṃhāśrama in *Tattvabodhinī* and Madhusūdana Sarasvatī in *Sārsañgraha* were consulted.

31. Amalānanda's *Kalpataru* and Appaya Dīkṣita's *Parimala*. There are a few others. See Dasgupta, Volume II, p. 108.

32. The work, entitled *Tattvasámīkṣā*, is referred to by Vācaspati himself, among others, but is not known to exist even in manuscript.

33. These passages are from *Saṃkṣepaśārīraka* (I.133). Cf. Sarvajnatman, pp. 75–76; *Samksepa*, pp. 663–664.

34. Sarvajnatman (I.135), pp. 76–77; *Samksepa*, p. 665.

35. But Madhusūdana, for example, takes it as a third kind of model. Cf. *Siddhantabindu*, p. 25 of the Sanskrit, p. 231 of the English.

36. Sarvajnatman (I.132), p. 75; *Samksepa*, pp. 662–663.

37. See *Bhamati*, pp. xxxiv–xxxviii. Dasgupta, Volume II, pp. 109–111, has a different interpretation.

38. At least one scholar has argued (in Bengali) that Vācaspati was as much a reflectionist as a limitationist. See Sengupta, pp. 255–256 and note 159 for the argument and a discussion of it. See also *Siddhantabindu*, pp. 231–232.

39. Although Sengupta, pp. 223–224, says it is.

40. But see Murti's chapter in *Ajnana*, p. 209 and second footnote; Hasurkar, pp. 207 et passim. *Bhamati*, p. xxii, seems to me to take the correct position.

41. *Avidyā* is said to be *jīvatvāpādika*, "the cause of selfhood." Padmapada, p. 67; *Pancapadika*, p. 98.

42. Reflectionism is defended at length in Padmapada, pp. 72–82; *Pancapadika*, pp. 104–117.

43. Padmapada (See Bibliography) has a useful index; by consulting it and the matching Sanskrit one can see what is involved. The point is illustrated in the next paragraph in the text.

44. *Pancapadika*, p. 71. My translation. Padmapada, p. 46.

45. *Pancapadika*, p. 288. My translation.

46. Padmapada, p. 254; *Pancapadika*, p. 289. Venkataramiah translates *ātmā* in the second passage as "Īśvara," which presumes more than is given.

47. On the two *lakṣaṇas* of Brahman, see Murti's contribution to K. C. Bhattacharya MV, pp. 135–150; also *Indian Philosophical Studies*, pp. 98–103.

48. See Madhusūdana's description in *Siddhantabindu*, p. 28 of the Sanskrit and p. 231 of the English. Also cf. *Advaitamoda*, p. 9.

49. ". . . barring a few distinctions . . . of little practical repercussions . . . there is no noteworthy difference in the outlooks held up by the Sṛṣṭi-Dṛṣṭi-vādins on one hand and the protagonists of Sāṃkhya school on the other, as is traditionally supported by a popular dictum—'vyavahāre tu Sāṃkhya-nayaḥ.' " Hasurkar, pp. 229–230.

50. Sengupta, pp. 249 ff., discusses this difficulty; see his references.

51. Sengupta, p. 240.

52. Padmapada, pp. 76–78.

53. *Samksepa* (II.160–161), pp. 674–675. My translation.

54. *Samksepa* (II.108), pp. 631–632 (II.170), pp. 683–685 and Sarvajnatman, p. 83.

55. *Samksepa* (II.187), p. 697; Sarvajnatman, p. 67.

56. *Samksepa* (II.190), p. 699; Sarvajnatman, pp. 68–69.

57. *Samksepa* (II.169), pp. 681–682; Sarvajnatman, p. 82.

58. *Samksepa* (I.303), pp. 298–299; Sarvajnatman, p. 89.

59. Sharma's translation of *Saṃkṣepaśārīraka* (II.239–240). *Samksepa*, pp. 745–746; Sarvajnatman, pp. 101–102.

60. *Samksepa* (II.227–232), pp. 736–740; Sarvajnatman, pp. 99–100.

61. *Samksepa* (II.183), p. 695; Sarvajnatman, p. 66.

62. *Pancadasi* (I.16–24), pp. 10–14; Vidyaranya, pp. 11–13.

63. *Samksepa* (II.215), p. 828; Sarvajnatman, p. 90.

64. *Samksepa* (II.218–219), pp. 730–731; Sarvajnatman, pp. 19–20.

65. *Samksepa* (II.129–131), pp. 737–738; Sarvajnatman, pp. 100.

10

NEGATION AND ERROR

The reader may recall that in all the chains which the classical systematic philosophers offered to explain the causes of bondage, the category of false knowledge or ignorance appeared. And in many if not all reverse chains (those leading to freedom) correct knowledge figures as the key type of event which leads regularly to freedom. A very real and constant source of doubt on the part of a seeker for freedom is this: can erroneous knowledge in fact be dispelled, and in such a way that it will not return? If complete freedom is a state from which one does not relapse, how can this state be achieved through human understanding which is known from experience to be regularly subject to relapse? What is the nature of false knowledge, then, that it can be removed for good? Is it not a recalcitrant, unavoidable fact of our existence that our viewpoint must be limited and therefore to some degree false? These are the sorts of questions Indian philosophers pose to themselves, and it is their answers to them that I shall be reviewing in this chapter.

The theories of negation and erroneous knowledge are properly understood as developed in answer to certain of the criticisms of the causal theories of the various systematic philosophies, some of which criticisms I have detailed in the previous three chapters. We shall want to examine each of the positions distinguished in those chapters, starting where we left off in the earlier expositions and following out each system's basic metaphysical stance into its epistemological implications. I shall start this time at the left-hand end of Figure 20, within the progress philosophy group, and work toward the right-hand end.

LEFT-HAND THEORIES

Apohavāda *in Buddhism*

In concluding my discussion of the Buddhist logicians' causal theory on pages 141–142, I mentioned two criticisms, the latter, which I called the "more serious" one, stemming from leap-philosophy and the former, "less disturbing" within progress philosophy as it stems from rival progress philosophers. My tags of "more serious" and "less disturbing" might equally well be reversed, however, if we consider that criticisms stemming from radically different presuppositions are not as serious as those stemming from critics who share the basic program of progress philosophers, and not as disturbing for one who sincerely believes in that program. The Buddhist's problems about co-ordination or similarity (*sārūpya*) are of the intramural variety and are grist for the progress philosophers' mill. It is as an aspect of these problems that the epistemologies of Yogācāra and the Buddhist logicians can most reasonably be understood.

The Buddhist logicians' difficulties about co-ordination stem from the fact that this relation appears to relate something real to something unreal, the real relatum being a point-instant of energy (*svalakṣaṇa*), the unreal relatum being our cognition of that point-instant as clothed with qualities. What, it is then asked, is the status of co-ordination itself? Does it exert force or not? Is it real or not? I suggested on page 142 that the Buddhist logicians try to meet this problem with a theory known as *apohavāda* or *bhedāgrahavāda*. It is now time to develop this theory in greater detail.

Vācaspati Miśra reminds us of Dharmakīrti's theory of *apohavāda* in the following words:

> Things that are extremely dissimilar are, indeed, rendered similar by their common contrast with other things. . . . Even though positive in its nature, external reality is indeed the negation of the non-silver. If the ideally-constructed object [silver] be also the negation of the non-silver, there would be in consequence similarity between it and external reality.[1]

Buddhist logic assumes that the world of efficient causality, of things which exert force and constitute reality, is made up of momentary but completely distinct events. These events are taken to be, in themselves, completely different from one another; they have nothing in common, they share no qualities. But as we saw, it is difficult to explain, on this basis, how our mental activities fit into the series of events about which we care—or indeed to explain anything whatsoever, since explanation itself presupposes recognizable or repeated characters shared by several things. In particular, insight (*prajñā*), which is held to destroy ignorance, does not seem to be a forceful element in the external world but to belong to a different chain, a chain of non-forceful elements, if you will. Thus the Buddhists develop a mind-body dualism, and co-ordination is the relation which is supposed to span the gap. But just because it is a relation one of whose terms is nonforceful and the other of which is forceful, its *own* status becomes dubious. Moreover, we can't say that the mind exerts force and orders the elements in the world, since this contradicts the presupposed character of the mind and the world; nor can we say that the world exerts force on the mind but not vice-versa, since this removes freedom from our control.

Dharmakīrti's solution to this problem is ingenious. Ignorance, he holds, is not a positive contribution of the mind, but a failure to see the ultimate differences between things (*bhedāgraha*). One may ask why, if one merely *fails* to see the difference between things, he in fact sees *something*, namely things with shared characteristics—i.e., qualities. The answer is that what we see is the nonotherness of several completely dissimilar things. When I see two cows, I say they share a common character and are therefore similar or belong to the same class. What is true is not that they share any positive thing but rather that they "share" the negative "character" of not being non-cows!

Thus it isn't that the mind has contributed anything positive to the world, exerting constraint upon it. However, Dharmakīrti can now explain how one is able to dispel ignorance or illusion. Although it falsifies reality to describe it as having a certain positive character (e.g., cowness), it does not falsify it to describe it as lacking a certain negative character (e.g., non-cowness). The mind has insight when it sees that its positive constructions are not the same as external reality; it is ignorant when it identifies these positive constructions with external reality. Co-ordination is the relation which effects this identification—it co-ordinates mental constructions, which are unreal since forceless, with negative constructions, which are also unreal since forceless but which nevertheless are in some sense not different from reality. Reality, for example, does have elements in it which are not non-cows, but has no elements which are cows; the cow-constructions of the mind, however, are similar to the non-non-cows in the world. Thus similarity is an unreal relation, to be sure, and yet its destruction constitutes freedom in a meaningful sense, since by breaking the unreal relation between mind and its constructions, one is able to destroy the conceptualizing faculty, the mind, and to achieve direct insight into the things-in-themselves which constitute the flux of reality. So runs Dharmakīrti's theory, according to which the "external" point-instants of energy, if that's what they are, are real, and our subjective impressions, since dependent on the point-instants, unreal.[2]

One difficulty with this explanation is that if one is to analyze "cowness" as "not non-cowness," then one ought also to analyze "thisness" as "not non-thisness." Consider the judgment "this is a cow." What is this judgment about? It denies the conceptual construct non-cowness to *this*, Dharmakīrti will say. But what is *this?* Is it not as well a conceptual construct, thus unreal and necessarily analyzable—by parity of reasoning—into the denial of a negative conceptual construct? And if so, is the subject or the predicate of the resulting judgment that which the judgment is about? The resulting judgment is "not non-this is not non-cow," and the subject and predicate appear to be on a par; the judgment could be converted without changing its meaning. If so, Nāgārjuna's point is once again made: since every judgment involves conceptualization, even the judgment "this is a *this*" is conceptual. Indeed, even "this" by itself is conceptual, and so there is no truth—only falsehood. In short, there are no logically proper names.

As a result, it would seem that the Buddhist, whether Yogācāra or Buddhist logician, will have to shift or modify his position somehow. Just as we saw in the case of the Naiyāyika and Advaita theories, for example, that there are several directions that these schools take on certain crucial criticisms, so in the Buddhists' case we can observe the same thing.

One can construe non-non-cow as having a third kind of status intermediate between positive and negative, as Maṇḍana does within the Advaita tradition. This would be to deny that negation signs when properly interpreted cancel out, and suggests an intuitionist-type logic.[3] One can try to make do with the interdependence between subject and predicate without capitulating to the conclusions Nāgārjuna draws, which is what the Bhāmatī type Advaitins apparently try to do.[4] One can espouse leap philosophy, as Sureśvara does among the Advaitins. Or one can try to find a way between the latter two alternatives, as the

Vivaraṇa school Advaitins try to. Although our knowledge of late Buddhist logic and post-Vasubandhu Yogācāra is still sketchy, one may hazard the guess that all these directions were tried by Buddhist philosophers in the latter days of Buddhism's reign in India. For example, we do know that after Dharmakīrti there develops a difference between two schools of thought called the Prāsaṅgikas and the Svātantrikas.[5] Whether the philosophers who belonged to these two schools, men such as Candrakīrti, Buddhapālita, Bhāvaviveka, and Śāntarakṣita, are to be classed as Mādhyamikas, as Yogācāras, or as Buddhist logicians is still an open question of scholarship.[a] But the analysis here offered of the problem which generates later Buddhist speculation suggests the likelihood that each of the four directions was tried by somebody.

A second point of attack on *apohavāda* leads to a consideration of the problems engendered by the common experience of empirical illusions, hallucinations, dreams, etc. To start with a common-sense distinction, we find that some of our perceptual judgments are true and some are not. Any theory of "the false" should surely be able to explain this obvious difference. And yet it would seem that the *apoha* theory is peculiarly unable to do so. For according to this theory, all judgments are *ipso facto* false. How on this theory shall we distinguish between "this is a cow" when faced with Bossie and "this is a piece of silver" when faced with a sea-shell? This criticism is urged by Vācaspati Miśra,[6] and indeed Dignāga and his followers seem to have trouble distinguishing common illusions (*pratibhāṣikī bhrānti*) from the general illusoriness (*mukhyā bhrānti*) of all perception.

The reason the Buddhist logicians have trouble with illusions is this. As we have seen, every judgment is negative and involves an activity of the mind which the Buddhist takes to consist in confusing the presence of an illusory positive character ("cow") with the negative similarity engendered by the fact of a group of particulars being different from something else ("non-non-cow"). Every act of classification, since it brings into play an abstractive element, an imposition of the understanding, involves a mistake. We are reminded of the Kantian doctrine of the imposition of the categories of the understanding upon the undifferentiated manifold of sensation. But if illusion is thus a function of the imposition of the understanding, surely a pure sensation, a knowledge without the imposition of the understanding (*nirvikalpaka*), must al-

[a] The Mādhyamika school will be discussed in the next chapter, and the philosophers here alluded to will be more fully introduced there.

ways be valid. Unfortunately, there are illusions, hallucinations, and dreams, showing that even the purest sensations which we are capable of experiencing are subject to error.

But, it may be suggested, we never in fact *do* have pure sensations—*all* our experience is interpreted and so vitiated by conceptualization. This is what Kant concluded. Experience, he held, consisted of a co-operation of intuition and understanding—without the former, "concepts are empty," and without the latter "intuition is blind." But even in that case, how are the Buddhists to distinguish illusions from valid perceptual judgments? All judgments are still in the same boat.

Furthermore, Kant, with different assumptions from the Buddhists about freedom and causation, was able to accept the notion that we never are knowingly in touch with reality as such in any way. The Buddhist logician on the other hand, as long as he remains a progress philosopher, is bound to allow that there is a way in which humans can mount to knowledge which is not invalidated through infection by concepts. There is an unhappy fence on which the Buddhist logician balances—he is unwilling on the one hand to fall over into idealism because this leads to leap philosophy, but he is not willing to fall back into realism for the reasons we have suggested in previous chapters.

Dharmakīrti appreciates this difficulty, though, and has an answer for it: "You ask what is the difference between empirical truth and empirical falsehood? I will tell you. The difference is in the fact that empirically true judgments are verified and empirically false ones are falsified." A true judgment, in the empirical sense, is one that works, and a false one is one that doesn't. The technical term that the Buddhist uses here is *arthakriyātva*, "the character of doing things," if you will, efficiency.

Unfortunately, it is not clear that this helps Dharmakīrti's case. To be sure, he has given a *criterion* of empirical truth. But he has not yet explained what it is about the world that is different when false judgments are produced rather than true ones—he still owes us an account of the *nature* of falsity, and it is that which concerns us most, as it is falsity that we wish to avoid. But there is a worse difficulty. The characteristic of *arthakriyātva* has already a use in Dharmakīrti's philosophy; it is used to distinguish the real point-instants, the pure "this's" (if there are any). So Dharmakīrti is using the concept of efficiency (previously called "forcefulness") overtime. He uses it to characterize ultimate reality as well as empirical reality. Does this mean that the two kinds of reality coincide? Certainly not, since even true empirical judgments are ridden with concepts and therefore false as compared with ultimate truth. Empirically true judgments are ultimately false, so that *arthakriyātva* cannot be the criterion for both.

In the face of these difficulties, Dharmakīrti develops an extremely complex theory of knowledge. If he denies that we can ever know ultimate reality at all, he capitulates to Nāgārjuna. He therefore holds that one *can* have direct intuitive knowledge of the point-instants of reality; he holds that there is an extraordinary kind of intuition, which he calls "[direct] mental experience" (*mānasapratyakṣa*). This mental experience mediates between sensation and conception; it may be thought of as occurring just after pure sensation (which is not a judgment) and just before the imposition of the concept (at which stage we have a judgment, and necessarily an erroneous one). However, although more direct than ordinary experience, this intermediate stage is still not quite the pure experience of the free spirit, since it is tainted somehow by the concept toward which it leads and whose relation to pure sensation it mediates. Therefore Dharmakīrti postulates a second sort of extraordinary intuition, which he calls "yogic experience" (*yogipratyakṣa*). This is an experience free from all limitations by the understanding or imagination—absolutely direct and unsullied by conceptualization.

Interesting as all this may be, it does not directly address our present problem, which is how to distinguish dreams, hallucinations, and illusions proper from the presumed general illusoriness of all judgments. Dignāga, in fact, would seem to have left this matter undiscussed on the theory that any answer would vitiate something he had already maintained.[7] The challenge is too obvious to be ignored, however.

Dharmakīrti's contribution here is to say that "knowledge which is exempt from such [conceptual construction], when it is not affected by an illusion produced by color-blindness, rapid motion, travelling on board a ship, sickness, or other causes, is perceptive [right] knowledge."[8] Let me comment on this a bit. First we must, as we have seen, distinguish between nonconceptual (*nirvikalpaka*) and conceptual (*savikalpaka*) knowledge. The latter is the only kind which can be called a judgment, but the former is a direct sensory experience, being "exempt" from any relation with concepts. In other words, the Buddhist here adopts the notion of a pure awareness of a sensory "given," reminding us of sense-datum phenomenalism in contemporary Western philosophy. Having made this distinction, Dharmakīrti must then admit that, although sense-data as such cannot be the subject matter of a *judgment*—i.e., there are no *nirvikalpaka* judgments—nevertheless a direct experience of a sense-datum is a kind of *knowledge* and, moreover, subject to error. As we know very well, we have erroneous perception when our sense-organs malfunction for some reason or other. When, for instance, we have jaundice everything looks yellow, or when, in the Buddhist's favorite example, the fire-brand is moving in a circular motion, it looks like a solid object.

Dharmakīrti assumes that if there are no causes of malfunction in the sense-organs, sensation is *ipso facto* right *nirvikalpaka* knowledge. The cause of valid sensory knowledge consists of a point-instant of reality together with a normally functioning sense-organ; the cause of an invalid sensory knowledge is the same point-instant together with an abnormally functioning sense-organ. But how do we find out that our sense-organs are functioning abnormally? By testing the knowledge, one might be tempted to say—that is the criterion. But how can one test a *nirvikalpaka* knowledge, since it makes no claim? To use the convenient analogy of a "sense-datum language" of the sort suggested by phenomenalists, a *nirvikalpaka* knowledge stands to a *savikalpaka* judgment somewhat as "red here-now" stands to "this is red at place *p* and time *t*." The difference is that the latter implies certain other judgments—e.g., "this is not blue at place *p* at time *t*"—which are not implied by the former, since "red here-now" doesn't imply anything. Only judgments can imply other judgments, one may submit, and "red here-now" isn't a judgment. Since verification presupposes that what is to be verified implies some other testable proposition, it would seem that a pure sense-datum report, or *nirvikalpaka* knowledge, cannot be verified. This conclusion is supported in addition by the general Buddhist ontological hypothesis of momentariness, for if everything is constantly in flux and nothing remains for more than a fraction of a second, there is no time to test any pure sensory knowledge before it has fled.

It might be thought that we could test the normality or abnormality of our sense-organs directly and then infer from the results of that test the validity or invalidity of a *nirvikalpaka* knowledge. After all, "my eyes are jaundiced" is a judgment even if "yellow here-now" isn't, and therefore it can be tested. However, the defect of Dharmakīrti's account now becomes clear. Since all judgments are *savikalpaka,* infected by conceptualization, they are all false, and therefore there can be no such thing as the verification of the truth of a judgment about our sense-organs, except in the *other* sense of "true," namely that it "does something" (*arthakriyātva*). Suppose we try to test a judgment about our sense-organs in this fashion. What will we look for to verify or falsify a judgment? Surely what a true judgment about a sense-organ ought to *do* is to predict accurately or imply unerringly a knowledge of ultimate reality! Against what other outcome can it be tested? But if that is so, then we are caught in a vicious circle, for we need to know what is ultimately True to know what is empirically true, but we need to know what is empirically true in order to know what is ultimately True. To get out of this circle, Dharmakīrti appeals to his theory of yogic perception as providing an additional criterion independent of efficiency. Phenomenalism, as we know, attempts a dangerous straddle between realism and idealism, and in Dharmakīrti's case at least seems forced to appeal outside the theory to an immediate intuition which it is very tempting to describe as mystical. With this appeal Dharmakīrti begins to fall off the fence toward leap philosophy.

We can appreciate Dharmakīrti's difficulties even better by examining account of yogic intuition as expanded by the commentator Dharmottara. Dharmakīrti writes:

> The intuition of the *yogi* is produced from the pre-*nirvāṇa* state of deep meditation on ultimate reality. . . .

Dharmottara comments on this:

> [This] reality is elicited after logical criticism of, e.g., the Four Truths of the *arhat*. The contemplation of ultimate reality means its repeated forcing into consciousness. . . . What is called a pre-*nirvāṇa* condition is that degree of clarity which precedes complete vividness. [A state of mind] is brought about by this pre-*nirvāṇa* knowledge, a knowledge apprehending with absolute vividness the contemplated [image], as though it were actually present before the meditator, and this is the *yogi*'s direct perception. . . . It has indeed the vividness [of direct perception] and just for this reason it [ceases to be] a construction.[9]

We should notice several things about this passage. First, note the introduction of reference to meditation and to logical criticism of, e.g., the Four Truths.[10] The suggestion is that one obtains yogic insight not by disciplining one's sense-organs so that they are not abnormal, but rather by sharpening one's understanding or insight by meditation and by dialectic. The answer to ignorance, then, would seem to be a turning inward of the self to contemplate a kind of truth which does *not* have to have its source in the pure sense-data of an external world. Dharmottara denies that this is the implication, holding that yogic knowledge is *avisaṃvādi,* "not contradicted by experience" and so a direct report of the point-instants of reality,[11] but he unfortunately gives no criterion for distinguishing a *report of a pure and vivid (internal) image* from a *pure and vivid report of (external) reality.*

The appeal to vividness (*sphuṭabhātva*) is a second thing to note. It is vividness which now serves as the criterion to distinguish yogic knowledge from ordinary *judgments.* But unfortunately, again, that is not the criterion we need: what we need is a criterion for telling valid yogic knowledge from invalid immediate knowledge. And no such criterion is offered.

The third thing to note is that the yogic knowledge is as vivid "as though it were actually present before the meditator." This presumably suggests that it is *not* in fact present before the meditator—indeed, if it were present, there would be nothing to distinguish yogic knowledge from *nirvikalpaka* sensory knowledge. But in that case it would seem that the ignorance we are trying to dispel has nothing to do with empirical reality at all. If that is so, moreover, there is no compelling reason for the Buddhist to believe in the reality of the external world. The Buddhist logician like Dharmakīrti would seem to have no strong epistemological reasons for not succumbing to the subjective idealism of Yogācāra. The entrance into the chain in which he is interested is, on his own pronouncement, to be effected in such a way that the existence or nonexistence of a world of point-instants "out there" rather than "in here" is gratuitous.[12]

The Yogācāra Theory of Error (ātmakhyāti)

As is well known to readers of Bishop Berkeley, the subjective idealist has strong arguments on his side. His position is familiar to all who have survived a standard introduction to philosophy: there is no "external" reality which operates as a causal factor in determining our cognitions, even the purest ones; the causal factors of sensation as well as cognition are exhausted by items within the knower. Knowing is a relation between the knower and himself. If it be objected that knowledge is never known to know itself, since it is always knowledge *of* something, the idealist has the handy example of dreams in his favor. When we dream we apprehend contents whose cause is not elsewhere than in the mind of the knower himself. Does this then mean that there is no difference between imagined and "real" experiences? No, replies Vasubandhu; although all experiences are our creations, some of them are not *present* creations, but rather stem from past traces (*vāsanās*) stored up in the unconscious or subconscious (*ālayavijñāna*). As Dharmakīrti rightly holds, error in knowing consists in attributing externality to the causes of our consciousness; where Dharmakīrti makes his mistake is in supposing there are exceptions to this. In truth, *all* the causes of our consciousness are ours, and although not all of them are under our direct control, they are all indirectly under our control since all experiences are the result of previous *karma* which laid down the traces. Therefore we don't need Dharmakīrti's yogic knowledge; to destroy ignorance one needs only realize the nonexternality of the causes of knowledge and he will consequently realize his own complete freedom. All *judgments* are indeed false, because a judgment is something which contains an element of prediction or implication concerning something assumed to be out of our control in an "external" world.

The main objection to the Yogācāra procedure arises from the fact that he must take *all* sensations at their face value in order to avoid making them too dependent on an imaginary external world. The objection runs as follows: if every sensation is self-revealing, i.e., doesn't refer to anything except itself, then what stops a sensation from revealing itself as what according to Yogācāra it is, namely, a creation of our consciousness? How can this theory ever explain the appearance of error in empirical hallucinations and illusions? And even if this difficulty is overcome and the appearance of empirical error accounted for, how can this theory explain our experience of rectifying our errors, of discovering that what we thought was a pool of water was in reality a mirage, for instance? Since all cognitions are self-revealing, i.e., do not refer beyond themselves, a given knowledge K cannot have its nature revealed by another knowledge L, since this would mean that L reveals something other than itself.[13] The difficulty, in short, is that the Yogācāra idealist has identified the criterion of validity with the nature of knowledge and thus rendered himself incapable of explaining the cause of empirical error. From this point of view, the Yogācāra has merely adroitly changed the subject when he says that all judgments are erroneous from some other standpoint, viz., as contrasted with the omniscience of a Buddha.

The idealist may be able to answer this argument, e.g., by appealing to efficiency (*arthakriyātva*) as Dharmakīrti tried to. But if one is dissatisfied, there seems to be nowhere to go from this theory except back to realism (no matter how qualified), or else on to leap philosophy, as in Mādhyamika. Either one takes the challenge of the critic in the previous paragraph seriously, or else he refuses to be subject to the demand for an explanation of empirical error. But if one goes back toward realism, he comes first to Dharmakīrti's phenomenalism, which as we have seen is also a rather unsteady position. And where else can one go without giving up the doctrine of similarity altogether? There is one more possibility to consider.

Prabhākara's Theory of Illusions (akhyāti)

We noted briefly in Chapter 7 that the Mīmāṃsā philosopher Prabhākara seems to stand somewhere between Buddhism and Nyāya-Vaiśeṣika on causation. However, his main philosophical contribution is in the field of epistemology, and it is an extremely important one.

Prabhākara holds, with the Buddhist, that error is essentially a lack, a non-grasping of the differences between things (*bhedāgraha,* i.e., *apoha*). Furthermore, he also agrees with Yogācāra that the nature of a simple, *nirvikalpaka* knowledge is self-validating (*svataḥ-prāmāṇya*). And he draws from these assumptions the same conclusion the Budhists do, that there really is no distinction between truth and error as far as the *nature* of simple knowledges are concerned. There cannot be, on these assumptions. But while Dharmakīrti draws the further conclusion that there are therefore no simple judgments at all, Prabhākara draws the conclusion that there are simple judgments and all of them are true! The difference lies in their definition of a "judgment." Dharmakīrti refuses to call anything a judgment unless it is *savikalpaka.* Prabhākara is willing to speak of simple judgments, i.e., *nirvikalpaka* ones.

Unlike the Yogācāra idealist, Prabhākara accepts the challenge of explaining empirical error. Prabhākara is a realist in his theory of relations and believes in an external world composed of objects which enter into knowledges as their subject matter. For him, *every* judgment must have as its subject matter actual objects in the world. This is as true for judgments of illusions as it is for true judgments. But what must be added is that in many situations we make *more than one* true judgment and frequently are unmindful of that fact. And this failure to distinguish between two or more true judgments is what we call error.

Specifically, when we mistake a shell for a piece of silver on the seashore, what happens? We make two simple judgments: (1) "this is silvery [colored]," and (2) "silvery things are [usually] silver." The former judgment is a true judgment of immediate perception, the latter one is a true judgment of memory, being a generalization from past immediate perceptions of silvery things which were silver. Then we collapse (1) and (2) into (3) "this is silver," and by so doing commit the error in question.

It is well to note that error need not involve memory. Consider the case where we are looking at a vase of transparent glass standing near a tomato on a table. We make the following true judgments, says Prabhākara: (4) "this is a vase," and (5) "this is red," and then collapse them into (6) "this vase is red." Here (4) and (5) are both judgments of immediate perception.[14]

What has happened is that the knower has failed to grasp the lack of relation between (1) and (2), or between (4) and (5). But it doesn't of course follow that *every* complex judgment constitutes error. Take for example (7) "this is silvery" and (8) "silvery things on the sea-shore are usually shells," leading to (9) "this silvery thing is a shell." Here we would say that (9) was true even though it involves a combination of two other judgments. What's the difference?

There is no difference, says Prabhākara, as far as the nature of (3), (6) and (9) are concerned, but there is a big difference as far as their practical value is concerned, and the criterion of truth or falsity, therefore, is just the practical test of whether predictions based on a complex judgment are verified or not. We reach for a piece of silver in the first case, but do not find it; we predict that the vase will be red tomorrow, but the cook recaptures the tomato. On the other hand, when we reach for a sea-shell we are not disappointed. The criterion of truth is just that expectations based on it are fulfilled; a complex judgment is false just when at least one expectation is not satisfied.

So far there is nothing other than a verbal difference between Prabhākara's theory of illusions and Dharmakīrti's; they both distinguish the nature of knowledge from the criterion of its validity or invalidity. Where Prabhākara differs from Dharmakīrti is, once more, in his attitude toward simple judgments. The Buddhists hold that simple, *nirvikalpaka* knowledges are not judgments at all, since they make no claims that can be verified or falsified. Nevertheless, they hold, these simple knowledges can be valid or invalid. That's where they get into trouble. Prabhākara takes a different tack: simple judgments are judgments all right, but can never be falsified—because if a judgment is falsified it isn't simple! Prabhākara puts us in the embarrassing position of not knowing whether a given judgment is a simple or a complex one until it has been falsified. Nevertheless, as I pointed out in Chapter 2, there is something about this situation which rings very true to the nature of empirical investigation and the accretion of knowledge.

Prabhākara is the most uncompromising realist in Indian philosophy in that he refuses to allow the human mind scope to create something which does not reflect an external object. The criticisms of his view stem largely, as a result, from those philosophers who think they need positive mental constructions to function as the avoidable necessary conditions of ignorance. In Prabhākara's own philosophy, as in that of the Buddhists we have been considering, the avoidable necessary condition of ignorance is a *lack* or privation, the non-grasping of the difference between things; ignorance is *ajñāna*, "non-knowledge," and it is destroyed by restoring the discrimination which is lacking. This discriminatory knowledge is discovered when we act purposively in response to our judgments. For example, when we discover that what we thought to be silver is really a shell, we learn to grasp the difference between shells and pieces of silver; a good habit of discrimination is set up which will guard us from similar mistakes in the future. And the conquest of *all* such good habits constitutes the sufficient condition for complete freedom. Prabhākara's way to freedom is essentially an experimental one—we conquer challenges by acting purposively and correcting our habits of action in the light of our success or failure.

The heaviest guns are directed at Prabhākara by his rival Mīmāṃsaka Kumārila, and it is Kumārila's arguments which are largely inherited by, for example, Vācaspati Miśra and other Advaitins who share with Kumārila the belief that the mind must be granted positive constructive powers in order to explain adequately the conditions of ignorance and freedom. Kumārila's arguments are summarized in Pārthasārathi Miśra's *Śāstradīpikā*.[15]

Prabhākara holds that there is error whenever we fail to discriminate two objects and act purposively toward the confused object which results. But, Pārthasārathi points out, we may discriminate two objects and still err in our purposive activity with respect to them. For example, I may know the difference between north, south, east, and west and still be mistaken about which direction I am facing now. Or again, if I press my finger against my eyeball I see two moons, and if I should act on the assumption that there are two moons I should be disappointed. This would constitute error, however, just as surely as Prabhākara's own examples do. The critic concludes that nondiscrimination is not a necessary condition for error, at least in the ordinary usage of "error." I can be in ignorance even though I am fully discriminative.

Secondly, according to Prabhākara knowledge is self-revealing[16] by nature, i.e., it doesn't need another knowledge to be appreciated. Presumably, then, if a single judgment arises in my mind, I should recognize it as a single judgment.[17] But Prabhākara's case rests upon my being able to confuse two single judgments. In that case he must give up his thesis of the self-revelatory nature of knowledge, since in cases of error the two knowledges apparently do not reveal their own number but depend on later verification or falsification for this revelation. So Prabhākara is caught in a dilemma: either he must give up the thesis of the self-revelatory character of knowledge or he must give up his theory of error.

Thirdly, if the materials of ignorance are merely several single judgments, why should there be any purposive activity at all? I would act so as to pick up the piece of silver I think I see on the beach only if I had *synthesized* the two judgments "this is silvery" and "silvery things are usually pieces of silver" into the (confused) judgment "this is a piece of silver." But this synthetic activity of the mind, which must be granted in order to explain purposive activity, shows that our minds *are* capable of constructing images which do not correspond to objects "out there."

An Advaitin argument[18] runs as follows: According to Prabhākara, when we have two knowledges error results because we fail to grasp the difference between "this" (the shell) and "piece of silver"; we fail to grasp the difference because the shell and pieces of silver are similar as regards their silveriness. But, points out Vācaspati, it is arbitrary on Prabhākara's part to identify the non-grasping of *difference* as the source of error: it is equally possible to regard the non-grasping of the ultimate *nondifference* of the two items as the source of error. Thus Prabhākara has not proved the superiority of his view to that of the Advaitin, who believes that error results from the failure to realize that everything is, in the last analysis, Brahman.

None of these arguments appear absolutely unanswerable. But even if Prabhākara had done nothing else in philosophy except espouse this theory, which is by no means the case, this contribution would alone place him among the great philosophers of India, for it is a daring defense of thorough-going realism.

Negation as an Entity: The Nyāya-Vaiśeṣika Theory of Negation and Error

Suppose we admit the force of at least the first three arguments against Prabhākara's theory which have just been summarized. What sort of position can be fashioned which still does not give way to out-and-out epistemological idealism? The Nyāya-Vaiśeṣika philosophers do admit the force of these arguments, and yet claim that they honor the realistic postulate that the objects entertained even in erroneous knowledge are really existent "out there."

Kumārila's first argument was that nondiscrimination is not a necessary condition for error. The Nyāya-Vaiśeṣika, unlike Prabhākara, is willing to admit that, even though the elements of a judgment be discriminated by the judger, he may still judge erroneously by selecting the wrong elements for synthesis. For an adequate explanation of this, we must elaborate the Naiyāyika's picture of the knowing situation, a task I shall essay in a moment.

Kumārila's second argument was to the effect that one cannot hold to a theory of error of a realistic variety without giving up the thesis of the self-revelatory nature of knowledge. Nyāya-Vaiśeṣika cheerfully admits that knowledge is not self-revelatory—though as we shall see this opens up new lines of criticism by the opponents of realism.

As to the third point, that the mind must be granted a synthetic function, Nyāya-Vaiśeṣika grants this too. Clearly this is a *prima facie* capitulation to idealism, and the Naiyāyika must defend his claim to hold a realistic view.

We begin the case for the defense with the basic point that the Naiyāyika does not accept the *apohavādin*'s contention that a negative judgment is privative, merely the appreciation of the lack of a certain property. Nor does the Naiyāyika think, as we shall see that the Advaitins do, that a negative judgment is simply a perverse way of expressing a positive one. The Naiyāyika takes all experiences very seriously; since people find it expedient to make negative judgments as well as positive ones, there must be negative facts to which these judgments refer, and these negative facts must be constituted of at least one negative entity (*abhāva*).

There are at least four different sorts of negative entities on the Naiyāyika's view. (1) There is the nonexistence of something before it comes into existence (*prāgabhāva*). In John's potting shed there are two pot-halves which he will put together tomorrow to make a pot: today there exists an entity called "antecedent nonexistence of [that] pot" (*ghaṭa*[*viśeṣa*]*prāgabhāva*). (2) There is the nonexistence of something after it has been destroyed. The pot John dropped yesterday has been replaced by its posterior nonexistence (*dhvaṃsa*). (3) John has a cloth in his shed, as well as a pot. He also has, according to the Naiyāyika, the difference between them, technically referred to as "reciprocal nonexistence" (*anyonyābhāva*). Reciprocal nonexistence is merely the absence of identity. (4) Finally, there is absolute nonexistence (*atyantābhāva*) of elephant in John's potting-shed. The shed is too small. There never was, is, or will be an elephant there.

The last two entities, reciprocal nonexistence and absolute nonexistence, have neither beginning nor end. Therefore the last two can neither be produced nor destroyed; they are not under our control, they are unavoidable. Therefore complete freedom cannot be identified with one or the other of the last two kinds of absence. But complete freedom can be defined in terms of the other two types of absences, and in later ("new") Nyāya a definition of complete freedom in terms of absences is preferred to other possible definitions on account of its precision. For example, Śaṃkara Miśra, commenting on the *Vaiśeṣikasūtras* in the fifteenth century, defines complete freedom (*niḥśreyasa*, i.e., *mokṣa*) as follows:

> Complete freedom is the final cessation of frustration. The finality of the cessation of frustration consists in its nonconcurrence with the antecedent nonexistence of frustration. An alternative definition is this: the finality of the cessation of frustration consists in its concurrence with the simultaneous posterior nonexistences of the special characteristics of the self, namely such things as agency (*adṛṣṭa*) and mental traces (*saṃskāra*).[19]

This pair of definitions is highly technical, and suggests how well developed the techniques of mapping were in Navya-nyāya of Śaṃkara Miśra's time. But it should also be evident that, granted the proper definitions of the key terms, the above definition is much clearer than the rather vague descriptions of complete freedom I have been suggesting heretofore.

With such a definition of freedom in mind it is clear that the Naiyāyikas must allow absences as entities, since absences enter into the causal chains we care about. They are among the ontological building-blocks we must grant being to in order to translate the sentences we care about into an adequate, accurate, consistent, and clear map. Allowing absences into its ontology, Nyāya-Vaiśeṣika claims the benefits of the *apohavādin*'s theory without his difficulties. Let us now review those difficulties and estimate the Naiyāyika's advantages.

The Buddhist introduced *apoha* to explain how causality could operate without constraint, to show how nonforceful causality was possible. But he was compelled to admit a relation between the real and the unreal which, it was charged, is incomprehensible. The Nyāya-Vaiśeṣika takes nonexistences as real, and thus for him the relations between existences and nonexistences are relations both of whose relata have an equal claim to reality. Where the Buddhist had a mind-body problem because one relatum was real and the other was not, the Naiyāyika has no such problem. Ultimately there can be no problem about the relation between a thing and its absence, since any absence must be the absence of *something*. The something which is absent is called, in Nyāya language, the counterpositive (*pratiyogin*). The relation between an absence and its counterpositive is a kind of self-linking connector (see page 128) and presents no special problems, granted the problematic character of the very notion of such a connector as explained earlier. Thus the relapse into idealism or leap-thinking which the mind-body problem seems to lead to in Buddhism is avoided in Nyāya-Vaiśeṣika. So, at least, the Naiyāyikas claim.

A second difficulty we noticed in *apohavāda* was its tendency to reduce to anti-conceptualization; insight seemed to require giving up conceptual thinking altogether. But the Buddhist was forced to this because he refused to admit universals, and absences, into the external world. This conclusion is only necessary for someone like the Buddhist who believes in the momentariness of everything which exists. The Naiyāyika sees no reason to accept the momentariness hypothesis, and considerable reason to reject it. He believes in the existence of things as well as of events.

The third source of difficulty was, we will recall, in the *apohavādin*'s theory of illusions and wrong knowledge in general. This problem is the most important of the three, since it bears directly upon the conditions of freedom. For various reasons, we found inadequacies in Dharmakīrti's, Vasubandhu's, and most recently Prabhākara's theories of error, and now we must ask whether the admission of negative entities by the Naiyāyikas will enable them to fashion a satisfactory theory of wrong knowledge.

The Naiyāyika is just as insistent as Prabhākara that the contents entertained in knowledges are in the world of reality, of things. Like Prabhākara and the Buddhists, he accepts the distinction between simple (*nirvikalpaka*) and complex (*savikalpaka*) perceptual knowledge. When we entertain simple perceptual knowledges, we are in direct contact with real objects. As to the question whether simple judgments make truth claims, there seem to be some Naiyāyikas (e.g., Śivāditya, the author of *Saptapadārthī*) who say with Prabhākara that simple judgments are always true, while others (e.g., Viśvanātha, author of *Siddhāntamuktāvalī*) deny with Dharmakīrti that the question of truth or falsity applies to *nirvikalpaka* knowledge.[20] In either case, simple judgments of immediate perception cannot be erroneous. Error can arise only in complex judgments.

But the Naiyāyika, unlike Prabhākara, is willing to grant that error is more than merely a sin of omission. Although all the elements of any cognition must be independently real, the combination of them in a given complex judgment may be valid or invalid. Prabhākara sought to explain error by saying that the mind merely fails to grasp a certain lack of relation between the subject ("this") and the predicate ("piece of silver"). According to the Naiyāyika, when we judge with respect to a certain shell "this is a piece of silver," we *commit* the sin of injecting a relation which is not *present* in reality. This relation is our old friend inherence (*samavāya*). To understand what happens, let us appeal to the following diagram:

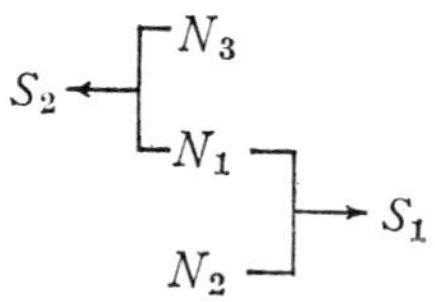

The simple relevant judgments are:

N_1 = this—inherence—silveriness
N_2 = silver—inherence—silveriness
N_3 = shell (on beach)—inherence—silveriness

The possible conclusions or complex judgments are:

S_1 = this is a piece of silver
S_2 = this is a shell

The simple judgments N_1 and N_2 are, of course, nonerroneous. And there really are in the world a "this" (the shell), the property silveriness, and inherence—so that nothing in either of these judgments is a mental construction. But when we draw the conclusion S_1, we are leaving out of consideration the third possible simple judgment, N_3. Why? Because of certain defects in the knower—generally speaking, either in his sense-organs or in his mental attitude. If N_3 *had* been entertained instead of N_2, the resulting complex judgment, S_2 ("This is a shell"), would have been valid. (Or else we would have been in doubt.) But since it was not entertained, due to the defects in the knower, and N_2 was entertained instead, the erroneous complex judgment S_1 is formed.

The elements of S_1 are (1) this, (2) inherence, and (3) piece of silver. Of these (1) is presented directly through the senses, (3) is remembered from past acquaintance with pieces of silver. What about

(2), inherence? The reader will recall that traditionally the Nyāya view was that there is only one inherence, a sort of pervasive glue as we pictured it. (See pages 119 ff.) Certain sorts of entities are capable of being stuck together by this glue. Both this shell and a piece of silver are capable of being related to silveriness, so that in judging either S_1 or S_2 we are in no way entertaining anything which is impossible. Nevertheless in judging S_1 we are injecting erroneously a *specific* (portion of the) inherence relation, a bit of glue whose function presupposes contemporaneousness and identity-of-location between "this" and a piece of silver, a juxtaposition which is not true to the facts of the case.

Our mistake, then, consists in positing relations of simultaneity and collocation which do not accurately reflect reality. Note that it is not that anything actually mentioned in either S_1 or S_2 is unreal—even inherence is real. But it will now be remarked, justly I think, that the appearance of one-to-one reflection between judgment and objects, an isomorphism which the Naiyāyika maintains and which he claims makes his system a realistic one despite its apparent capitulation to the mind's powers to construct, can only be made plausible as long as the judgments in question are not properly expanded. If we represent the spatial and temporal references implicit in the judgment "this is (here-and-now) a piece of silver" it will become plain that the mind has, in fact, projected the relations referred to by the "(here-and-now)."

This once again moves the Nyāya-Vaiśeṣika philosophers to a consideration of space and time, crucial concepts in their philosophy. Unfortunately, an investigation of these notions is beyond my compass here,[21] but let me at least remark that according to the Vaiśeṣikas (though not according to some Naiyāyikas) spatial and temporal judgments are not perceptual at all, but inferential, the inferences having to do with the respective relations of the object to be located to certain standard objects (e.g., the location of the sun as it first touches the horizon). This is one of several reasons why (as has already been suggested) the topic of the nature of inference becomes of major concern in Navya-Nyāya.

What is the bearing of all this on the search for complete freedom? We need to return to the questions posed at the outset of this chapter. These were (1) what are the necessary conditions of false knowledge? And (2) how is at least one of them avoided?

The necessary conditions of an erroneous judgment, e.g., S_1, include N_1, N_2, and what we have so far been calling "defects in the knower." Now N_1 and N_2 are unavoidable, according to Nyāya-Vaiśeṣika; they arise automatically from experience, and making no claims they cannot be "corrected." But the cause of the erroneousness of S_1, as we have seen, might be described as the knower's *forgetting* N_3—not in the sense that he does not know or believe N_3 to be true, but rather in the sense that he *overlooks* it. N_3 was the memory-judgment "shells (on the beach) are silvery." If the knower had not overlooked it, he would not have made the erroneous judgment S_1. The overlooking of N_3 is, then, a necessary condition of S_1, and although N_3 cannot be avoided, the overlooking of N_3 can.[b]

The overlooking of N_3 is caused by what we have called "defects in the knower." What does the Naiyāyika have in mind by this? The *Nyāya-sūtras* say:[22] "Defects have urging or inciting for their distinguishing feature." Vātsyāyana tells us in his commentary on this passage that the defects are "attachment and aversion"; that these are in turn caused by "ignorance"; that they produce agency (*karma* or *adṛṣṭa*) and mental traces (*saṃskāras*). As we saw from the Navya-Nyāya definition of complete freedom, it is precisely these last two things—agency and traces—whose connection with the self has to be destroyed to obtain freedom. The "ignorance"—elsewhere called "wrong notion"—is identified later in the same work as ". . . the notion of what is not-self as 'self'—appearing in such forms as 'I am'; this is the notion of 'I.'" The Sūtra then says "From the True Knowledge of the 'Cause of Defects' follows the cessation of the notion of 'I.'" That is to say, the proper understanding that the causes of defects such as desire and aversion lie in the misidentification of the Self with the body, the senses and other things which are not-Self, is sufficient to eradicate those defects. And when the defects are eradicated, there will be no more overlooking of N_3's—one will be aware of all relevant simple judgments. True knowledge is obtainable by human effort, through meditation which is the result in part of previous merit and wisdom but which (since one can backslide from meditation) is in our control. The merit and wisdom are attained by

> . . . embellishment of Soul by means of restraints and observances and such other methods of internal discipline as may be learnt from the science of Yoga; [from] repetition of the study of the Science [of Nyāya] as also friendly discussion with persons learned in the Science.

[b] The reader may well wonder what the difference is between the Nyāya-Vaiśeṣika's "overlooking N_3" and the Prabhākara's "failure to grasp the lack of relation between N_1 and N_2." The difference, as far as I can tell, lies in the implications of the two views about the contribution of the knower to the knowledge situation. "Overlooking" is a positive function of consciousness, while "failure to grasp" is a negative qualification, a privation of consciousness.

Specifically, Vātsyāyana is suggesting, it is our greed for a piece of silver rather than a shell which causes the "defect" of entertaining N_2 ("pieces of silver are silvery") rather than N_3 ("shells on the beach are silvery"). Nyāya thus nicely takes account of the evaluative element in knowledge. We are told in the Sūtras that "Color and other objects, when they form the subjects of wrong notion, become the cause of defects. Regard for the object as a whole becomes the cause of defects." By associating certain colors with desirable things and other colors with disagreeable things, Vātsyāyana explains, we set up habits of attachment and aversion. Again, by admiring the pleasant aspects of, e.g., the female form while disregarding the unpleasant aspects, we set up habits which misguide us.[c] We see more correctly when we see adequately, and it is the bad habits born of attachment and aversion that produce the inadequacy. If for instance we had not been the victim of greed on the beach, instead of reaching for silver and experiencing the pangs of disappointment we might well have experienced doubt leading to experimental verification of the judgment "this is a shell" and consequent reinforcement of the good habit of adequate consideration of the relevant possibilities.

Of the two major sources of arguments in opposition to the theory I have just described one is from the left (Prabhākara) and the other from the right (Advaita). I shall also consider some modern critics.

As we have seen, the most important distinction between Prabhākara's *akhyāti* theory and the Naiyāyika's *anyathākhyāti* theory is that the latter believes that S_1 ("this is a piece of silver") is a unified judgment, that is, that N_1 and N_2 actually coalesce to form S_1. The Prabhākarite fails to see how this coalescence can occur. The Nyāya-Vaiśeṣika is ready with an answer, for whatever it is worth: there is a type of perception in which the eye, for example, *sees* an object even when it is not presented to it directly; it does this through the force of the mental trace laid down by a past experience of that object.[d] But, the Prabhākarite points out, in such awareness we are always aware that the object we are seeing is *not* presented here and now but *was* presented there and then. How is it that we are not aware of the "elsewhereness" in this

[c] Vātsyāyana recommends "conceiving of the Female as only made up of hairs, bristles, flesh, blood, bone, tendons, arteries, phlegm, bile, ordure, and so forth" in order to remove these bad habits.

[d] This (*jñānalakṣaṇasannikarṣa*) and two other sorts of perception are regularly referred to, somewhat unfortunately for the Naiyāyika, as "extraordinary perception" (*alaukikapratyāya*). It is perhaps fairer to say that the Nyāya is of the opinion that we should use the term "perception" to cover more than merely awareness of directly presented data.

case? "Because of the defect in the eye," says the Naiyāyika; "since we are attracted by silver, we are prone to see silver here where it isn't." "But," the Prabhākarite fights on, "if this defect is the cause of the trouble why doesn't it cause us to see things we've never seen at all—it might just as easily, you know." "Then how," replies the Naiyāyika, "could the mental trace ever have gotten into the mind?" "Ah well, if that's necessary, all right, why don't we import any old attractive remembered object into the situation—why *silver* in particular?" "Because," the Naiyāyika patiently replies, "there must be some similarity between what is presented now and the trace that is excited; in this case, both objects are silvery."[23]

The Advaitin difficulties with the Nyāya theory can be appreciated from an argument in the form of a dilemma which is most thoroughly expounded in the *Vivaraṇa* of Prakāśātman. The dilemma has three horns. The question is raised, "What do you Naiyāyikas mean by 'elsewhere' (*anyathā*) in your theory of error as *anyathākhyāti*? Literally, *anyathākhyāti* ought to mean 'knowing [something] as otherwise.' Now by this do you mean (1) that the *form* (*ākāra*) of one thing is known as belonging to something else? Or (2) that one object is known as a different object? Or (3) that an object transforms itself into something different?" There are difficulties in each case.[24]

As to interpretation (1), how can the form of one thing appear somewhere else? On your view, Naiyāyika, every thing which is contained in knowledge is existent "out there"; since the perception of a form, say, the shape of a piece of silver, is gained through the contact of the eye with an object which has that shape and only in that way, it cannot be gained by contact of the eye with the shell. Shells produce shell-forms, and pieces of silver produce pieces-of-silver-forms. As to interpretation (2), two objects can only be confused if there is a relation between them. But is that relation itself real or unreal? If it is real, where is the error? If it is unreal, the theory reduces either to subjective idealism or to the Advaitin position, both of which the Naiyāyika is trying to avoid. As to interpretation (3), that the object actually changes its form, this is not the Nyāya view but the view of Bhedābhedavādins like Bhāskara. It is untenable in any case because when an object changes its form, e.g., when milk becomes curds, we don't suppose we have discovered an error when we discover that what are now curds were once milk!

S. K. Maitra[25] offers several considerations against the Nyāya position, most of them drawn from the classical Advaita sources. He points out that when we reject an illusion, we don't just reject the *relation* between this and piece-of-silver; we reject piece-of-silver. Strictly, it seems to me he ought to say that what we reject is piece-of-silver here-and-now, for the Naiyāyika's position rests on the assumption that we don't entertain absolutely nonexistent entities—therefore we don't reject piece-of-silver altogether, but only as being present at this time and place. Again, he complains, if it is a *relation* that is rejected when we correct error, then this relation must be unreal. (If it were real, we would have Bhedābhedavāda as argued above.) But what is unreal is, for the Naiyāyika, nothing, and the rejection of nothing is no rejection. Therefore error can never be corrected. It seems to me that the Nyāya view of negative entities (*abhāva*) as real is intended to answer this sort of objection. Nothing, for the Naiyāyika, is something!

Mysore Hiriyanna[26] argues against the Nyāya theory that the criterion of truth and error consists in verification or falsification. On the one hand, he suggests, verification can never guarantee correspondence of a judgment with reality, since there is a vicious infinite regress involved. To verify a judgment one must make another judgment, and verifying that one requires still another, etc. We must know at least one judgment to be true independently of verification in order to verify anything. Furthermore, we cannot depend on verification to discover error, as it is possible to dream that one is verifying. In short, verification can at best guarantee consistency within a set of judgments; it can never guarantee accuracy. These objections apply against any empiricist theory and have been exhaustively scrutinized in twentieth-century Western analysis. They remain compelling to some.

Perhaps the most original modern criticism of the Nyāya-Vaiśeṣika theory of truth is to be found in Kalidas Bhattacharya's work.[27] He asks the relevant and probing question: "what sort of a thing is the piece-of-silver entertained in S_1? Is it a universal or a particular?" The Nyāya-Vaiśeṣika must answer "neither." It is not a universal, clearly; we do not judge that this is silverness, but that this is a *piece* of silver. But equally clearly it isn't a particular, since particulars are spatio-temporally determinate. If this piece of silver is the same piece I saw when the trace was first etched in my brain, then I should see it now as a *past* and *elsewhere* piece of silver. But I don't. The Naiyāyika therefore holds that it is an entity seen as "mere silver," stripped of its other properties. In that case, Bhattacharya submits, N_2 cannot be a judgment of *memory,* for when we remember something we remember it *as past* and *as in the shop* (or wherever it was). So what is presented in N_2 is not the remembered piece of silver; it is something dreadfully abstract, "an abstract universal with its axones and dendrides all shaven off. Such desolate creatures cannot for a moment endure." The implication is that the piece of silver so understood is no real entity—and once this is admitted, the Naiyāyika's grip on realism is broken.

Kumārila Bhaṭṭa's Theory of Error (viparītakhyāti)

The other great Mīmāṃsaka philosopher besides Prabhākara is Kumārila, whose followers are frequently referred to as "the Bhāṭṭa school." He accepts the Nyāya-Vaiśeṣika account of negative entities as real; he also accepts in the main the Naiyāyika's theory of illusions. However, there are three important differences between the Bhāṭṭa and the Naiyāyika views. (1) Kumārila espouses a different name for the view, *viparītakhyāti*. Thus he may hope to avoid the Advaitin argument mentioned above, which was directed at the use of the word "elsewhere" or "otherwise" (*anyathā*) in the Naiyāyika's name for his view. "*Viparīta*" means "opposite" or "contrary"; "*viparītakhyāti*" means the theory that an erroneous knowledge is contrary to reality—something the Bhāṭṭa hopes no one would deny. (2) Kumārila does not agree with the Naiyāyika that the word "perception" (*pratyakṣa*) ought to be used to cover knowledges like N_2—in fact, he doesn't believe there is any such type of knowledge as N_2. Consequently, he has to explain how the piece of silver gets into S_1 at all. (3) That brings us to the only really crucial difference. The Bhāṭṭa doesn't believe in inherence as an independently existing entity. He doesn't believe in relations as entities at all. Like the Jain, he thinks that everything is a unity-in-difference.

> Everything both is and is not. It *is* as itself; but it *is not* as another. If an object is shell in a positive sense, it is silver, say, in a negative sense.[28]

The result is that the Bhāṭṭa analyzes simple knowledges not into three entities (as the Naiyāyika does) but into two entities in relationship to one another. Thus our N_1 has to be represented as "this (both-the-same-and-different-from) silveriness," and instead of N_2 we shall have (N_4) "piece-of-silver (both-the-same-and-different-from) silveriness." (N_4 is not a perceptual knowledge but a judgment of memory.) This gives the knower a choice in combining N_1 and N_4: he can emphasize the difference and get a true judgment, or emphasize the sameness and get a false one. Which he does depends on the presence or absence of defects, as before.

There are special difficulties about this account, however. For one thing, since the piece of silver in N_4 is a *remembered* piece of silver, when we discover our "error" we ought to say "Ha! That piece of silver I remembered *isn't* the same as this object on the beach." But we never thought that it was; we didn't confuse *that* piece of silver with this object but rather we thought that there was a *new* piece of silver here and now. The Naiyāyika tried to get around this with his theory of mental traces, and Kumārila by rejecting it leaves a gap in his own theory. The critic can then argue that the gap can only be filled by supposing that the defects in our knowing apparatus actually *create* a new, "unreal," piece of silver. But that is idealism; it gives up realism by allowing that some contents of judgments do not correspond to objects in the world.

If the Bhāṭṭa should try to save his position by insisting that the shell is actually the-same-with-and-yet-different-from the remembered piece of silver, this will mean in effect that everything is the same with and yet different from everything else, and the Bhāṭṭa position begins strongly to resemble either Jainism or Bhedābhedavāda. Kumārila himself appears to hedge here; he needs external and independently existent relations like inherence, and yet doesn't want to admit them.

Finally, the Advaitin urges the following argument in contention that the Bhāṭṭa is logically bound to accept a "levels of reality" position like Śaṃkara's. Consider the Bhāṭṭa counterpart to S_1, "this (both-the-same-as-and-yet-different-from) piece-of-silver." What is in the parenthesis, the relationship between this and piece-of-silver, is a construction of the mind, "unreal" in the sense that it does not correspond to anything distinct in the objective world. But even if we admit that neither "this" nor "piece of silver" are unreal in this thorough-going sense, we must still admit that "this" has a different status from "piece of silver," since when we discover our error, it is the latter which is rejected and not the former. Therefore there are three "levels" of reality: the highest is the one on which the shell—"this"—stands; the middle one is where "piece of silver" rests; and the relationship between them constructed by the mind belongs below either of the other two. This view, as we shall see, is something like the Advaita view of error.[29]

Kumārila's special difficulties seem to stem from his inability to decide—or, more kindly, his attempt to steer between, the Nyāya-Vaiśeṣika type of ontology and the Jain sort. Kumārila accepts part of the Nyāya-Vaiśeṣika ontology, including the thesis that there are negative entities, but he rejects that part which depends upon the independent reality of inherence. He doesn't seem to be able to have it both ways. One must posit some sort of relation—independent entity or not—to connect the reals in the universe, and if one is unwilling to accept inherence there is apparently no choice but to appeal to some form of the identity-in-difference relation. This, however, sets restrictions upon one's theory of negation. It follows, then, that the next set of views we shall want to consider will be those which do not accept inherence but rather accept identity-in-difference as the basic model of relation, and as a consequence reject the category of negative entities.

THE CENTER

The Jain Theory of Negation and Error

We are brought, then, to the Jain position. For the Jain, negation is an essential aspect of every real. Everything, on his view, is a unity in multiplicity; as a unity, it is different from everything else, while as a multiplicity, it resembles and is to that degree the same as everything else. Negation is merely the former aspect. It is not an independent entity as the Nyāya-Vaiśeṣika holds, nor is it an "unreal" mental construction as, for example, the Advaitin holds. It has as much reality as any aspect of things has.

As a result, error can be explained in only one way. When Indian philosophers review the various theories of error, it is interesting to note, the Jain position is rarely given. If it is mentioned at all, it is lumped together with Nyāya-Vaiśeṣika, Prabhākara, and Kumārila. The fact is that the Jain has no particular theory about the shell and the piece of silver over and beyond saying that every judgment, inasmuch as it is partial, is erroneous. If we say that x is not y, we have omitted to indicate that as regards property F they are the same; they share F. If we say that x and y are the same, we have failed to indicate that x lacks property G which y has. Complete truth, it would seem, could only be gained by taking x's relations of sameness and difference with every other thing into account, and this, the Jain submits, goes beyond the abilities of language and conceptual thinking. The conclusion would seem to be that "this is a shell" and "this is a piece of silver" are both false, since inadequate.

The obvious retort is that this was not the sense of "true" that had to be explained; what we want clarification of is the difference between the two judgments above. The Jain has no analysis of this difference except through appeal to verification and falsification, which he sees once more in pragmatist terms. In this common, unphilosophical (to him) sense of "true" and "false," a judgment is true just so long as it leads us to what we are expecting, and false just when it doesn't and we are disappointed. The Jain's query is just this: why do we need any *more* of an explanation than that? If we use "science" as the name for the activity of getting ahead in worldly matters and "philosophy" for the contemplation of the ultimate nature of things, we must admit, he claims, that they have little to do with one another. A scientific truth may be a philosophical lie. This bifurcation of scientific knowledge and metaphysical wisdom is fashionable in Western thought also. And why not? The Jain might argue that nothing is lost by the bifurcation, and if nothing else, a great simplification is effected, since all the troubles over the nature of error that we have seen torturing Buddhists, Mīmāṃsakas, and Naiyāyikas are avoided. For example, the Jain makes no distinction at all between simple and complex knowledges. He can and does eschew the endless debates within Vaiśeṣika about whether this or that (e.g., inherence, negation) is or is not a category in itself or just a special case of something else.

It may be charged that the Jain has lost sight of the considerations which determine philosophical relevance. The topic of error was significant for Buddhists, Mīmāṃsakas, and Naiyāyikas because they all accepted the doctrine that ignorance is a necessary condition of bondage and its eradication the path to freedom. To show that ignorance is avoidable is, for them, to show that freedom is possible. But this criticism is not to the point, for the Jain accepts the same doctrine. He is not saying that knowledge is not relevant for the attainment of freedom—on the contrary, he thinks it essential. But he doesn't think that the kind of knowledge that is essential is the kind of knowledge that we seek in every-day situations. Where the others assume that the proper understanding of common illusions like the shell-silver case could serve as a model for the proper understanding of the metaphysical illusion which breeds bondage, the Jain makes no such assumption.

Jain philosophers tend to distinguish at least five "levels" of knowledge, of which only the first two are capable of literal linguistic expression in the form of judgments. Arranged in an ascending series, these five "levels" are (1) the level of sensory cognitions (*matijñāna*); (2) the level of revealed knowledge (*śrutajñāna*); (3) the level of knowledge of modes (*avadhijñāna*); (4) the level of knowledge of mental states (*manaḥparyāyajñāna*); and (5) omniscience (*kevalajñāna*). By (1), we are able to make judgments of sensory perception, more or less adequate as our sense-organs are more or less well-trained. By (2), we become able to make general judgments about the nature of the things known by (1), the difference being that (2) allows us to make universal judgments whereas (1) properly speaking is limited to specific reports of presented sensory contents.[e] When we get to (3), however, there is no appropriate verbal means of expression. Through (3) we know the shapes of things not given to us through the senses. Through (4) we come to know the essential nature and interrelationships of such subtle items as minds, light, speech (conceived as neither auditory nor visual but as that which lies behind speech-sounds and written words), and *karma,* that subtle stuff of infinite variety which constitutes the material of bondage. Finally, in (5) we come to know the exhaustive interrelationships of all the contents entertained in the previous four levels. These five kinds of knowledge are not levels in the sense that one graduates from one to the next; each one is capable of greater or less adequacy in a given individual.[30]

Besides these five varieties of knowledge (*jñāna*) there are several varieties of intuition (*darśana*). The difference between knowledge and intuition seems to be that knowledge is outer-directed while intuition is inner-directed. Most Jain writers seem to agree that in the fifth stage knowledge and intuition coincide, but that they are distinct outside of that stage.[31] In any case, as we have seen, right intuition or "attitude" (as I translated it previously) is prior to right knowledge in the chain leading to complete freedom.

The complexities of the Jain epistemology are fascinating and devious, and I cannot do justice to the details here. The relevant point for our present purposes is that, at any level of knowledge or intuition, the model is not that of common "scientific" knowing. As far as we can know, the *verification* of a knowledge on the first level has nothing to do with its *adequacy* metaphysically, i.e., in terms of self-realization. We are reminded of Dharmakīrti's introduction of yogic perception and his consequent inability to provide a criterion for distinguishing valid yogic knowledge from invalid empirical knowledge. The path to a more adequate knowledge is for Jainism primarily *moral* and not intellectual at all. One prepares himself for freedom by practising such all-important virtues as *ahiṃsā* (non-violence), celibacy, and the like, but in Jainism there is no suggestion that one can see how well one is succeeding by testing his judgments by experimental means. For all we can see, a scientifically *false* theory may well be the theory the holding of which leads to metaphysical *truth.*

[e] There is some disparity in the treatment of the distinction by various Jain authors.

It is presumably because of this uncompromisingly moral bent of Jainism that none of the other schools include accounts of the Jain theory of error or essay criticisms of it; perhaps they are aware that such criticism would completely miss the Jain position. Nevertheless, one may at least remark that although there is apparently nothing that compels a philosopher to make intellect prescribe to conduct, there is presumably the general requirement that if a philosopher sets forth a pattern of realization (*sādhana*) he should be able to explain how one knows he is succeeding in its accomplishment. Even if the path is non-intellectual, intelligence is needed by the practitioner in appraising his performance, and therefore judgments, truth, and falsity do become relevant and cannot be avoided. To be sure, the Jains admit this requirement and set forth a lengthy, fourteen-step account of the stages (*guṇasthānas*) on the path to freedom. But on examination this turns out to be not a path of conduct after all but a path of successive stages of intuition, and the description of these stages is, strangely, too figurative and too literal at the same time. I shall illustrate this by considering the first stage.

The first thing that happens to the soul in its search for freedom, it is said, is that it comes "face to face with what is known as *granthi* or the Gordian knot of intense attachment and repulsion."[32] This is spiritual awakening, an intuition of the possibilities for the self through challenges and discipline. Then follows a "struggle" consisting of two processes. In the first of these (*apūrva-kāraṇa*) "the soul passes through such states as it never experienced before (*apūrva*)." But, as psychologists know, failure at this point might result in withdrawal and fantasies, during which one might also pass through states never before experienced. How can we tell the right sort from the wrong? Instead of an answer to this in terms of recognizable experiences or analogies with experience, the answer is couched in terms of "the duration and intensity of *karmans*." The soul must "reduce the duration and intensity and also the mass of the karmic matter associated with it." But how can it know that it is doing so and be able to direct its efforts toward the reduction of the intensity and duration of *karma*? The trouble is that we don't properly understand *karma* until we have adequate understanding of the fourth sort (*manaḥparyāyajñāna*). Therefore our understanding at this primary stage must be very shaky indeed. One would like to have a *test* suggested whereby one could know that the intensity and duration of *karma* are being reduced. But this is precisely what the Jain has avoided giving us. And it is hard to see, given his theory of relations and the nature of things, how he could give us a criterion or propose a test. Apparently we must depend on guess-work at this stage, or read accounts written by people who have succeeded. That is the human predicament, the Jain may retort—but the fact remains that the task that the other progress philosophers set themselves is a task from which, wisely or unwisely, the Jain has begged off.

Though this may be unfair to Jainism, I do not want to press the issue further at this point. But one more remark seems in order, since it applies in one way or another to all the other right-hand theories we are about to discuss as well as to the Jains. The right-hand theorist characteristically abandons empirical or ordinary knowledge in favor of some superior variety not modelled after scientific knowledge at all. Yet one cannot help suspecting that these philosophers believe that this superior variety of knowledge is available to us *before* realization. The general question that needs to be raised, then, is how we, in our mundane, limited way, can distinguish this superior and therefore true knowledge from inferior but imaginative false knowledge. The general answer, from Jains and Hindus alike, is that we are all somewhat divine. True, one may reply, but what if we can't recognize which part of us is divine until no part of us isn't, that is, until we are free? The right-hand theorist, by concentrating on superior knowledge, helps us only when we don't need it, unless he can somehow hook up mundane, empirical knowledge (with its pragmatic criteria of truth and falsity) with the superior knowledge. We shall want to keep our eyes out for any such connections in the discussion of the philosophical schools which constitutes the remainder of this chapter. The bifurcation we mentioned between scientific and metaphysical truth is dangerous, since it reopens an old source of doubt, namely, that even if there is a way to complete freedom we are incapable of knowing what it is or recognizing it even when it's right under our noses.

RIGHT-HAND THEORIES

The Sāṃkhya Theory of Error (sadasatkhyāti)

The classical Sāṃkhya and Yoga texts do not tell us anything which would lead us to distinguish their view from that of the Mīmāṃsakas or Nyāya-Vaiśeṣika on the problem of common illusions. Their analysis is not carried to the point where we wonder how the remembered silver gets here and now presented. This is probably because, as in Jainism, metaphysical ignorance was not consciously modelled after common illusions.

The avoidable necessary condition of bondage is specifically said to be the nondiscrimination of the *puruṣa* from the *buddhi* of cognitive mechanism. This is avoided when the *buddhi* achieves discrimination, and that happens when it gets to know all about *prakṛti* and *puruṣa*. Truth with a capital "T" is, as in Jainism, completely adequate knowledge, and not just knowledge which works.

Professor Hiriyanna has nevertheless essayed to relate truth with Truth, and error with Ignorance, but is forced to admit that "in the latter [the metaphysical realm], truth stands for *complete* knowledge; in the former (the realm of everyday or 'scientific' knowledge) complete knowledge is neither attainable nor necessary, so that truth signifies such knowledge as does not leave out of account that feature of the given object which is *relevant*. . . ."[33] It is precisely this limitation of *relevance* which allows us to set forth criteria of truth and the lack of which makes it difficult to set forth criteria of Truth. In order to set forth criteria of Truth we should have to have already discriminated the *puruṣa* from the *buddhi*, and it's at that point that we no longer need a criterion.

Rāmānuja's Theory of Error (satkhyāti; yathārthakhyāti)

Rāmānuja proposes a novel way of meeting the Naiyāyika's and Mīmāṃsaka's difficulties about how the elsewhere and elsewhen silver gets to be here and now. Rāmānuja was a great student of the Upanishads, and discovered there an interesting theory about the makeup of things. According to this theory, there are five elements—earth, water, fire, air, and "ether" (*ākāśa*).[34] Every existing entity is a mixture of all five of these elements, the differences between entities being explained by the difference in amounts of each element present in the respective entities.

Armed with the authority of the Upanishads, Rāmānuja is able to hold that in effect illusory judgments are true judgments as far as they go, and that when I think I see silver on the beach I actually *do* see silver on the beach! The mistake I make is not in saying I see silver, but in not saying I see shell. In the other views—e.g., Prabhākara's, the Naiyāyika's, and Kumārila's—it will be recalled that the similarity between shell and silver insofar as they were silvery constituted the source of confusion. Rāmānuja interprets similarity as part-identity. To say that x is similar to y is to say that a part of x is part of y.[35] The piece of silver I see is a part of the shell, the silvery part. Only it's not a piece of silver anyone would give money in return for, or that would look nice as a spoon on the dining-room table. That is because this object is more shell-y than silver-y.

This doctrine enables Rāmānuja to combine the strong points of the pragmatic test of truth with the logicality of the adequacy theory of Truth. And best of all, he can link the two together, as we suspected the Jains and the Sāṃkhya could not. For to find out that this object is shell and not merely silver is to rise to a more adequate understanding of things, and it is marked by verification as well. Scientific truth and metaphysical Truth, although they are distinct because they answer to distinct criteria, coincide at least up to the level of omniscience, so that we can use the mark of truth to prove the acquisition of Truth.

Apart from the out-datedness of the five-fold theory of elements, this is not an easy view to criticize. Jadunath Sinha reports some Advaita criticisms as sketched in a late Advaita work, *Advaitāmoda* by Vāsudeva.[36] A good deal of it is directed toward the archaic physics. A more relevant point that Vāsudeva mentions is this: how does Rāmānuja propose to explain why we see this object on the beach as a piece of silver and not as anything else which is silvery-colored—e.g., a piece of glass? Several possible replies on Rāmānuja's part are considered and rejected. (1) He might say that certain elements (mainly fiery ones!) combine and produce a piece of silver which we actually see. But, Vāsudeva points out, this is a gratuitous theory since it remains unverifiable: when we look closer, we don't find a piece of silver, we find a shell. (2) Rāmānuja might say, then, that the very fact that we see a piece of silver here shows there is a piece of silver here. But that commits the fallacy of the vicious circle.

However, Rāmānuja probably wouldn't say either of these things (this is no longer a report of Vāsudeva's remarks). Rather, he would appeal, as the Naiyāyikas and the rest do, to the distortive effects of attachment and aversion, to the "defects in the knower." Since we want to find pieces of silver and care little for pieces of glass, we see the piece of silver in the shell rather than the piece of glass.

As regards the thesis that similarity is part-identity, one might argue in the following fashion. There are cases where no one could reasonably claim that similarity is part-identity. For example, I might think (mistakenly) that General DeGaulle is wearing my trousers, but no one would suggest that a part of the General's trousers are mine, as would be the case if similarity were always to be construed as part-identity. And since the general thesis won't do, the particular one won't do either—for Rāmānuja has no reason to think the shell-silver case is not a case of similarity in the DeGaulle's trousers sense. This argument at least suggests the need of a more penetrating analysis of similarity.

One criticism which might occur to the reader but which is more easily answered than he may expect is this: when we reject a judgment as illusory we reject either the subject or the predicate or the relation between them (e.g., when we say "this *isn't* a piece of silver, it's a shell" we are rejecting either the illusory piece of silver or the relation of the piece of silver to this time and this place), but Rāmānuja's account leaves nothing whatever to reject. But the answer to this criticism is not hard to find. We know from experience that when we discover that something has produced an illusion we don't guarantee that it won't produce another illusion subsequently to someone else or even to ourselves if we should forget our present experience. We may mistake this shell for silver next year when we return to the beach, or if we don't, someone else may. Therefore experience tells us that in fact we *don't* reject any entity in the world; our mistake was in confusing a part of "this" (the piece of silver part) with more of it (the shell part), but correction does not involve rejecting either object or even a relation but rather in appreciating the inadequacy of the *interpretation* of this as a piece of silver.

This answer announces a subtle and important change in attitude toward the nature of omniscience and of complete freedom. In considering the Nyāya-Vaiśeṣika and Mīmāṃsā theories, we have supposed with them that freedom involves at least the adjustment of the knowing subject to an external world. Even the Sāṃkhya seems to grant to the *buddhi,* i.e., to *prakṛti,* the power of creating a bond between itself and *puruṣa* which has to be broken in gaining omniscience. All these theories assume that the knower and the known interact or influence each other in some fashion or other. For Rāmānuja and the theories to his right, however, freedom is wholly confined to purification of the knowing subject itself. It is not a question of adjusting to the world, but of expanding the Self by enlarging its interpretation. To put it another way, whereas the other theories claimed that the correction involved the *rejection* of one content in favor of another, Rāmānuja and the theories to his right make the correction out to be a matter of *adding* something to the illusory perception. One should not reject the illusory judgment, but catch it up in a new synthesis—"this *is* a piece of silver, to be sure, but it is also, and more importantly, a shell." Why more importantly? Not only because to see this as shell leads to success in our purposive activities, but for some more basic reason having to do with the purification of the

Self. The former is of philosophical importance only insofar as it is a mark of the latter. Once more we find science and philosophy distinguished as to their nature, although here at least success in the one is thought to parallel success in the other.

Bhāskara's View of Error

Suppose we cannot swallow Rāmānuja's assumption that similarity is part-identity. How can we maintain essentially his position without involving ourselves in his difficulties or those of the other theories I have discussed? The Bhedābhedavādin Bhāskara apparently intends to hold some such theory, but it is difficult to make out how he answers the crucial question of the status of the illusory piece of silver. According to Hiriyanna,[37] Bhāskara holds that the silver, although not a part of the shell, nevertheless "springs up" where the shell is for the limited time of the illusion. How it gets there we aren't told, and evidently the problem is a difficult one, particularly for a *pariṇāmavādin* like Bhāskara. This piece of silver of temporary duration is not unreal for Bhāskara—he gives temporarily enduring objects as much reality as permanent ones. As we have seen, the Bhedābhedavādin endows the aspects of Brahman with as much reality as Brahman itself—and thereby occasions the criticism of Advaita. The present epistemological theory is merely the logical outcome of Bhāskara's metaphysics. Its difficulties are those we noted in the previous chapter. But at this time we have very little textual material to work on in the case of Bhedābhedavāda. I turn without further ado, then, to the question of the status of the silver in Advaita.

The Classical Advaita View of Error (anirvācanīyakhyāti)

Advaita has been represented to the world as idealism, and so perhaps it is in some sense, but any good Advaitin will deny vehemently that he holds the mind capable of projecting illusions which are unreal or "have no being." Short of extreme *dṛṣṭisṛṣṭivādins* like Prakāśānanda, all Advaitins admit that even the illusory silver has some being and is not nothing. Surely, they point out, this illusory silver has a different status from a barren woman's son or a hare's horn. A false knowledge, therefore, is not a non-knowledge, since unlike a hare's horn it does occur. Nor is it a knowledge of a non-entity. Thus we must guard against confusing negation with falsity. The Advaitin is particularly unhappy with Prabhākara on this account, for, he charges, Prabhākara thinks a false knowledge is knowledge of *nothing*—since, as we saw, the

Prabhākarite makes no attempt to synthesize the *nirvikalpaka* judgments neither one of which contains the presented illusory silver. Advaitins see in Prabhākara's position an implicit capitulation to *apohavāda* and thus to Buddhist fluxism, and we have seen that they are quite right about the former, though perhaps not about the latter. They are less unhappy with the Naiyāyika's account of negation, since the Naiyāyika does not see either the content of false knowledge or false knowledge itself as a *lack*. Where they differ with Nyāya-Vaiśeṣika is in the latter's elevation of negation (*abhāva*) to a co-ordinate status with positive being (*bhāva*). This, they submit, is taking negation *too* seriously!

The upshot is that falsity must have a status above negation but below reality. It is not real (*sat*) like Brahman, but it isn't unreal (*asat*) like nonsense either. It is *sadasadvilakṣaṇa,* "other than real or unreal." Otherwise expressed, it is *anirvācanīya.*

But, asks the ultra-realist such as the Nyāya-Vaiśeṣika or Rāmānuja, why *isn't* the piece of silver real like Brahman? One might think immediately of answering that inasmuch as it at best has an inadequacy about it one may say that it is unreal since it is only a *part* of reality. But this would surely be an odd use of "real." If something is, in ordinary usage, said to be real, a part of it would be admitted to be real too, though partial. So the question now becomes: what is the point of introducing a technical, un-common-sensical use of "real" at this juncture? The Advaitin has more in mind by calling something "unreal" than merely that it is part of Brahman. Everything is part of Brahman (or nothing is, depending on the meaning of "part"), it being a ticklish but perhaps inconsequential point whether Brahman is part of itself.

Specifically, the "real" is defined frequently in Advaita as *trikālābādhya,* "unsublated through the three times (past, present and future)." That is to say, the real is that which we don't ever entertain and subsequently reject. Better, the real is that which we couldn't possibly ever entertain and subsequently reject. It is, by definition, eternal. The unreal is, therefore, the non-eternal. It is that which comes into and goes out of existence, while the real—Brahman—is not subject to change at all. But this is still not the ordinary use of "real." Again, what is gained by this technical term?

What is gained is this. By defining "reality" as that which is never entertained and subsequently rejected, the Advaitin paves the way for his celebrated identification of Brahman and the true Self (*ātman*). The Upanishads say "Tat tvam asi"—"that art Thou." What this means for the Advaitin is that "Brahman" is another name for the Self, and this identification is justified by pointing out with a Cartesian *cogito* argument that, no matter what one *can* reject in knowing, one *cannot* reject the knower. Brahman, it is concluded, is not only *sat* ("real") ; it is also *cit* ("pure consciousness"), that which is never sublated in *knowledge.* The Advaitin adds that Brahman is also *ānanda* ("bliss"). Thus the Advaitin's first defense of his technical use of "real" is that it allows him to interpret the Upanishads correctly.

But what are the necessary conditions of bondage, and can they be avoided at all? The Advaitin proposes to use his account of ordinary illusion to illustrate by analogy the answers to these two central questions. That is his second point in defense of his technical usage of "real."

The Advaitin locates the inadequacy of falsehood not, as does Rāmānuja for instance, in the erroneous *judgment* but in the falsely-perceived silver itself. What's wrong in error is that the *object* of illusion is inadequate—the silver, in our example. It is inadequate since it is not eternal, disappearing when illusion is corrected. In this way the Advaitin thinks he can liken metaphysical inadequacy (bondage) to epistemological inadequacy (illusion), where we saw Sāṃkhya, for example, having trouble keeping up the analogy.

The Advaitin's theory of error as the presentation of an *anirvācanīya* object is easy enough to state, though it may be hard to understand. When we look at the shell and see a piece of silver, there comes to be a piece of silver there. The piece of silver is *not* a mental construction. Negation (*asat*) is a mental construction, but a false object is not a negation. The piece of silver is not real, however, since it comes into being when we look at the shell and goes out again when we discover our mistake or, if we don't discover it, when we look away and pass on. But, it may be objected, the shell itself is *also* something which comes into and goes out of existence; why is the piece of silver made out to be false, while the shell is not? "Yes indeed," cries the Advaitin; "quite so. You've discovered the truth for yourself. The shell isn't real either. So *it's* false! But it isn't *as* false as the piece of silver, as you can see for yourself. When the silver disappears, the shell carries on."

So far it all sounds as if to be more real is to last longer, and this would be a rather naive view. But it is not, on the Advaitin's view, merely smaller duration which constitutes the inadequacy of the piece of silver; in cases of error, this temporal inadequacy is symptomatic of a more profound inadequacy. What the Advaitin wants us to understand is that the piece of silver *depends* for its existence on the shell's being here on the beach; if the shell were not here, there wouldn't be any silveriness to cause us to produce this false piece of silver. The existence of the piece of silver is dependent upon the existence of the shell, but not vice-versa; therefore relatively speaking the shell has more reality. But when we consider the shell, we come to realize that its existence depends in turn upon something *more* real, and the limit of this series of more and more adequate sorts of being is Brahman, the perfectly real, on which everything else depends and which is not dependent upon anything else.

We saw in the previous chapter how Śaṃkara distinguished three levels of being—the highest level (*paramārthika*), which consists of exactly one entity, completely real, Brahman; the empirical level (*vyavahārika*), containing the objects we common-sensically call "real" like the shell; and the illusory level (*pratibhāṣika*), containing objects like the piece of silver. We may be tempted now to wonder whether the distinction between the latter two levels is not rather arbitrary. From the account just offered, it would seem there ought to be a continuous scale of more or less from Brahman as the limit at the upper end to negation (*asat*) as the limit at the lower end. (Remember that negation doesn't reside in the *pratibhāṣika* level but below it.) For example, according to Śaṃkara the objects confronted in dreams belong on the illusory level. But now suppose I have a dream in which I am walking along the beach and think I see a piece of silver, only to be disappointed in finding it only to be a (dream) shell. This dream piece of silver must surely be relegated to an even lower level than the *pratibhāṣika*.

More interesting than a continuous series of more and more illusory phenomena is the possibility of a continuous gradation of more and more perfect ones. And this brings us back to the major questions of the chapter. For the Advaitin, gaining knowledge is like finding that silver is really shell, or like waking up from a dream. It is important to ask how we know we have discovered an object to be more adequate than another. What is the *test* of the relatively more true (real, adequate) according to Advaita?

It is not at all obvious that the correction of common illusions like the shell-silver case is the same process as correcting dream-illusions. To test the former error, we bend down and reach for the object; if we are still deluded, we carry it to the market and try to get a metallurgist to assay its worth. When do we perceive our error? We may perceive it when our senses show us that its qualities are different on closer examination than we had thought previously, but we may not—sometimes it will take the force of public or trained opinion, e.g., the metallurgist's, to convince us that we are the victim of an illusion. (This analogy may help to explain the importance of the expert opinion of the *ṛṣis* or wise men who wrote the Vedas and Upanishads; they are to Truth what the metallurgist is to truth in our stock example.) Discovering an illusion, then, is a more drawn-out process, frequently, than waking up from a dream. Yet the Advaitin ought to explain all error in a parallel fashion, for otherwise we may controvert his theory by claiming that there are several varieties of error corresponding to different criteria, an admission the Advaitin cannot allow without giving up hope of using his account of ordinary error to illuminate his doctrine of bondage and release.

It appears that either the shell-silver case must be assimilated to the dream-case, or vice versa, for the Advaita theory to succeed. If the Advaitin assimilates illusions to dream, he comes close to suggesting that the gaining of freedom is not something we can effect by our efforts. For it is not as a result of any conscious decision on the part of either the dream-self or the waking self that we wake up from dreams—this seems just to happen. The analogy with respect to gaining release ought to be that it just happens, and this leads fairly directly to leap philosophy, perhaps of that type which makes release dependent upon the grace of God. This would seem to be the tendency in Sureśvara's brand of Advaita, consonant with his general theory of relations.

On the other hand, if we take the eradication of error in all cases, including dreams, to be modelled on the pattern of discovering that the shell isn't a piece of silver, we admit the importance of conscious effort in the activity of testing. In this case it is difficult to see how the Advaita position differs in any important respect from, say, Kumārila's or that of the Nyāya-Vaiśeṣika. There is of course a metaphysical difference between the Advaitin, who says that a false piece of silver springs up into existence during the illusion and pops back out of existence when the error is discovered, and the denial that this happens by the Mīmāṃsakas and Naiyāyikas. But this now appears as a metaphysical difference in that bad sense properly exposed by the pragmatists and logical positivists—it is a difference which makes no difference. For the putative piece of silver serves no function in respect to anything we care about; it might just as well *not* be there. Truth will still consist in a more adequate account, whether the inadequacy rests in the object or in the judgment. It is thus to be expected that the most "conservative" branch of Advaita is sympathetic with Kumārila and Nyāya. Maṇḍana is quite happy with the theory of *viparītakhyāti*;[38] in some respects he is as much a Bhāṭṭa as an Advaitin and is attacked by other Advaitins for precisely that reason. Vācaspati Miśra and the Bhāmatī school take the line that the Bhāṭṭa theory, as well as the Naiyāyika's and Prabhākara's, necessarily imply *anirvācanīyakhyāti.*[39]

There remains the possibility of assimilating both illusions and dreams to some more penetrating model, and this seems to be the aim of Padmapāda and the Vivaraṇa school of Advaita. I shall assume in the rest of the discussion that this last-named branch of Advaita is the peculiarly original type of progress Advaita. Whether it properly represents the meaning of Śaṃkarācārya is an issue I need not explore here.

The Vivaraṇa School's Theory of Error

To steer between the Bhāmatī line and the Sureśvara line means in effect to steer between the view that philosophical truth is gained by scientific method and the view that philosophical truth has nothing to do with scientific method. Again, it is to avoid the extremes—on the one hand of taking the method of realization to depend on the well-known pragmatic tests of verification and falsification used in every-day life and in science, and on the other of taking the method of realization to stem from the authority of scripture or the mystical experience of God without any testing on our part being in the last analysis relevant at all. Still again, the Vivaraṇa school criticizes the Bhāmatī school for making of *anirvācanīya* an empirical concept and criticizes the Sureśvara tradition for making of *anirvācanīya* a non-rational concept. Padmapāda and his followers would like to see philosophy as utilizing a peculiar method of cognition, unlike that of science and ordinary affairs but for all that rational. Such a method would be a kind of direct experience, not necessarily conceptual or expressible, but at least in some sense cognitive. This, Padmapāda thinks, is what Śaṃkara has in mind, rather than the more mystical intuition which Sureśvara found in their common teacher's somewhat obscure pronouncements.

This direct experience, which we may call "insight," is something we all have. Like Plato's recollective intuition (*anamnesis*), it is always present in our subconscious or unconscious; it rises to consciousness at unexpected moments. When we wake up from a dream, for example, this insight rises to consciousness, and also when we discover that the silver is really shell. The problem of assimilating the two kinds of error to a common model is solved. The difference between the two cases lies not in the method but in the causes which activate it. Though this insight sometimes arises unexpectedly, we *can* train ourselves to use it constantly—and when we have succeeded in this, we shall be completely free. Yogic meditation is precisely this training. Through it we throw off the bonds of ignorance and replace ignorance with insight.

There remain difficulties about the sliding scale between Brahman and negation. *Anirvācanīya*, it may be charged, is used in Advaita in both an absolute and a relative sense. It is that which is different from Being and non-Being (*sadasadvilakṣaṇa*), but it is also that which, *relatively* to a more adequate object, is inadequate. The Vivaraṇa theorist would like to find a common characteristic which unifies these senses; in fact, if he doesn't, as was indicated above, we are left in a puzzle about what constitutes insight. The problem is really this: granted that it doesn't much matter in general whether an object *x* is more real than an object *y*, what does matter is which way lies freedom! We need some criterion for knowing that we are going toward Being and not toward non-Being. This is not a gratuitous doubt. There is one very influential Upanishad, the Māṇḍūkya, in which the path to freedom is said to consist of four stages, the waking state, the dream state, the state of deep sleep, and finally "the fourth" (*turīya*)—complete freedom. How seriously are we to take the order of these stages? The logical outcome of the sequence assumed in this Upanishad will be the identification of complete freedom with the attainment of non-Being, unless the Upanishad means that the dream-objects are more real than waking ones. There is a side of Advaita, associated with the authority of Gauḍapāda, which takes the Māṇḍūkya categories very seriously indeed. At the time of this writing, a scholarly controversy rages over whether Gauḍapāda is more of an Advaitin than a Buddhist. The historical question need not concern us, but the doubt which the Māṇḍūkya scheme and Gauḍapāda's espousal of it generates needs careful consideration. Śaṃkara refers respectfully to Gauḍapāda, despite his Buddhist affinities.

A way of addressing ourselves to this doubt is to consider more carefully the meaning of the term *anirvācanīya*. We have already seen it described as "other than Being or non-Being," but we now perceive that this doesn't go far enough. Perhaps by a more careful examination of the nature of falsity we can elicit a criterion for relatively greater adequacy. One hint was dropped above: the less real is not only temporally inadequate compared to the more real, but is *dependent* upon it. Let us see whether the Vivaraṇa theorist can expand this notion of dependence into a definition of *anirvācanīya* which contains a criterion for its application.[40]

Consider first Padmapāda's own definition of *anirvācanīya*—"not to be the locus of either Being or non-Being."[41] This might mean one of two things.

It might be taken to mean that the false is the contradictory of Being-and-non-Being.[42] But this won't do. "Being-and-non-Being" is an impossibility, and the false for the Advaitin is not to be considered as merely something which is not impossible. Vyāsarājā points out that to define it in this way would commit the fallacy of proving what the opponent already accepts. Furthermore it would have the unhappy consequence of proving Brahman to be false, and so from the Advaitin's own point of view it overextends.[43]

But perhaps Padmapāda means that the false is any object which has these two properties: (1) absolute nonexistence of Being, and (2) absolute nonexistence of non-Being.[44] But this plausible interpretation won't do either, says Vyāsarājā. It is self-contradictory. The absolute nonexistence of Being *is* non-Being, and non-Being cannot reside in the same locus as its own nonexistence. The Advaitin has a reply for this, however, and that is that the absolute nonexistence of Being *isn't* non-Being but falsity. Vyāsarājā has assumed the very point to be proved.

There are other criticisms of this interpretation which get rather involved. The most important is once again that the definition will include Brahman, who lacks all properties whatever, including the properties of Being and non-Being. It is apparently in order to forestall this objection that Prakāśātman, author of *Vivaraṇa*, comes forward with an improvement on Padmapāda's definition. Not that he thinks Padmapāda's definition can't be defended; one could defend it, for example, by arguing that since according to the definition anything which is false must have at least two properties and Brahman has none, the definition certainly can't apply to Brahman. Nevertheless, the definition though defensible is not complete enough, primarily because as far as we have gone Brahman and the nonexistent (e.g., a hare's horn) are on a par, and though we are hoping for a criterion as well as a logically impeccable definition, we apparently aren't going to get one out of Padmapāda's definition as it stands.

Therefore Prakāśātman suggests that falsity be defined as that which is the counterpositive of an absolute nonexistence in the very same locus where that counterpositive appears.[45] The silver is the counterpositive of its absolute nonexistence in the shell, which is to say it appears where it is not, was not, and never will be. This differentiates the piece of silver from the hare's horn, for the former appears where it is not while the latter doesn't appear at all. But leaving aside the difficulty about a something which is here and yet is not here—which we have already touched on—this definition still tells us nothing much about *dependence,* nor offers any other criterion for telling the less false from the more false.

Prakāśātman offers another definition. The false, he says, is that which ceases upon knowledge of its locus.[46] Criticism of this definition brings us closer to our point. The critic points out that the new definition is both over-extensive and under-extensive. It is over-extensive since it makes *any* cognitive state false inasmuch as it passes over into a subsequent one. And it is under-extensive since jars are false, according to Advaita, and yet they are destroyed not by knowledge but rather by their suddenly meeting a hard object, like a hammer. In answering these criticisms, the Vivaraṇist brings out his distinctive interpretation of knowledge as insight. Since cognitive states succeed one another whether insight is involved or no, the definition of falsity doesn't apply to them. Furthermore, the word "ceases" in the definition has been misunderstood. Physical smashing doesn't destroy the jar, for it continues on as the potential cause of possible effects. Yet the jar will eventually cease in the required sense, when there is the insight that there is no jar, only Brahman. Therefore the definition does apply to the jar after all.

This added detail brings down other difficulties on the head of the Vivaraṇist. Some of these were indicated in the discussion of relations in the previous chapter. Others center around the recalcitrant notion of *possibility*. But we are looking for a criterion of greater reality or adequacy, and additional details are helpful in the search. Let me then emphasize one other facet of this definition—the insight which brings about actual as opposed to apparent ("physical") cessation is said to have an object, the locus of the illusion. Perhaps this is the clue to our desired criterion.

The locus (*adhiṣṭhāna*) of an object x is the object in which x resides. But the "in" here is not to be taken merely spatio-temporally, as we have already seen. How then is it to be taken? Another prominent sense of "in" is the sense used when we say that a certain property is "in" a substance (e.g., "there's red in autumn leaves"). Here "in" indicates a relation between a universal and the particular which it characterizes. Can we then say that the object of an illusion is to its locus as a universal is to a particular it characterizes, or, alternatively, vice-versa? There are certainly points of similarity. For example, just as a certain particular may have now one property and now another, so a given locus may manifest now one illusion and now another. More important, universals and particulars *depend* on each other, and it is a relation of dependence we are looking for. Thirdly, universals may plausibly be classified as abstract or concrete, and a continuum might be worked out of more and less concrete universals. This will parallel and so explain the continuity of falsity from Brahman to non-Being.

I turn, then, to a necessarily brief examination of the possible use of the notions of universal and particular in Vivaraṇa thought.

It is often supposed that there is a problem of philosophy called the "problem of universals," and that it might be posed as follows: we make both singular judgments and general ones. It seems clear that some singular judgments are reports about particular entities we have confronted; general judgments, however, do not share this characteristic of referring to something confronted in experience. Does this mean that there are no entities referred to by general judgments other than the particulars referred to in singular judgments? Or are there "general" entities (universals) as well as particulars? Or does the human mind construct new entities—concepts—when it forms general propositions? Affirmative answers to each of these three questions yield the three positions usually known respectively as nominalism, realism, and conceptualism in Western philosophical circles.

But this problem does not arise for Indian philosophers, at least not in just this way. For one thing, it seems unnecessarily restricted. We start out assuming that we are confronted with particulars and ask about the status of universals; why not start out assuming that we are confronted with universals and ask about the status of particulars? It's not true that common sense is unreservedly on the side of the former assumption: common sense is not on either side, since it informs us that in making any judgment, singular or general, if we confront anything at all we confront a substance and a quality. For example, in the singular judgment "this is red" we confront a substance, "this," and a quality, "red"; in the general judgment "all the books on the shelf are red" we confront a set of particulars (the books) and a universal (the red color). If it is objected that the red color isn't a universal, we shall be forced to investigate the meanings of the terms "universal" and "particular"—an investigation we shall in any case want to make in the interests of clarity. And if it is said that there are some judgments in which substances only are confronted (e.g., "this is a table") it can equally well be retorted that there are some judgments in which universals only are confronted (e.g., "this shade is blue"). In short, the formulation of the problem in the preceding paragraph jumps too far too fast. Let us start out, rather, with an analysis of the terms "universal" and "particular."

At least three different distinctions have been wrapped up together in the use made of these two terms in Western thought. Although these distinctions are not unconnected, it will be useful to separate them for the purposes of this discussion.

First, there is the distinction between a repeated entity and an unrepeated one (and, by extension, between a repeatable entity and an unrepeatable one). A repeated entity is one which occurs at more than one moment of time, at more than one position in space, or both. An unrepeated entity is one which is momentary and has no spatial parts. This is, by itself, not the usual philosophical usage of "universal" and "particular," but it seems to be connected with that usage.

Second, there is the distinction between an abstract entity and a concrete one. A concrete entity is "filled in"; an abstract one is "empty." Or again, the abstract is unactualized, the concrete is actualized; the concrete thick, the abstract thin.

Thirdly, there is the distinction between the clear and distinct on the one hand, and the vague and flexible on the other. We may call this the distinction between the definite and the indefinite. It also comprises the difference between the determinate and determinable, although the term "determinate" is sometimes also used—confusingly—to designate the "concrete" in the sense of the previous paragraph.

No one of these three distinctions by itself answers to the "ordinary" distinction between universal and particular, yet all of them are involved in the discussion of the problem of universals in Western thought. Likewise, every Indian philosopher seems to have a theory about their interconnection. These theories differ. For example, the Naiyāyika holds that comparative definiteness is a function of comparative abstractness, while the Advaitin thinks just the reverse, that definiteness is a sure sign of concreteness. Again, whereas the Naiyāyika thinks that an entity must be definite to be repeated, the Jain takes repetition of an entity as a mark of its indefiniteness. The Buddhist holds that the concrete is that which is momentary and extentless—i.e., unrepeated—while the Jain takes the concrete to be that which is repeated everywhere and everywhen.

The Advaitin takes reality to be concrete and definite. Brahman is, it has been suggested, comparable to the Absolute of Hegel or of Bradley's *Appearance and Reality*, although I do not wish either to endorse or dispute the comparison. This Absolute is sometimes said to be a "concrete universal." Notice, however, that as to the repeatedness of Brahman, the Advaitin must in strict consistency say that it is not repeated. Brahman does not occur in space or time at all, and therefore *a fortiori* does not occur at more than one position in space and time. The distinction between repeated and unrepeated just doesn't apply in the case of Brahman. So it is not yet clear what might be intended by calling Brahman a "universal."

Since he cannot use the first distinction—between repeated and unrepeated entities—to explicate his problem about dependence, the Vivaraṇist must look to the second and third distinctions if he is to find a clue as to his desired criterion.

The abstract certainly depends upon the concrete. Who ever saw a shape without something shaped? How can there be color without extension? We laugh when Lewis Carroll writes of the smile of the Cheshire Cat floating disembodied over the head of Alice. Unfortunately, however, the concrete equally depends upon the abstract. Who could imagine an object without any qualities whatsoever? The Cheshire Cat must have *some* expression. If the relation in question is this kind of relation—between more or less abstract or concrete—then the shell depends for its qualities upon the piece of silver, and the objects known in the waking state depend for their qualities upon what we see in dreams. And worst of all, Brahman depends for its qualities upon the nature of the empirical world. This poses a vicious problem of evil—Brahman is dependent upon the ignorance and sin of men as well as upon their adequate insight into its nature. If the Advaitin seeks to save the analogy by claiming that Brahman is qualityless (*nirguṇa*) and thus not dependent upon qualities at all, one of two conclusions follow: either (1) the world does not depend on Brahman, or (2) the dependence must be of another sort than this one. So we turn to the third distinction for a clue.

Determinables depend upon determinates. Being red implies being some determinate shade of red; a thing cannot be hot without being some specific temperature or other. It is not easy to see how the stock cases of error can be fitted into this sense of dependence, but we may try. The piece of silver, it may be suggested, is more indefinite than the shell, and the dream more indefinite than the waking world. But in what sense? And how do we know? What is involved is some sense of definiteness in which Brahman is completely definite. But this seems just the wrong way around—if anything, Brahman is complete *in*definite!

Perhaps, then, the dependence is parallel to the way in which particulars depend upon universals, determinates upon determinables. In that case, Brahman is completely determinable, and non-Being completely determinate. But that makes little sense, since non-Being is just as vague as Brahman.

There may be a criterion of dependence lurking behind or within our notions of "universal" and "particular," but I haven't been able to discover it. If no criterion can be discovered, a Vivaraṇa Advaitin must either revert to the view of Maṇḍana and the empiricists, which is hardly distinguishable from that of Kumārila or Nyāya-Vaiśeṣika, or else give up progress philosophy and espouse the nonrationalism of Sureśvara. There is, in addition, another reason why Padmapāda's school is always in danger of capitulation to Sureśvara's. Even if the Vivaraṇists *should* find a definition of falsity which yields a satisfactory criterion of dependence, there is still the difficulty that Brahman or Being (*sat*), like nothing or non-Being (*asat*), is a *limiting* notion. Neither Brahman nor negation is false, though they limit the range of things which are false. Now just as one cannot get to sheer negation no matter how far down the range of falsity one may erroneously wander, so, it would seem, one cannot get to sheer reality no matter how far up the scale one may insightfully climb. The curve of *anirvācanīya* or falsity seems to be asymptotically related to its limits; to get from even the most perfect empirical truth to a realization of Brahman will require a nonrational leap. But if that is so, why does it matter what the criterion of improvement is? What is important is the leap, as Sureśvara thinks. From Sureśvara's point of view Padmapāda seems an intellectual dilettante, frittering his energy away answering unanswerable doubts.

CONCLUSIONS

The search for a dependence relation, in its epistemological consequences, generates an interesting pattern among Indian philosophical systems. I shall conclude this chapter by briefly alluding to some points of comparison and contrast among the theories of negation and error we have been discussing.

If the reader will once more examine the chart given in Figure 20, he will see that the relationships between those systems which appear equidistant from the center suggest some useful comparisons. For example, just as we found the Buddhist logicians and Yogācāra having difficulty justifying the dependence of either ideas on objects, or objects on ideas, so Advaitins find it difficult to justify the dependence of falsity on Brahman. In certain important respects the differences between Dharmakīrti and the Yogācāra idealist are like the differences between Vācaspati and Prakāśātman.

In meeting the problem of relating the real to the unreal, Dharmakīrti and Vācaspati appeal to the theory that the mistake lies in the non-grasping of something (the something being difference [*bheda*] for Dharmakīrti, nondifference [*abheda*] for Vācaspati), whereas the Yogācāra and Prakāśātman are not sympathetic to the *apoha* theory in either version. This is because Dharmakīrti and Vācaspati are both interested in emphasizing the relatively independent reality of objects, while the Yogācāra and Prakāśātman are interested in emphasizing the relative dependence of objects upon the knowing subject.

The Yogācāras and the Vivaraṇists hold that sensations are self-revealing, not needing to be tested against an external reality by another judgment. They both are forced, therefore, to look elsewhere than to empirical testing for their criterion of relative validity. Since Dharmakīrti and Vācaspati hold, on the other hand, that sensations can only be known to be valid by appeal to other knowledge about the world, empirical knowing is a proper model for discovering truth.

Thus Dharmakīrti and Vācaspati are known as great masters of logic, while the Yogācāra and Prakāśātman tend to downgrade logic or, like Nāgārjuna and Sureśvara, to limit its use to a negative, critical function.

The comparison between Prabhākara and Bhedābhedavāda (which appear at the same distance from the center) is not easy, since we know so little about the latter. However, they are both emphatic in granting reality to everything positively entertained in knowledge, and to this extent their interests coincide.

The resemblances between Nyāya-Vaiśeṣika and Rāmānuja's system have already been emphasized sufficiently. Kumārila's theory differs from theirs only in being more sympathetic to certain features of Jain ontology. All these theories, along with Īśvarakṛṣṇa's primitive one, grant the knower the ability to synthesize complex judgments out of simple ones, but deny the knower the ability to create *new* entities by thought alone.

The Jain, as we saw, has no epistemological theory to speak of, thinking as he does of the gaining of freedom as primarily a moral progression rather than an intellectual one. He represents a limiting position epistemologically, as contrasted with Nāgārjuna and Sureśvara at the other extreme, who think of the gaining of freedom as primarily a change of understanding rather than a metaphysical change. The very conceptions of freedom are in sharp contrast. Jainism thinks of freedom as the physical dissociation of *karma* from *jīva*. Nāgārjuna and Sureśvara think of freedom rather as the discovery by the Self of the purity which it has always possessed after all. The Hindu and Buddhist progress philosophies fall in between these conceptions, as typified by the Bhedābhedavādin's *samuccayavāda,* for instance, and the willingness of the others to construe progress toward freedom as involving elements of both moral and intellectual realization. This correlation between speculative and path philosophies has been alluded to before, in Chapter 3.

NOTES

1. Quoted by Sen in *Hir Comm Vol,* p. 177, with Sanskrit.
2. Cf. Sen, *ibid.,* and *Buddhist Logic,* Volume I, p. 555, references under "Reality."
3. Ingalls₁, p. 68, note 135, points out that Raghunātha Śiromaṇi, the neo-Naiyāyika, also adopts such a position. See Chapter 9, note 15 above.
4. See Sen in *Hir Comm Vol,* p. 180; cf. *Buddhist Logic,* Volume II, p. 424.
5. Cf. Murti, pp. 102–103 and note 4.
6. *Buddhist Logic,* Volume I, p. 158.
7. *Buddhist Logic,* Volume I, pp. 155–159.
8. *Buddhist Logic,* Volume II, p. 24.
9. *Buddhist Logic,* Volume II, pp. 30–32. Translation revised slightly.
10. For the Buddha's Four Truths, see *Source Book,* pp. 275–278.
11. *Buddhist Logic,* Volume II, pp. 32–33.
12. This account of Dharmakīrti's epistemology depends entirely on the *Nyāyabindu* and its commentaries as expounded by Stcherbatsky. But Dharmakīrti's maturer thought is probably to be found in his *Pramāṇavārttika,* which will shortly be presented to us in translation by Professor Masatoshi Nagatomi. Cf. M. Nagatomi, "The Framework of the Pramāṇavārttika, Book 1," *Journal of the American Oriental Society,* 79, No. 4, 263–266 (1959).
13. Hiriyanna's introduction to *Istasiddhi,* pp. xxii–xxiii.
14. *Indian Philosophical Studies,* pp. 32–33.
15. Parthasarathi₁, p. 73. See also *Doctrine of Maya,* pp. 15–24.
16. *svataḥprakāśa.* Cf. Saksena, p. 63, and also in his index, s.v. *svataḥ-prakāśa.*
17. This argument is also found in *Istasiddhi,* p. 43.
18. *Doctrine of Maya,* pp. 18 ff., puts this argument in several ways, with references.
19. My rendering of Sinha's translation of *Vaisesika Sutras,* p. 8. *adṛṣṭa* is the unseen force or agency (see p. 120 above). My rendering of this text substitutes "complete freedom" for Sinha's "nihsreyasam," "locus" for his "substratum," "mental traces" for "samskara," "agency" for "adrsta," and "concurrence" for "simultaneousness in the same locus."
20. *Indian Philosophical Studies,* p. 21, note 5.
21. For a discussion of Nyāya-Vaiśeṣika theories of time and space, cf. Bhaduri, pp. 183–225.
22. The following remarks are based on and quoted from *Nyayabhasya* (I.1.18, IV.2.1–3, 38–41, 46–47), pp. 43–44, 467–472, 494–496, 498–499. See also Tatia, p. 103.
23. Padmapada, pp. 24–25, note 53. Cf. also *Vedanta-paribhasa,* pp. 35–36.
24. *Vivarana,* p. 144; Sengupta, pp. 61–63. The three horns, in Sanskrit, are (1) *anyākāram jñanam anyālambanam,* (2) *vastuno vastvantarātmanāvabhāso,* (3) *anyathā pariṇate vastuni jñānam.*
25. Maitra, pp. 255–263.
26. *Indian Philosophical Studies,* pp. 19–24.
27. *Alternative Standpoints,* pp. 127–128.
28. *Istasiddhi,* p. xviii.
29. *Istasiddhi,* pp. xix–xxi.

30. Tatia, pp. 27–70.
31. Tatia, p. 75.
32. See Tatia, p. 270 ff. for the material on which this paragraph is based. Quotes are from Tatia.
33. *Indian Philosophical Studies*, pp. 25–30. This quote is from p. 28.
34. The theory was, therefore, called *pañcīkāraṇavāda*.
35. Some recent Western philosophers have proposed treating similarity as part-identity. See, for example, Nelson Goodman, *The Structure of Appearance* (Cambridge, Mass.: Harvard University Press, 1951), p. 191.
36. *Advaitamoda*, pp. 146 ff.; Sinha, pp. 296–297.
37. *Indian Philosophical Studies*, pp. 39–44.
38. Cf. Mandana, pp. 136–150.
39. *Bhamati*, pp. 20–32.
40. A lengthy controversy over the definition of *anirvācanīya* is recorded in Madhusūdana Sarasvatī's *Advaitasiddhi*. The opponent's role is taken by Vyāsarājā, a skillful logician of the Dvaita school of Madhva. This controversy is summarized in detail in *Post-Samkara Dialectics*, pp. 179–207, as well as in *Self and Falsity*, pp. 119–176. The present account follows these latter expositions.
41. *sadasadanadhikāraṇatvam*. *Post-Samkara Dialectics*, p. 180.
42. *sattvaviśiṣṭa-asattvābhāva*.
43. See pp. 75 and 87 for these fallacies.
44. *sattvātyantābhāva-asattvātyantābhāvarūpam dharmadvayam*. *Self and Falsity*, p. 124, formulates it slightly differently, but the difference is not important. For "absolute non-existence," see p. 201.
45. *pratipannopadhau traikālikaniṣedhapratiyogitvam*. "Counterpositive" was explained on p. 203 above.
46. *jñānanivarttyatvam*.

11

LEAP PHILOSOPHIES

Leap philosophers are those who believe in *ajātivāda*, the theory that nothing is ever born, created, or caused—"no causation." When we become free, nothing comes to be; therefore, none of the problems about becoming that puzzle progress philosophers arises for the leap philosopher.

Nevertheless, even if we are all in one sense free already, as the leap philosopher likes to say, there is *another* sense in which we are *not* all free—the sense in which we are not fully appreciative of our freedom in the first sense. There must be some such second sense of "free," or leap philosophy is indistinguishable (except verbally) from skepticism or fatalism.

With respect to this second sense, in which there *is* change from "not free" to "free," leap philosophers may conveniently be divided into "do-it-yourself" and "non-do-it-yourself" philosophers. I shall treat Nāgārjuna, Sureśvara, and Prakāśānanda as typical of do-it-yourself leap philosophy, which holds that a man's gaining knowledge of his freedom depends on his applying himself, an application which he has the choice of performing or not performing. As typical of the non-do-it-yourself philosophers, who think that a man's gaining knowledge of his freedom depends on something superior to him, say God's grace, I shall discuss Madhva, Vedānta Deśika, and some modern Advaitins.

Nāgārjuna and Mādhyamika Buddhism

We have had occasion to notice how uncomfortable a position (in certain respects) is occupied by the Yogācāra idealist. By confining reality to momentary mental states he seems to render the distinction between ideas and objects inexplicable; by talking of a "storehouse" of ideas he seems to contradict the doctrine of momentariness. And if he refuses to allow the question "What becomes free?" on the ground that there is no becoming, he rejects causation in general and capitulates to leap philosophy. The relation of similarity (*sārūpya*) doesn't seem to help him out of his predicament, for the acceptance of it depends, among other things, upon a solution to the problem of erroneous knowledge—and we saw that the Yogācāra is forced to hold that all judgments are False and seems unable satisfactorily to distinguish empirically true knowledge from empirically false knowledge.

On the other hand, as we saw, the Buddhist logician such as Dharmakīrti, who makes ideas subordinate to things-in-themselves, is no better off than the Yogācāra. His difficulties are complementary to those of the Yogācāras.

Nāgārjuna, the most famous exponent of the Mādhyamika school of Buddhism, contends that there is no basis on which one can posit a dependence relation of the asymmetrical sort sought by Vasubandhu and Dharmakīrti. When the Buddha said that everything was interdependent he meant just what he said. He did not mean that some things depended on other things which were themselves independent—a theory which other philosophers, both Buddhist and Hindu, have espoused; he meant that all things are on a par, dependent on one another. Nāgārjuna develops a rather unusual terminology for the status of all things. Since they are interdependent, he says, and since to depend on something else is to have no nature of one's own (no *svabhāva,* to use the technical Buddhist term), they must be without any nature, that is to say "void" (*śūnya*). Nāgārjuna's philosophy is frequently called *śūnyavāda,* the doctrine of the void.

Nāgārjuna harps upon the concept of dependence. That which depends upon something else is less real than that something else. This, argues Nāgārjuna, is accepted by all philosophers. But all the other philosophers conclude that there must be some positive reality upon which other things depend but which does not depend on anything else. For example, the Nyāya-Vaiśeṣikas and Mīmāṃsakas think that substances—atoms, Selves, and the like—do not depend on anything else, while other things

—qualities, for example—depend on substances. The Sāṃkhyas think that the manifested evolutes which make up the empirical world depend upon the unmanifested *prakṛti,* but not vice-versa. The Jains think each thing really depends on everything else. (They are *almost* right!) The Bhedābhedavādins and Advaitins think that everything depends on Brahman, but that Brahman doesn't depend on anything else. Even among the Buddhists, the logicians think there are elements which do not depend on others but are depended on, and the idealist Yogācāras suppose that everything else depends on consciousness but not vice-versa. But these theories are all wrong, says Nāgārjuna, and proceeds to show by a masterly dialectic that they are.

Is Nāgārjuna a skeptic? No, since he allows that causality has a limited play—that is what the dialectic itself shows. Causality is what the dialectic demonstrates, since causality is interdependence. The skeptic, such as the materialistic Cārvāka, does not even go so far as to admit the interdependence of things. Nāgārjuna may with reason claim that if the empirical world were not ordered by the principle of dependent origination even the dialectic would fail. Nāgārjuna is not anti-rational; in fact, he elevates reason to the position of the prime means of attaining freedom. Unlike skepticism, his is a philosophy of hope: we *can* achieve freedom by our own efforts, through remorseless application of the dialectic.

Yet freedom is release from the conceptual, for Nāgārjuna as for all Buddhists. This seems to be an insoluble paradox. How can we free ourselves from the conceptual by indulging in a dialectical play which is conceptual through-and-through? The answer is that through application of the dialectical method we convince ourselves that everything is interdependent, and we develop a special kind of insight (*prajñā*) into the void itself. This insight has no content—i.e., its content is the void. It is nonsensuous and nonconceptual, although it is rational in the sense that it is *developed* through a rational procedure.

We have seen other schools of thought espousing a kind of rational intuition or insight—for example, the Vivaraṇa school of Advaita and certain Buddhist theories. But the difference between Nāgārjuna's insight and theirs is that while Prakāśātman and Vasubandhu seem to suppose that insight can be attained by degrees, Nāgārjuna does not. We have seen that the Vivaraṇa type of Advaita used the analogy of reflectionism to suggest how the relatively True could be distinguished from the relatively False. Vasubandhu supposes that insight is one of the elements, and that it can be developed.[1] Both seem to agree that, as we may say, there is some reality in the world; they agree on a doctrine of immanence, in which development is possible, a means of removing from the pure insight the obscuring ignorance which partly, but not entirely, covers it. This notion of the immanence of reality in appearance is not shared by Nāgārjuna. He seems to be a transcendentalist. It's not that there's a certain quantity of confusion that must be unloaded—this quantitative model is inapplicable. There is, in fact, a kind of unexplained leap from the use of the dialectic to the acquisition of insight.

Professor T. R. V. Murti writes:

> The Madhyamika conception of Philosophy as Prajñaparamita (non-dual, content-less intuition) precludes progress and surprise. Progress implies that the goal is reached successively by a series of steps in an order, and that it could be measured in quantitative terms. Prajña is knowledge of the entire reality once for all, and it does not depend on contingent factors as a special faculty, favourable circumstances, or previous information. . . . The concept of progress is applicable to science, not to philosophy. It is, however, possible to conceive of the progressive falling away of the hindrances that obstruct our vision of the real. But there is neither order nor addition in the content of our knowledge of the real. The modern conception of philosophy as a universal science, co-ordinating and weaving the findings of the various sciences into a coherent system, is at variance with the Madhyamika conception of philosophy as Prajñaparamita.[2]

In this passage Murti seems to waver to a certain extent. He says that *prajñā* is not reached by steps, but adds that it is possible to see it as a progressive series providing we do not draw the wrong inferences from that way of looking at the matter. This wavering is symptomatic of the issues which divide Nāgārjuna's Mādhyamika descendents. It would seem that what we may call the "pure" Mādhyamika position holds the no-progress interpretation, but there *are* attempts to construe the gaining of insight, *śūnya, nirvāṇa,* freedom—for these are the same, according to Nāgārjuna—as a progressive approximation, too.

The matter was thrashed out between two schools of thought called the Prāsangikas and the Svātantrikas. The Prāsangikas, championed by Buddhapālita and Candrakīrti,[3] held that insight into *śūnya* neither affirms nor denies the "lower" (*saṃvṛti*) truths. The empirical world is not illogical in itself, "for if there is no logicality there is no illogicality either."[4] From the higher (*paramārthika*) standpoint, the lower, since it's void, just doesn't exist. That is to say, there is no stepladder progression from the lower to the higher standpoint; the two are incommensurable. The Svātantrika school, led by Bhāvaviveka, found in the Prāsangika interpretation an utter disregard for logic. As Bhāvaviveka sees it, the use of logic made by Buddhapālita is a sham, since logic can be put to no use on Prāsangika grounds. If nothing is denied, there is no logic. Since there must be positive arguments for *śūnya*, as well as the purely destructive dialectic Nāgārjuna suggests, there must be some middle ground between the higher and lower truths. Bhāvaviveka therefore distinguishes a higher and lower within the empirical truths and a higher and lower within the void, and identifies the higher empirical truth with the lower (i.e., conceptual) void.

The Svātantrika position suggests the possibility of a midway position between Yogācāra or Buddhist logic and Mādhyamika. And this was apparently attempted by Śāntarakṣita and Kamalaśīla, whom we have met previously in the roles of critics. In any case we can see that the "pure" Mādhyamika position required constant vigilance on the part of its defenders from inroads made by those who wanted—like Bhāvaviveka—a criterion of success. If insight is nothing like empirical knowledge, how can we know that it will in fact follow upon completion of the dialectical appreciation of the apparent contradictions in the world? And if those contradictions are only apparent, how can we tell a contradiction from a garden-variety confusion? Bhāvaviveka suspects that there is no way to tell good reasons from bad on the Prāsangika view.

Other critics, speaking, unlike Bhāvaviveka, from the outside, voice the same kind of doubts. The masterful tenth-century Naiyāyika Udayana, in his thoroughgoing attack on Buddhism, *Ātmatattvaviveka,* challenges the Mādhyamika to say whether the void is something or nothing.[5] The Jain logician Malliṣena asks the Mādhyamika by what means of proof (*pramāṇa*) he establishes *śūnya*—perception, inference, authority, or what?[6] The attitude of Advaitins, whose own position has been claimed by some scholars to show remarkable affinities with Nāgārjuna's, is interesting. Śaṃkara dismisses Mādhyamika Buddhism as "not worth refuting."[7] The author of the *Iṣṭasiddhi,* Vimuktātman, as well as the author of the *Sarvasiddhāntasārasaṃgraha,* points out that the Mādhyamika convicts himself every time he opens his mouth—his only defensible line is silence.[8] This is a classic line for dealing with mystics, and a mystic is clearly what many Hindu philosophers conceive Nāgārjuna to be. Nāgārjuna answers these questions fairly straightforwardly in his *Vigrahavyāvarttinī,* for instance: the answer is that it is possible to use bad reasoning to prove true propositions. All reasoning is bad, to be sure, but human beings are prone to reason, and thus if one is to teach them the truth he must use the reasoning that people recognize. This answers all of the above criticisms, except perhaps Udayana's.[9]

Other criticisms center around Nāgārjuna's putative theory of relations and his theory of error, called *asatkhyāti*. Padmapāda and Vimuktātman put forward objections to the theory of the void as if it were an alternative which had to be removed from contention. For example, Vimuktātman asks "How can the void, the nonexistent, show itself as existent?"[10]—a typical query echoed by all critics who attempt to take Nāgārjuna seriously. The Mādhyamika answer (when it is even thought to be worthwhile giving one) is merely, "Well, it does. You can see that for yourself!" No explanation is necessary for something being experienced. In fact, no explanation is necessary for anything, since there is nothing to explain.

That is the clue to Mādhyamika—it doesn't try to explain. The challenge of explaining the world has been abandoned as not worth attempting to meet. Nāgārjuna has no theory of relations or of error—he has no theories at all. We may well ask, then, what Nāgārjuna intends to do about the nagging doubts that many serious would-be saints experience? Does Nāgārjuna simply not believe in the occurrence of these doubts? Or is it that he doesn't care? One might think that, although Nāgārjuna's leap theory is not, properly speaking, skepticism, it nevertheless comes to the same thing in that it breeds an irresponsibility about moral endeavor. Nāgārjuna, however, is held up by Buddhists as a venerable example of morality, and although his teaching is negative with respect to reasoning it is quite positive on the moral side: Mādhyamika Buddhists, as all Buddhists, must respect the "three jewels" (the Buddha, the Law, and the monastic Order) and practice the five virtues of the *pañcaśīla*—giving, morality, patience, manliness, and meditation.[11] If Nāgārjuna was teaching irresponsibility he covered it up well.

The answer is rather, I think, that Nāgārjuna quite appreciates the nature and force of the doubts and takes them very seriously indeed. Like many a Western sage, however, he does not believe in the power of the human mind to unravel the mysteries of the universe. That being the case, resolution to the doubts can only come when one becomes free. One does not (indeed cannot) first resolve the doubts and *then* achieve freedom. Obtaining freedom *is* the resolution of the doubts. Philosophy is not a movement of thought prior to our embarking on a path to freedom. It *is* the path. By applying the dialectic we follow the only path we can follow. We are forced to it by our predicament. And, since they signify a conscious awareness of the desirability of freedom on the pupil's part, doubts, far from being something to be explained away, are to be encouraged.

The Advaita of Sureśvara

The reader will recall that as we worried through the various branches of Advaita Vedānta metaphysics we became more and more impressed with the presence in the background of a commanding figure who consistently takes a dim view of the uninhibited speculations of the Bhāmatī and Vivaraṇa philosophers. This figure is Sureśvara, one of Śaṃkara's two known pupils.

Sureśvara's efforts were directed not so much to justifying by argument the possibility of freedom as they were to interpreting properly the words of the sacred scriptures, which, one can imagine him saying, are the only fit source for the resolution of the trainee's perplexity. His most comprehensive work is a gigantic commentary on the longest of all the Upanishads, the Bṛhadāraṇyaka Upanishad, a text containing a large proportion of passages crucial for Advaita monism. Sureśvara's commentary, however, makes hard going for those not thoroughly familiar with the very complex methodology that Sureśvara assumes acquaintance with, exegetical practices associated to a large extent with the earlier Mīmāṃsā teachers such as Jaimini and Śabara.

A less formidable and, indeed, charming work by Sureśvara is his *Naiṣkarmyasiddhi,* a beautifully written, compact introduction to what its author considers the essentials of Advaita. Here problems of interpretation are confined to the first of four parts. The other three discuss various philosophical topics with a minimum of references to the sacred texts.

What is perhaps most significant is what Sureśvara does *not* discuss. He *does* discuss the alternatives of ignorance-resides-in-selves and ignorance-resides-in-Brahman and declares, against Maṇḍana, that ignorance resides in Brahman. But he doesn't even let Maṇḍana's own criticisms of the residing-in-Brahman view arise. For example, Maṇḍana had pointed out that if Brahman were the seat of ignorance then it would be Brahman that would have to be freed and, furthermore, since Advaita holds Brahman to be one, when Brahman was freed everyone would have to be freed at the same time. In any case, Maṇḍana concluded, Brahman, being perfect, cannot be infected by ignorance. Sureśvara's attitude toward this kind of criticism is short and sweet. For example, here he deals with an objector who is attempting to open the question of whether it is Brahman or *jīva* that gets freed:

> *Question:* "Is the teaching for the highest Self or the lower self?" *Answer:* "What are you driving at?" *Question:* "If the teaching is for the highest Self, then because it is already liberated anyway without the teaching, the teaching is useless. But if the teaching is for the lower self, then, the lower self being irrevocably *saṃsārin* [bound] by nature, the teaching has no chance to succeed." *Answer:* "Listen! [quoting Śaṃkara] 'If the scripture refers to both the higher and the lower self in their nondiscriminated condition it is intelligible.' . . . The teaching of 'That thou art,' however, is to be directed to one who through lack of deep discrimination has made superficial intellectual discrimination between Self and not-Self. The holy sentences are meaningful to those who know the difference between the Self and the not-Self. When that difference is not known, pronouncing the holy text is about as useful as singing songs to an assembly of the deaf!"[12]

Sureśvara's explanation of how one comes to be free is equally pithy. There are two (and only two) parts to the path: first, as we have just been told, one must differentiate between the Self and the not-Self through negative dialectic and, second, one must then hear a great utterance from the scripture. Freedom will dawn all of a sudden, and, because the world of appearance will disappear altogether and with finality, one will no longer be victim of fanciful distinctions. The world will be sublated like the piece of silver when the illusion is over or, even better, like a dream after waking up.

Whereas the Bhāmatī and Vivaraṇa Advaitins took enlightenment to consist in the realization of identity of the self with the Self, Sureśvara takes enlightenment to consist in the absolute destruction of even the appearance of not-Self. While I am ignorant the whole world of not-Self, including you, appears "as the lights that appear when the eyes are closed and the eyeballs pressed with the fingers";[13] as soon as I am free the question of your bondage or freedom doesn't arise. All talk about "you" and "I," about an "external world," even about "God" (Sureśvara hardly mentions Him) is appearance-talk only and has no relation whatever to reality and freedom. "Between the world and the rock-firm Self there is no connection except ignorance itself, and wherever a positive connection or identity is affirmed [by scripture] between the two, that is to be interpreted as forming part of an injunction to perform symbolic meditation. . . ."[14]

This theory, like Nāgārjuna's, is something of a speculation-stopper. The only development that seems possible from it is in the direction of improving the reasoning process which leads on to the point at which, impelled by hearing the Word, he leaps to complete freedom. As I have mentioned, this improvement is taken up by other Advaitins, notably

Śrīharṣa, author of *Khaṇḍanakhaṇḍakhādya*. Śrīharṣa owes a great deal to Nāgārjuna and the Mādhyamika dialectic.[15]

Prakāśānanda's Solipsism

We have spoken of Prakāśānanda before, as the arch-solipsist (*dṛṣṭi-sṛṣṭivādin*) of the Advaita tradition. Sarvajñātman, we saw, had certain leanings toward the Vivaraṇa position and seemed to qualify the apparent solipsism he inherited from his teacher Sureśvara. Prakāśānanda's solipsism is unqualified, and he is not afraid to disagree with Sarvajñātman on some issues.

One point on which he differs from Sarvajñātman is in his theory of the number, abode, and object of ignorance. The reader will remember that Maṇḍana and Vācaspati hold that there are many selves, and that the self is the locus of ignorance that covers over Brahman, the object. Prakāśātman apparently holds that there are many selves, but that Brahman is both the locus and object of ignorance. Sureśvara refuses to let the question arise. Sarvajñātman interprets his teacher's silence to mean that there is only one self, but he raises the question of the locus of ignorance and insists that it resides in Brahman, not in the self. As a result, we saw, Sarvajñātman is able to maintain that there is an external world, and also a God (albeit one lower than Brahman). However, he pays for this by interpreting liberation not, as Sureśvara does, as the complete extinction of the world-appearance, but as the realization of identity with Brahman on the part of the self.

Prakāśānanda, on the other hand, holds a simple and unalloyed monism: there is only one real entity; it is named "Brahman"; and we call it the "self" under the influence of ignorance. Since the self and Brahman are absolutely identical, the question of the abode and the object of ignorance is easily solved: they reside in both self and Brahman, since they are the same.[16] Prakāśānanda will have none of Sarvajñātman's ontology. There is no external world, and there is no God; there is Brahman and nothing else. Even ignorance itself is simply constituted. While others (including Śaṃkara himself) divide the world of *māyā* into at least two grades of *anirvācanīya*—the *vyavahārika* world of waking experience and the *pratibhāṣika* world of illusions and dreams—Prakāśānanda interprets this distinction as propounded by Śaṃkara and Sarvajñātman as a crutch for weak minds. He writes:

> *All* experience is like dreams. . . . Nor is the view of a twofold existence contradictory of the older view of a threefold existence; for while ancient teachers . . . did not abandon the position that the

> existence of a dual order of things is dependent upon the perception of it, they taught a third kind of existence (the so-called *practical,* i.e., *vyavahārika*) to satisfy the deluded vulgar. For although the *esse* of the world is *percipi,* there is no contradiction in maintaining the *practical* as a third kind of existence, if attention is had to those intermediate differences which the unphilosophic are persuaded of.[17]

This signalizes, as the reader will appreciate, the abandonment of the search for a criterion whereby we can tell when we're getting closer to freedom. Everything here is ignorance, and when we are liberated there will be nothing at all. On this point Prakāśānanda quotes Sureśvara with hearty approval: "Nescience with its products was not, is not, nor will be, whenever perfect knowledge is produced from sentences as 'that thou art.' "[18] When we wake from dreaming the dream is completely gone—and one doesn't wake by stages. Or so Prakāśānanda holds. He assails the whole notion that there could be stages (or criteria), on the grounds that such a position would "overthrow Vedāntic monism."[19] The crucial point is that "this conviction . . . consisting in the destruction of *all* that is not Brahman is destruction, inasmuch as it includes itself [within the *all*]."[20] When we wake up, not only does the dream in question disappear, but *dreaming* also disappears. That is to say, not only the content of the dream, but also the very attitude or cognitive activity of dreaming is destroyed. So it is in liberation according to Prakāśānanda.

But it is on the theory of causation that Prakāśānanda departs most significantly from his predecessors. Śaṃkara had spent some effort in arguing that Brahman is both the material and efficient cause of the world. This signalizes the naïve Advaita attitude toward causation in which one does not take the implications of *vivartavāda* too seriously and talks easily about cause and effect. The Bhāmatī and Vivaraṇa schools typify a second, more mature stage in which one is aware of the implications of *vivarta* as distinct from *pariṇāma* and appeals to analogies to ease the tensions set up by the possibility of solipsism. We may think of Sarvajñātman's as a third stage of ripe maturity in which the analogies are still used, but the author is careful to indicate that there are different levels of understanding, that the thoroughgoing *vivartavāda,* being incompatible with anything but solipsism, is too uncompromising an attitude for any but the most advanced to adopt. Sureśvara represents even a fourth stage, in which one chooses to emphasize the positive requirements of liberation and minimize ontology—thus the acerbity of Sureśvara's handling of such critics as find their way into his pages.

Prakāśānanda, finally, represents the death of *vivartavāda,* which in him becomes indistinguishable from *ajātivāda.*[21]

Where the others try more or less seriously to explain Śaṃkara's doctrine of the causality of Brahman, Prakāśānanda bluntly says that it is merely a metaphor. "To Brahman causality does not pertain."[22] What is the cause of the world then? An objector points out that the sacred texts talk glibly enough about the cause of the world: if that cause is not Brahman, presumably it can only be that ignorance is the cause. "No," says Prakāśānanda:

> Nor does Śruti imply that Nescience . . . is the cause of the world. For causality is affirmed as simply due to error. . . . A theory of cause and effect lies outside the Upanishads, in that these confine their teaching to that of illusory manifestation (*vivarta*) . . . the statement that Nescience is the cause of the world is made with the view merely of obviating the awkward silence . . . that ensues when one is asked the question: What is the cause of the world?[23]

A final look at Prakāśānanda's theory of error, then. In what way does his theory of error differ from Nāgārjuna's so-called *asatkhyātivāda,* the view that the False is nonbeing? Since the true meaning of *vivarta* is that the erroneously cognized silver is nothing but the shell, and the erroneously perceived self, or world, is nothing but Brahman, how can Advaita say that its view is different from *śūnyavāda,* the theory that everything is void? Prakāśānanda doesn't have an answer for this. He says that he has refuted the theory earlier, but in fact he hasn't. It turns out that an opponent had![24] But he doesn't care, really.

> "Now after error has been discovered, one says, "this rope looked like a snake to me." "But didn't he see a snake?" "Certainly not!" "Then experience is contradicted." "No; because the contradiction of the experience of a deluded man is no contradiction at all, since he doesn't discriminate between what he sees and what he doesn't see; and the undeluded man has no experience at all, so there can't be any contradiction of it!"[25]

Prakāśānanda wraps up into one bundle both the negative side of Sureśvara, as in Śrīharṣa, and the positive side, as perhaps found in Ānandabodha and Citsukha. His position represents the logical resting place of Advaita *vivartavāda* in *ajātivāda* and solipsism. But he himself admits that the whole view "serves only to instruct the uninitiated"; since everything is false (except undifferentiated Brahman), the *vivarta* theory itself is false as well.[26] The Advaitin is cornered finally in his own illusion—and one suspects that most people are unable to proceed to liberation along the road of the solipsist. We shall not be surprised to find, then, that as the extreme implications of solipsism became more and more apparent to Advaitins, they turned away from do-it-yourself philosophy to the possibility of another road to freedom.

Non-do-it-yourself Philosophies

We have discussed some of the leap philosophers who are so in virtue of their *ajātivāda,* but who still believe in man's ability to find a path to complete freedom. Now I turn to those who not only deny that human beings can through their own choice enter into causal chains and affect them significantly, but who also deny that man *alone* can find his way to freedom in any fashion. Although this denial does not necessarily imply an acceptance of theism, it nevertheless is associated in Indian thought with belief in a personal deity.

The philosophical relevance of devotion to God (*bhakti*) may not be altogether clear. We have been arguing that philosophy is developed in answer to the doubts that assail a seeker for freedom, doubts which threaten to render him incapable of applying himself along an appropriate path prescribed by his *guru* or otherwise discovered. These doubts we have represented as intellectual doubts—e.g., "Is the world such that freedom is possible?" But there is at least one other way of reading doubts, a way familiar to students of religion; doubt can be seen merely as the loss of faith, a kind of fall from grace. If one sees doubts not as intellectual vacillation but as moral and spiritual backwardness, then he may also be inclined to think that the antidote for doubt is not clarification (as do-it-yourself philosophers suppose), but the grace of God itself. In keeping with this line of thinking, a leap philosopher advising a student who is afflicted with doubts may be moved to inspire the student to pray rather than to study.

It may be fruitful here to review the attitude toward God on the part of both the progress and leap philosophers we have met, showing how each distinct type of theory is developed by certain of its proponents into a non-do-it-yourself theory emphasizing grace and devotion. For the devotionalizing of philosophy is not confined to theories which grow from *ajātivāda.* Particularly in later times, after the fourteenth century or so, the major philosophers were synthesizers, men who tried to make room both for the intellectual satisfaction of doubts as well as for satisfaction through devotion—and even, in some cases, through overt activity, reinstating the ideal of *karmayoga* as it is found expounded, for example, in the first few chapters of the Bhagavadgītā. Men such as Madhusūdana and Appaya Dīkṣita, as well as others within each of the major schools of progress philosophy—and leap philosophy, too—comment at length upon the Bhagavadgītā and other texts like the Bhāgavatapurāṇa which preach a reconciliation between the various paths, *jñāna, karma,* and *bhakti.*

I shall take up the theories running from left to right in our diagram. Buddhism's theistic development took place largely in other countries of Asia outside India. However, even while Buddhism still flourished in India during the period of Dharmottara, Śāntarakṣita, and Ratnakīrti, Buddhism was becoming involved with what is known as Tantrism, a burgeoning of devotional fervor in which the various *bodhisattva*s were personalized and divinized, endowed with *śakti*s or energies (symbolized as feminine images), and treated as objects of worship whose grace was necessary for the attainment of complete freedom. Little is yet known of Buddhist Tantrism, for the textual materials of Indian Buddhism are still largely extant only in Tibetan and Chinese, and the work of restoring them into Sanskrit or translating them into Western languages is as yet in its infancy.

Turning next to Nyāya-Vaiśeṣika, we must note that neither the *Nyāyasūtra*s nor the *Vaiśeṣikasūtra*s themselves have much to say about God. The *Vaiśeṣikasūtra*s, in fact, don't mention God, and later commentators have to work hard to substantiate their reading of Vaiśeṣika as a theistic system. The *Nyāyasūtra*s mention God in only one passage,[27] and there the word is apparently put in the mouth of an opponent. As early as Vātsyāyana, however, attempts are made to introduce theistic readings into otherwise innocent passages. For example, both Nyāya and Vaiśeṣika sometimes appeal to a vague sort of entity called *adṛṣṭa,* one of the *guṇa*s, which seems to be thought of as somehow connected with the good and bad forces of attached action which produce the continuity characterized in the Law of Karma. As Nyāya-Vaiśeṣika progresses in its early stages, God is mentioned as being one of the Selves and *adṛṣṭa* is peculiarly associated with Him as a causal power that allows him to function as a kind of indirect cause of the creation, sustenance, and destruction of the world. God's *adṛṣṭa* is not the direct cause, but a kind of general, necessary condition, like time and space, which must be there in order for change to occur at all. As Nyāya-Vaiśeṣika develops, God becomes more and more important, to the point where, in the tenth century, Udayana devotes a whole work (the *Nyāyakusumāñjali*) to the proof of God's existence. In the fifteenth century, Raghunātha conceives of God as being not only a Self, but also Space and Time. But by this time Nyāya-Vaiśeṣika is largely a logician's system, and although there is a party-line metaphysics occasionally expounded (e.g., by Viśvanātha and Annambhaṭṭa in their handbooks *Siddhāntamuktāvalī* and *Tarkasaṃgraha*), Navya-naiyāyikas tend to separate their philosophical activities as logicians from their devotional activities as Śaivites or, less frequently, Vaiṣṇavites.

The linking up of a Nyāya-Vaiśeṣika type of ontology with theism is carried out by a remarkable philosopher named Madhva, who founded a whole school of dialecticians whose main purpose in philosophy was, apparently, to controvert monism of the Advaita variety. Madhva himself reads the Upanishads, the Bhagavadgītā, and the Brahmasūtras as propounding a pluralistic metaphysics closely resembling the Naiyāyika's in some details, although Madhva is something of a syncretist, incorporating elements of Sāṃkhya (*prakṛti, guṇa*s) and Mīmāṃsā (similarity as in Prabhākara and Kumārila's handling of inherence and universals). But God takes a place quite unlike that found in any of these systems.

Madhva believes in what he calls the "fivefold difference" (*pañcabheda*). These are differences which cannot be overcome, even in complete freedom. God is different from the world; God is different from the selves; the selves are different from the world; each self is different from the next; and the world itself is made up of different entities. The central point to notice here is that, for Madhva, complete freedom involves neither direct knowledge of Brahman nor the experience of oneness with Brahman. Brahman is God. Madhva will have none of the downgrading of God found in Śaṃkara and many of his followers. What, then, is complete freedom if not the essential union of man with the divine? Complete freedom, says Madhva, is release from the bondage of *prakṛti;* it is effected by God and by the knowledge of God's superiority. But God remains completely independent of man. Otherwise he would not be superior and so worthy of devotion.

Theologically, leaving aside the question of a savior, Madhva's metaphysics strongly resembles that of Calvinism. One may ask, then, what is the function of philosophical inquiry for Madhva? He is uncompromising about release; it is entirely dependent upon God's grace. He goes so far as to divide selves into three kinds: those who are chosen and who will eventually be liberated (*muktiyogya*s), those who are doomed to eternal circling in *saṃsāra* (*nityasaṃsārin*s), and those who are condemned to eternal damnation (*tamoyogya*s). This doctrine seems to breed doubt rather than resolve it. But Madhva disagrees; he thinks instead that the realization of the awful possibility that one may never be able to achieve salvation will constitute the kind of stiffening of faith necessary to eradicate the doubts. One must affirm without wavering that one *is* the first kind of soul. Philosophical inquiry into the nature of the world, the selves, and God has the function of preparing one for redemption through grace by bringing the individual to the realization that he is entirely dependent (*paratantra*) upon God, whereas God is quite independent (*svatantra*) of him. The function of reason is to remove the sources of doubt present in the temptations of erroneous theories—particularly the sacrilegious theory of Advaita, which drags God down to man's level. After such erroneous theories are refuted, the remaining function of reason is the proper understanding of scripture, which results in the incessant drumming into one's consciousness of the truth of God's superiority. At this point one is ready for freedom, and nothing more has to be done by the individual. God will do the rest.

As we have mentioned, Pūrvamīmāṃsā started out as a method of interpreting injunctions in the sacred texts. One might suppose that its philosophical tradition would therefore be theistic, but in fact that is not the case. The early Mīmāṃsā apparently held that man ought not to perform actions because he hoped for liberation; he should rather act because the Vedas say so and because the Vedas are authoritative. Thus there is no purpose in philosophical investigation into the nature of God, the self, or the world since nothing is to be gained by such investigation. Reading between the lines, one might add that much is to be lost, since philosophical inquiry presupposes doubts about the validity or authority of what one has been told. The way to avoid such doubts is to keep one's eyes and ears firmly on the Vedas, following their instructions just because they *are* their instructions. This firmly parental air of "do what I say because I say so, and don't ask questions" on the part of orthodoxy in Hinduism was, by reaction, largely responsible for the rise of Buddhism and Jainism. And the *philosophical* development of Mīmāṃsā, long after the Buddha, was in turn largely a reaction to Buddhism's inroads on Hinduism.

The philosophers who liberated Mīmāṃsā from this procrustean attitude are Kumārila and Prabhākara. On the existence of God, however, they remain noncommittal. Kumārila takes up the question of God in three connections—as the author of the Vedas, as the creator of the world, as an omniscient being like the Buddha. He has no use for any of these functions for God, and Prabhākara quite agrees with him on the matter, being indeed even more emphatic than Kumārila. However, their position is attended by a halting description of freedom, a concept treated with discretion and largely in negative terms by both philosophers. The result was that Mīmāṃsā came to be incorporated into various theistic streams as their exegetical part. For example, in Advaita, once the distinction between the two parts of the Veda—one injunctive, the other informative—has been accepted (orthodox Mīmāṃsakas do not accept it), the injunctive portions can safely be left to Mīmāṃsist interpretation.

The story of Sāṃkhya is similar. Originally atheistic in the hands of such as Īśvarakṛṣṇa, it gets incorporated into leap theories both by way of Rāmānuja's development and by its use in Advaita.

In the case of Rāmānuja it may well be questioned whether he is not a leap philosopher himself, and indeed many understand him to be so. Rāmānuja, we have seen, elevates God to the supreme position in his ontology and elevates *bhakti* to the supreme position among the paths. In the last analysis, it is God's grace alone that can obtain freedom for us. Then what is the function of philosophy? Apparently Rāmānuja takes philosophy to be not the resolver of doubts, but rather the path of knowledge itself. This implies that doubts are to be encouraged, as they lead one to embark upon the path of knowledge. But that path doesn't lead to freedom, or at least all the way. Where does it lead?

Rāmānuja is somewhat ambiguous on this point. Vedānta Deśika, however, understands him to mean that there are in fact two kinds of freedom, and that one is more worthwhile than the other. The less worthwhile is what Vedānta Deśika calls *kaivalya,* which is the experience of being in unique control of all that surrounds one. This is the freedom-to-cum-freedom-from that we tried to characterize at some length in earlier chapters; it is the freedom the possibility of which we have been supposing all philosophers to be committed to in one way or another. Vedānta Deśika, however, although he seems to think *kaivalya* important, finds another state even more so. That is the state of *kaiñkārya,* servitude to God. This, we might say, is the side of freedom which involves submission to discipline. In Chapter 1 we pointed out that paradoxically the freedom we were describing there, though it is essentially spontaneous and, therefore, "controlling," is also gained through discipline, and is, therefore, "controlled." We proceeded on the assumption, however, that the discipline involved submission only from our limited point of view. From the point of view of the completely free man, he is not submissive to discipline but master of it. The conception of freedom as *kaiñkārya* brings this assumption into question. To be sure, slavery to God does not yield the same feelings of inadequacy as slavery to another man; only the completely adequate can be God's servant. Nevertheless, the free man of the *kaiñkārya* variety is submissive where the *kaivalin* is not. And Vedānta Deśika cannot argue, as the Advaitin might, that since God *is* the Self the distinction between being a slave and being master does not arise. For Rāmānuja does not believe that God and a Self, even when realized, are identical; they are, as they always have been, related by identity-in-difference as is the soul to the body.

For Vedānta Deśika, therefore, *bhakti* becomes all-important, and a new note creeps into it. *Bhakti,* which regularly connotes adoration of God, seems to admit of a sensation of enlargement of self and a consequent overflowing of greater love because of one's greater identification with the holy, not as servant to master but as Self to Self. Vedānta Deśika emphasizes, instead, a particular kind of *bhakti* called *prapatti,* the kind which involves self-abasement before God and an emphasis on the unworthiness of the finite self before the Infinite. It is this sort of *bhakti* that enables even the most insignificant person to win the grace of God and become His servant.

With the entrance of this notion of *prapatti* as a path, the role of doubts in self-realization becomes completely reversed. Whereas other philosophers take doubts as stumbling blocks to be removed through clarification, Vedānta Deśika has a tendency to treat doubts as stimuli to greater awareness of the vast gap between the individual self and God. Where others recommend clarification of the relation between God, man, and the universe, Vedānta Deśika emphasizes their lack of relation to one another. As with Madhva, good reasons are relevant only to discomfit the opposition; when actually proceeding toward freedom, explanations are out of point. Viśiṣṭādvaita grows into a fervently devotional religion, and in Śrīvaiṣṇavism of the present day, an exceedingly influential sect in parts of the South, Rāmānuja's personality and organization of ritual comes to be seen as more important than his philosophical writings. With its emphasis on *bhakti* and *prapatti,* this development of Rāmānuja's tradition can be said to represent one of the main arteries through which philosophy reached down to the masses, and it may be that Viśiṣṭādvaita is today the most powerful philosophy in India in terms of numbers of adherents, whether they know themselves by that label or not.

Viśiṣṭādvaita is not, however, the philosophy which the West associates with India, nor is it the avowed position of the large proportion of nineteenth- and twentieth-century professional philosophers in Indian universities. The philosophy which is commonest among the Western-educated of India (those who can read and write English and with whom the West has been able to come into contact) is a synthetic leap-theory variety of Advaita. The influence of Advaita on English-speaking Indians and Westerners is not something one can attribute to the activities of any one organization. But there are certain figures who stand out among recent exponents of Advaita, such as Rāmakrishna and the important South Indian teacher Ramaṇa Mahārṣi.

The Advaita espoused by these philosophers is synthetic, by which I mean that it deviates from Śaṃkara's exclusive emphasis on *jñānayoga* by allowing the equal importance of other paths. For example, Ramaṇa Mahārṣi is reported to have answered a student in the following manner:

> *Disciple:* "But is it not necessary to understand His (God's) nature before one surrenders oneself?"
>
> *Mahārṣi:* "If you believe that God will do for you all the things you want him to do, then surrender yourself to Him. Otherwise let God alone, and know yourself."[28]

Rāmakrishna and Vivekānanda not only allowed that the various paths spoken of in the Bhagavadgītā were appropriate in the proper context, the former at any rate embraced and experimented with all the religions of the world. Rāmakrishna, however, is mainly a *bhakta*: his teachings largely pertain to God.

> There is no distinction between Impersonal God (Brahman) on the one hand and Personal God (Śakti) on the other. When the Supreme Being is thought of as inactive, He is styled God the Absolute (Śuddha Brahman); and when He is thought of as active—creating, sustaining, and destroying—He is styled Śakti or Personal God.[29]

This is not classical Advaita; it is bhaktized Advaita. Rāmakrishna frequently refers to the grace of God. But, furthermore, his Advaita is so comprehensive that it includes the other types of Vedānta as well.

> There are three different paths to reach the ideal, the path of "I," the path of "Thou," and the path of "Thou and I." According to the first, all that is, has been, or ever will be, is I myself. In other words, I am, I was, and I shall be, to all eternity. According to the second, Thou art, O Lord, and all is Thine. And according to the third, Thou art the Lord, and I am Thy servant or Thy son. In the perfection of any one of these three, God is realized.[30]

These are the paths of *jñāna, bhakti,* and *prapatti,* respectively. Rāmakrishna took a dim view of book-learning. He held that he had direct vision of God: "All this has been revealed to me; I do not know much about what your books say."[31] All in all, Rāmakrishna was a very unusual

Advaitin, if one judges Advaita from the point of view of its classical exposition in Maṇḍana, Śaṃkara, and their close followers.

The Western Orientation

The synthetic proclivity of latter-day Advaita, which is to say its ability to absorb elements of disparate philosophies (Mīmāṃsā, Sāṃkhya, Buddhist idealism, Viśiṣṭādvaitic *prapatti,* theism, Tantra) has helped to give rise to the commonly accepted notion that the genius of India is its tolerance of many points of view. The final phase of this development may be found in the philosophers of the very recent past and present, such as Aurobindo, Gandhi, and Vinoba Bhave. These philosophers take as their texts the Bhagavadgītā, the Bhāgavatapurāṇa and other works which appear to preach tolerance among paths and disciplines. Success in philosophy has come to be measured in terms of how many different positions one can incorporate into one's own world-view without their apparent contradictions becoming any more than apparent. The peculiar and rigorous purposes and presuppositions of classical Indian thought have become lost in other ends and objectives. For example, philosophy is put to ends such as the peaceful co-existence of nations. Arguments are taken to be useful only insofar as they subserve social ends; what is important is no longer the resolution of doubts nor even the enticing of pupils onto one or another path leading to freedom.

A new dimension has entered Indian philosophy in the most recent period, the dimension marked out by the distinction between altruism and egoism. It is a dimension that is not recognized in the classical period, at least in the way that we have it in the West. Indians no longer believe that the most they can do to help others is to improve themselves. They suppose they must find first a social philosophy satisfying to everyone, and only then can they attend to their own salvation. With this new end for philosophy the very conditions of the teaching context are withdrawn (the context that we have been taking as defining the scope of philosophy in India). The social philosophies of Gandhi and Aurobindo may be couched in language drawn from India's past, but they are addressed to problems posed in the Western present.

As in the sphere of political and religious philosophy, so also in academic philosophy the problems are nowadays Western. The academic philosophers of the British-founded universities are many of them graduates of English schools; most know more of classical Western than of classical Indian philosophies. There remains a backlog of Sanskrit scholars painstakingly working over the details of the classical systems, but little in the way of original contributions within the confines of these systems can be found among the publications of recent years. The attitude of many Indian scholars, as well as of their Western counterparts, is that the very framework of classical Indian thought is outmoded, so that practically all books written on Indian philosophy are out-and-out historical in their orientation, with no suggestion that the matters they are talking about have any relevance to contemporary problems.

In fact, philosophy in India for the moment has degenerated into mere scholarship, the description, classification, and comparison of Indian or Western schools of thought. Philosophers no longer talk problems; they talk about problems. This, I venture to think, is because they no longer are sure what matters. They find themselves caught in a sort of limbo between the attitudes of the Indian past, of which they have lost hold, and the attitudes of the Western present, in which they are still not at home. They are defensive about both sides of the coin; they wish to make out that India has something unique to offer, but at the same time they want it thought that they are *au courant* with the latest developments in positivism or existentialism. From this limbo there is little forthcoming at the moment. The plight of the young Indian philosopher is that he cannot find anyone who can initiate him into the problems of classical Indian thought in a way that will make them live for him and his times. And yet on the other hand he feels a need to find something unique in his own heritage, something which will give him the right to say honestly that Indian philosophy can contribute to the world at this juncture and which will inspire him in the knowledge that he is a living part of a functioning tradition. Lacking such inspiration, it is hard for a young man to become really engrossed in philosophy, and one is forced to the realization that the quality of philosophy teachers and scholars in India is steadily declining.

What is the answer? Very few practising philosophers in India nowadays know the details of the classical systems, and when they do they know them by rote and not in such a way as to make them relevant to living problems. Yet this is strange, for the aims of classical Indian thought are such as to guarantee the relevance of philosophy to a human predicament and longing which does not change through the ages. It is because this predicament and these aims are not clearly understood and appreciated by present-day philosophers, I feel, that they cannot make out the relationship between what was said by the philosophers we have studied and the problems they themselves face.

NOTES

1. Stcherbatsky, pp. 41–42.
2. Murti, p. 220.
3. Murti, p. 95.
4. Y. Kajiyama in *NNMRP*, p. 298.
5. *Post-Samkara Dialectics*, p. 259. *Ātmatattvaviveka* is edited in the Chowkhamba Sanskrit Series, 1925–37, Nos. 338, 361, 392, 417, 450, 480.
6. Mallisena (17), pp. 115 ff.
7. Ingalls$_3$, pp. 302–303.
8. *Istasiddhi*, p. xxiv; *Post-Samkara Dialectics*, p. 259.
9. *Vigrahavyavarttini*$_{1 \text{ and } 2}$.
10. *Istasiddhi*, p. xxiv.
11. *dāna, śīla, kṣānti, vīrya* and *dhyāna*, known in Mādhyamika as the Pāramitās. See Murti, p. 222.
12. *Naiskarmyasiddhi* (IV.19–21), pp. 208–210.
13. *Naiskarmyasiddhi* (II.95), p. 97.
14. *Naiskarmyasiddhi*, p. 111.
15. See, for instance, S. Mookerjee in *NNMRP*, pp. 1–175.
16. Prakasananda, pp. 6 ff.
17. Prakasananda, p. 25.
18. Prakasananda, p. 134. The text quoted is from Sureśvara's commentary on *Bṛhadāraṇyaka Upanishad* (III.183).
19. Prakasananda, p. 126.
20. Prakasananda, p. 130.
21. The history of *vivarta* is brilliantly reviewed by Paul Hacker in *Vivarta*.
22. Prakasananda, p. 116.
23. Prakasananda, pp. 117–118.
24. Prakasananda, on p. 168, says: ". . . moreover, we have overthrown him who holds to a universal blank." But on page 130: ". . . because the holder of the *anyathākhyāti* view has shown that neither error nor the destruction of it can be satisfactorily accounted for on the view of . . . *asatkhyāti*, no attempt has been made here to discuss these views for fear of extending our book . . ."
25. Prakasananda, p. 170. My translation.
26. Prakasananda, p. 171.
27. *Nyayasūtras* (IV.1.19–21). See Ingalls$_4$.
28. *Maharshi's Gospel*, p. 54.
29. Diwakar, p. 213.
30. Diwakar, p. 214.
31. Diwakar, p. 193.

12

CONCLUSIONS AND OUTSTANDING PROBLEMS

I believe that many Indian philosophers and practically all Western ones are under the impression that Indian thought has nothing relevant to say to the kinds of problems that the Western tradition in philosophy has developed over the centuries. Furthermore, so strong is the domination of Western ways of thinking over most Indian thinkers who are writing and teaching in India that there is, I am afraid, a real danger that the relevance of classical Indian thought to recurrent problems of philosophy may be lost sight of and the whole tradition lapse from want of attention.

In concluding this book, then, I would like to point out the numerous problems that lie beyond or outside this preliminary study of the presuppositions of Indian thought, to indicate how rich a field of philosophical investigation classical Indian thought presents—not to the Orientalist but to the philosopher himself. Indians all too frequently take the attitude that their own classical thought is merely interesting as a historical phenomenon or as something to be compared with other kinds of thinking in much the same spirit in which one investigates the history of thought. This is unfortunate. What is needed are philosophers who are willing to push to the limit the presuppositions of Indian thought, to work along original lines either to refute or to justify them, but at any rate to address them as living ideas and not as dead ones.

In the following few reminders of problems which have been alluded to during the present study and which open exciting avenues of philosophical analysis and construction, I am trying to remind Indian philosophers, as well as to inform educated Westerners, about the truly challenging nature of classical Indian thought. I am not going to order these by importance, nor do they exhaust the field; they are merely the beginning. What I do claim is that they are crucial philosophical problems for any philosophical tradition, not merely for the Indian tradition.

1. In Part One the concepts of *artha, kāma, dharma,* and *mokṣa* were discussed in such a way as to suggest the relevance of these concepts to certain ideas in current psychoanalytic and depth psychological theories. This connection has been somewhat developed by Jung and Fromm, but there is much room for philosophical endeavor here.

2. What is the relation between freedom—complete freedom, freedom from or freedom to—and what we in the West call "morality" or "virtue"? The Indians' emphasis on freedom or *mokṣa* as superior to *dharma* makes possible a reassessment of our traditional assumptions, e.g., the assumption that the best life is the one in which the reason controls the passions.

3. Bringing up to date the old classification of paths (*mārgas*) would be a task worthy of considerable effort. How can nonattachment be practised in contemporary situations? Is there any worth in the attitudes of Buddhism or of Krishna, i.e., of pacifism and activism? Which is to be preferred?

4. Does faith come from conviction or conviction from faith? Here is a problem on which the classical Indian thinkers have a lot to say, at least by implication.

5. Is there really such a gulf as we are nowadays prone to think between ethical reasoning and scientific reasoning? Isn't it true that any investigation, properly carried out, involves the techniques of empirical hypothesis, verification, and falsification which we think of as appropriate to factual inquiries and which the classical Indian philosophers thought of as appropriate to all inquiries—seeing no difference between knowing oneself and what one ought to do and knowing the world, which is thought of as essentially or ideally an extension of the self?

6. Can we get along without freedom from and freedom to, and if not what requirements stemming from these concepts must philosophy fulfill?

For example, Western philosophers have argued both that freedom requires determinism and that it requires indeterminism. Can we find a new way through this tangle by attention to the kinds of questions the Indians found it natural to ask in this connection?

7. What exactly is the point of the distinction between analytic and synthetic, between *a priori* and *a posteriori*, between formal and inductive logic? The Indians did not find the distinctions relevant. Might it not be that we have worked ourselves into a cul-de-sac on this issue, drawn there under the domination of the scholastic and Aristotelian tradition which in other respects we have come to reject?

8. In Western philosophy, too, we can find progress philosophers and leap philosophers, those who believe that philosophy opens up and points the way to progress of some sort and those whose conception of philosophy is quite different, who think of it as the clarification of issues which will in some mysterious way suddenly lay bare man's true nature or who encourage doubts rather than discouraging them, claiming the function of philosophy to be the heightening of awareness and not the resolution of tensions. The Indians wrestled with both sorts of philosophies of philosophy for many centuries; their conclusions are certainly worth considering.

9. Progress philosophers in India have searched for a dependence relation as a model for causation. Is this not what Western philosophers have frequently been doing, too? Why the continuing dissatisfaction with the Humean account of causation, for instance, as well as with the alternative account along the lines of logical necessity? Are not the aims of both Indian and Western philosophy very similar at this point? If so, a consideration of the details of the Indians' investigations of the problems surrounding dependence relations should shed light on our concerns.

10. So accepted is the distinction between egoism and altruism that it hardly seems possible to question its legitimacy. Yet the Indians did not recognize this distinction as particularly important and certainly not as obvious. Their assumption is that the good of all is served by the enlargement of a person's concern for himself, for his self eventually encompasses all selves. The importation of the egoism-altruism distinction seems to be foreign to the spirit of Indian philosophies of life. Can we learn something from them?

These are quite general problems. We have in addition had occasion to notice specific ones that required further attention. I remind the reader of the Nyāya-Vaiśeṣika's self-linking connectors, the mind-body problem of Buddhism and Sāṃkhya, the definition of pervasion, the question of whether there may be no simples as in Jainism, the implications of the models of reflectionism and limitationism in Advaita, the analysis of similarity in Rāmānuja, Prabhākara's problem in avoiding granting the knower any constructive capacity, the Bhedābhedavādin's difficulties over visiting Brahman with bondage, the Vivaraṇa Advaitin's search for a criterion of greater truth and his appeal to universals, the proper analysis of space and time, the number of *pramāṇas*, and many other problems we have touched upon in this discussion. These are all problems requiring acute philosophical judgment, and none of them is altogether foreign to Western philosophy; there are parallels with all of them in somebody's philosophy in the European tradition.

It is time that Western professional philosophers—and Indians, too—stopped ignoring the contributions of classical Indian thinkers to their pet problems. The contributions of the Indians are in many cases available, although admittedly difficult to find.[1] But they can be reprinted, collected, and presented in new translations if there is sufficient interest to warrant it. Fortunately, India has a proficiency in English which makes it possible for Indians to transmit to us in our language the contributions of their philosophers. They should be encouraged to do so.

NOTES

1. The writer hopes that he will be able to publish in the near future a large and fairly comprehensive bibliography, containing editions and translations of major works of systematic Indian philosophy as well as books and articles dealing with the systems and problems.

APPENDIX
SOME SUGGESTIONS FOR TEACHERS

Here are a few suggestions for collateral readings to accompany assignments from the present volume. In many cases it should be noted that the translations here recommended need improvement.

Chapter One. Students should certainly read the Bhagavadgītā. The most accurate translation is Edgerton's (s.v. Bibliography, *Bhagavadgita*). Radhakrishnan's translation is not bad; it is available in *Source Book.* For further discussion of the four "attitudes" or "aims of life," several of Hiriyanna's papers are helpful, especially "The Indian Conception of Values" (pp. 21–35) and "Philosophy of Values" (pp. 101–112) in *Quest After Perfection,* and "The Aim of Indian Philosophy" (pp. 19–24) and "The Idea of Purusartha" (pp. 65–68) in *Popular Essays.* On *karma* and transmigration some more Hiriyanna papers may be helpful, "Karma and Free Will" (pp. 30–34) and "Reincarnation: Some Indian Views" (pp. 43–48) in *Popular Essays.* Chatterjee provides an excellent discussion of all these matters in *Fundamentals of Hinduism.*

Chapter Three. Chapters viii–xii of *Fundamentals of Hinduism* develop the theory of paths beyond the text. *Source Book* contains a translation of Patañjali's *Yogasūtras.*

Chapter Four. One might here have students read brief essays on

Cārvāka and the Ājīvikas from one or another of the general works mentioned at the end of this Appendix.

Chapter Five. For a discussion of the nature and number of *pramāṇas* according to some of the schools, a good source is Chatterjee, pp. 49–68 and pp. 358–376. Book Two (pp. 115–229) of the same work is probably the best single source on perception. From the vast literature on Indian logic it is hard to choose; the references given in footnotes to the text provide a guide. No one account seems to me superior, although *Buddhist Logic* is probably the most thorough. On *tarka* the most complete account is that in Bagchi, particularly pp. 151ff. On *śabda* Chatterjee, pp. 317–356, is recommended.

Chapter Six. With the reading of this chapter should go an introduction to a very few important *sūtras* relating to causal chains and models. The Buddhist twelve-fold chain is found in *Source Book*, pp. 278–280, the Jain chain on p. 252, Gautama's chain on p. 358, Īśvarakṛṣṇa's chain on p. 434. For the *satkāryavāda* model the student should read the *Sāṃkhyakārikās* in *Source Book*, pp. 426–445; for the *asatkāryavāda* model, there is no easily available single text, but there is an excellent discussion in Bhaduri, pp. 271 ff.

Chapters Seven to Nine. On inherence, see Bhaduri, pp. 229–270, and Hiriyanna's paper "What is Samavāya?" in *Indian Philosophical Studies*, pp. 107–120. An excellent discussion of Nyāya ontology which follows a text (Annambhaṭṭa's *Tarkasaṃgraha*) is found in Kuppuswami Sastri, pp. 3–187. One might also assign the *Source Book* readings on Vaiśeṣika, pp. 386–423, though they need plenty of explanation. Ingalls$_1$, Part II, is excellent but extremely technical.

For the *Abhidharmakośa* one should use Stcherbatsky, particularly pp. 17–36, as well as *Buddhist Logic*, Volume II, pp. 346–347. The Yogācāra selections in *Source Book*, pp. 328–337, are readable. The first three chapters of *Indian Realism* may be used to supplement the present account. *Buddhist Logic*, Volume I, pp. 79–145 and 506–529 are generally helpful on the Buddhist logicians' ontology and causal theory.

On Jainism see Tatia, pp. 220–232. Even better is Mookerjee, particularly pp. 25–105 and 195–233.

An interesting paper on Sāṃkhya is found in Maitra, pp. 202–217. *Rāmānuja's Theory of Knowledge*, particularly pp. 103–165, also covers Rāmānuja's metaphysics. For Bhedābhedavāda Hiriyanna's paper on Bhartṛprapañca in Indian Philosophical Studies, pp. 73–94, is indispensable.

The Advaita literature is plentiful but confusing. A good locus for material is Das, particularly pp. 149–172 and 219–243. One would like to be able to assign texts at this juncture, but good translations are hard to find. The translation in *Bhamati* is usable, and the one in Padmapada; H. P. Shastri's translation in Vidyaranya is readable but almost too free. The *Source Book* selections cannot be used easily unless considerable time for explanation and interpretation is allowed for.

Chapter Ten. A direct and exceptionally helpful account of much of the crucial material in this chapter is found in Hiriyanna's introduction to *Istasiddhi*, particularly for Yogācāra, Prabhākara, Kumārila and Advaita. His Indian Philosophical Studies contain clear papers on Mīmāṃsā (pp. 31–38), Nyāya (18–24), Sāṃkhya (25–30) and Bhāskara (39–44), as well as a reconstruction of Advaita (1–18). In addition, on Buddhism see *Buddhist Logic*, Volume II, pp. 1–46; on Jainism, Tatia, pp. 268–275; on Rāmānuja, Sinha, pp. 295–297; and on Advaita, Das, pp. 14–122.

Chapter Eleven. On Mādhyamika, see Murti, Robinson, and *Vigrahavyavarttini*$_2$ (in French). For Sureśvara, have students read *Naiskarmyasiddhi* and Prakasananda (now very hard to get). A little work possibly suitable for students on Dvaita is *Visnutattvanivnaya.* There is a fairly large literature on Ramaṇa Mahārṣi, and of course a great amount on Rāmakrishna.

In addition to these specific suggestions, use can be made of the several introductions to and histories of Indian philosophy. Among these, the most complete is Dasgupta, but this is difficult going for the beginner. For introductions, this writer prefers Sharma, Chatterjee and Datta, and Hiriyanna's two volumes, *Outlines* and *Essentials.*

PRONUNCIATION

An excellent guide to the pronunciation of Sanskrit words can be found in *Source Book,* pp. 638–39. We do, however, call attention to the pronunciations of the following letters here:

a like *u* in but
ā like *a* in father
i like *i* in pin
ī like *i* in police
u like *u* in pull
ū like *u* in rude
r like *r* in red
ṛ like *Ri* in Rita
t like *t* in water
ṭ like *t* in time
ṃ semi-nasal sound
ñ like *n* in singe
c like *ch* in check (*ch* is thus like *chh* in Churchhill)
d like *d* in dice
ḍ like *d* in drum
s like *s* in since
ś (palatal) like *sh* in shut
ṣ (sibilant) like *sh* in shut but with tip of tongue turned backward
h like *h* in him
ḥ final *h* aspirate sound
ph and *th* like *ph* and *th* in uphill and boathouse (in combination with various consonants, the result is like that in English words such as: lo*gh*ut, in*kh*orn, a*bh*ore, a*d*-*h*ere; *jh* is like *dgeh* in he*dgeh*og)

BIBLIOGRAPHY

This is a bibliography of works cited in the text. Items are arranged alphabetically according to the key word or phrase used to refer to it throughout the book.

Abhidharmakosa: Sphutārtha Abhidharmakośa-vyākhyā of Yaśomitra, N. N. Law, ed. Calcutta Oriental Series No. 31. London: Luzac & Co., 1949, 1957.

Advaitamoda: Advaitāmodaḥ of Abhyaṃkaropahya Vāsudeva Śāstri, H. N. Apte, ed. Anandasrama Sanskrit Series No. 84. Poona, 1940.

Advaitasiddhi: The *Advaitasiddhi* of Madhusūdana Sarasvatī with the *Guruchandrikā,* D. Srinivasachar and G. Venkatanarasimha Sastry, eds. Three volumes. University of Mysore Oriental Library Publications, Sanskrit Series 75, 78, 80. Mysore, 1933, 1937, 1940.

Ajnana: Ajñāna, by G. R. Malkani, R. Das and T. R. V. Murti. Calcutta Oriental Series No. 26. London: Luzac & Co., 1933.

Alternative Standpoints: Kalidas Bhattacharya, *Alternative Standpoints in Philosophy.* Calcutta: Das Gupta & Co., Ltd., 1953.

Bagchi: S. Bagchi, *Inductive Reasoning.* Calcutta: Sri Munishchandra Sinha, 1953.

Basham: A. L. Basham, *History and Doctrines of the Ajivikas.* London: Luzac & Co., 1951.

Belvalkar: The *Brahma-Sūtras* of Bādarāyaṇa with the Comment of Śaṇkarāchārya, Chapter II, Quarters I & II, ed. and tr. by S. K. Belvalkar. 2nd edition. Poona: Bilvakunja Publishing House, 1931.

Bhaduri: Sadananda Bhaduri, *Studies in Nyāya-Vaiśeṣika Metaphysics.* Bhandarkar Oriental Series No. 5. Poona: Bhandarkar Oriental Research Institute, 1947.

Bhagavadgita: The Bhagavad Gītā, translated and interpreted by Franklin Edgerton. Part I: Text and Translation. Harvard Oriental Series No. 38. Cambridge, Mass.: Harvard University Press, 1946.

Bhamati: The *Bhāmatī* of Vācaspati (Miśra) on Śaṃkara's *Brahmasūtrabhāsya* (Catuḥsūtrī), ed. and tr. by S. S. S. Suryanarayana Sastri and C. Kunhan Raja. Adyar, Madras: Theosophical Publishing House, 1933.

Bhasapariccheda: Bhāṣā-Pariccheda with *Siddhānta-Muktāvalī* by Viśvanātha Nyāya-Pañcānana, tr. Swami Madhavananda. Almora: Advaita Ashrama, 1940.

Brahmasutrabhasya: The *Brahmasūtrabhāsya* (of Śaṃkara), Narayan Rama Acharya, ed., 3rd ed. Bombay: Nirnaya Sagara Press, 1948.

Buddhist Logic: Th. Stcherbatsky, *Buddhist Logic.* Two volumes. 'S-Gravenhage: Mouton & Co., 1958.

Chatterjee: S. C. Chatterjee, *The Nyāya Theory of Knowledge.* 2nd ed. Calcutta: University of Calcutta, 1950.

Chatterjee and Datta: S. C. Chatterjee and D. M. Datta, *An Introduction to Indian Philosophy.* Calcutta: University of Calcutta, 1950.

Das: Saroj Kumar Das, *Towards a Systematic Study of the Vedānta.* Calcutta: University of Calcutta, 1931.

Dasgupta: Surendranath Dasgupta, *A History of Indian Philosophy.* Five volumes. Cambridge: Cambridge University Press, 1922, 1932, 1940, 1949, 1955.

De Smet: R. V. de Smet, S.J., *The Theological Method of Śaṃkara.* Ph.D. thesis, Pontifical Gregorian University, Rome, 1953 (unpublished).

Diwakar: R. R. Diwakar, *Paramahansa Sri Ramakrishna.* Bombay: Bharatiya Vidya Bhavan, 1956.

Doctrine of Maya: A. Ḳ. R. Chaudhuri, *The Doctrine of Maya.* 2nd ed. Calcutta: Das Gupta & Co., Ltd., 1950.

Essentials: Mysore Hiriyanna, *The Essentials of Indian Philosophy.* London: George Allen & Unwin, Ltd., 1932; New York: The Macmillan Co., 1949.

Fundamentals of Hinduism: S. C. Chatterjee, *The Fundamentals of Hinduism.* Calcutta: University of Calcutta, 1950, 1960.

Gaudapada: *The Āgamaśāstra of Gauḍapāda,* ed. and tr. by V. Bhattacharya. Calcutta: University of Calcutta, 1943.

Gitabhasya: The *Bhagavad-Gītā* with the commentary of Śrī Śaṇkarāchārya, tr. A. Mahadeva Sastri. 4th ed. Madras: V. Ramaswamy Sastralu & Sons., 1947.

Hacker: Paul Hacker, "Eigentumlichkeiten der Lehre und Terminologie Śaṇkaras: Avidyā, Nāmarūpa, Māyā, Īśvara," *Zeitschrift der Deutschen Morgenlandische Gesellschaft* 100: 246–286 (1951).

Hasurkar: S. S. Hasurkar, *Vācaspati Miśra on Advaita Vedānta.* Darbhanga: Mithila Institute, 1958.

Hir Comm Vol: Professor M. Hiriyanna Commemoration Volume, N. S. Sastry and G. H. Rao, eds. Mysore, 1952.

Hiuan-tsang: *Vijñaptimātratāsiddhi: Le Siddhi de Hiuan-tsang,* tr. L. de la Vallée Poussin. Paris: P. Geuthner, 1928–29.

Indian Philosophical Studies: Mysore Hiriyanna, *Indian Philosophical Studies 1.* Mysore: Kavyalaya Publishers, 1957.

Indian Realism: Jadunath Sinha, *Indian Realism.* London: Kegan Paul, Trench, Trubner & Co., Ltd., 1938.

Ingalls$_1$: Daniel H. H. Ingalls, *Materials for the Study of Navya-Nyāya Logic.* Harvard Oriental Series No. 40. Cambridge, Mass.: Harvard University Press, 1951.

Ingalls$_2$: do, "Śaṃkara on the Question: Whose is Avidyā?" *Philosophy East and West* III, No. 1, 69–72 (1953).

Ingalls$_3$: do, "Śaṃkara's Arguments against the Buddhists," *Philosophy East and West* III, No. 4, 291–306 (1954).

Ingalls$_4$: do, "Human Effort Versus God's Effort in the Early Nyāya," in *Dr. S. K. Belvalkar Felicitation Volume,* 228–235. Banaras, 1957.

Istasiddhi: Iṣṭasiddhi of Vimuktātman with extracts from the *Vivaraṇa* of Jñānottama, M. Hiriyanna, ed. Gaekwad's Oriental Series No. 65. Baroda: Oriental Institute, 1933.

K. C. Bhattacharya MV: *Krishna Chandra Bhattacharya Memorial Volume.* Amalner, 1958.

Karikavali: Kārikāvalī-Muktāvalī-Dinakārī-Rāmarudrī (of Viśvanātha and commentators), Rāma Śukla Nyāyācārya, ed. Kashi Sanskrit Series No. 6. 2nd ed. Banaras, 1951.

Kumarila: *Ślokavārttika* (of Kumārila) translated with extracts from the commentaries of Sucarita Miśra (*Kāṣika*) and Pārthasarathi Miśra (*Nyāyaratnākara*) by Ganganatha Jha. Bibliotheca Indica. Calcutta: Asiatic Society, 1906.

Kuppuswami Sastri: S. Kuppuswami Sastri, *A Primer of Indian Logic according to Annambhaṭṭa's Tarkasaṃgraha.* 2nd ed. Madras: Kuppuswami Sastri Research Institute, 1951.

Madhava: *Sarvadarśanasaṃgraha* of Mādhava, tr. E. B. Cowell and A. E. Gough. London: Kegan Paul, Trench, Trubner & Co., Ltd., 1904, 1914.

Maharshi's Gospel: Maharshi's Gospel, Books I and II. Tiruvannamalai: Sri Ramanasrama, 1957.

Maitra: S. K. Maitra, *Studies in Philosophy and Religion.* 2nd ed. Calcutta: the author, 1956.

Mallisena: The *Syādvādamañjarī* of Malliṣena, A. B. Dhruva, ed. Bombay Sanskrit and Prakrit Series No. 83. Bombay, 1933.

Mandana: *Brahmasiddhi* by Ācarya Maṇḍanamiśra with commentary by Śaṅkhāpani, S. Kuppuswami Sastri, ed. Madras Government Oriental Manuscripts Series No. 4. Madras, 1937.

Mookerjee: Satkari Mookerjee, *The Jaina Philosophy of Non-Absolutism.* Bhāratī Mahāvidyālaya Publications, Jaina Series No. 2. Calcutta, 1944.

Murti: T. R. V. Murti, *The Central Philosophy of Buddhism.* London: George Allen & Unwin, Ltd., 1955.

NNMRP: The Nava-Nalanda-Mahavira-Research Publications, Volume I. Nalanda: Navanalandamahavira, 1957.

Naiskarmyasiddhi: The *Naiṣkarmayasiddhi* of Sureśvara, tr. A. J. Alston. London: Shanti Sadan, 1959.

Nyayabhasya: Gautama's *Nyāyasūtras* with Vātsyāyana's *Bhāṣya,* tr. Ganganatha Jha. Poona Oriental Series No. 59. Poona: Oriental Book Agency, 1939.

Nyayasara: The *Nyāyasāra* of Acharya Bhāsarvajñā, with commentary and notes, V. Abhyankar and C. R. Devadhar, eds. Poona: Oriental Book Supplying Agency, 1922.

Nyayasutra: Nyāyadarśana. The *Sūtras* of Gautama and *Bhāṣya* of Vātsyāyana with two commentaries, Ganganatha Jha and D. S. Nyayapadhyaya, eds. Chowkhamba Sanskrit Series. Banaras, 1925.

Nyayavatara: Nyāyāvatāra: The Earliest Jaina Work on Pure Logic by Siddhasena, ed. and tr. S. C. Vidyabhusana. Arrah: Central Jaina Publishing House, 1915.

Outlines: Mysore Hiriyanna, *Outlines of Indian Philosophy.* London: George Allen & Unwin, Ltd., 1932, 1956.

Padmapada: The *Pañcapādikā* of Padmapāda, tr. D. Venkataramiah. Gaekwad's Oriental Series No. 107. Baroda: Oriental Institute, 1948.

Pancadasi: The *Pañcadaśī* of Vidyāraṇya, with commentaries, Mahesvaranando Mandalesvara, ed. Bombay: Nirnaya Sagara Press, 1949.

Pancapadika: The *Pañcapādikā* of Śri Padmapādācārya with *Prabodhapariśodhinī* of Ātmasvarūpa and *Tātpāryārthadyotinī* of Vijñānātman, S. Srirama Sastri and S. R. Krishnamurti Sastri, eds. Madras Government Oriental Series No. 155, Part I. Madras, 1958.

Parthasarathi$_1$: *Śāstradīpikā* (Tarkapāda) of Pārthasarathi Miśra, tr. D. Venkataramiah. Gaekwad's Oriental Series No. 89. Baroda: Oriental Institute, 1940.

Parthasarathi$_2$: *Shastra Deepika* of Partha Sarathi Miśra, with two commentaries, L. S. Dravida, ed. Chowkhamba Sanskrit Series. Banaras, 1913.

Philosophy of Bhedabheda: P. N. Srinivasachari, *The Philosophy of Bhedābheda.* 2nd ed. Adyar, Madras: The Adyar Library, 1950.

Popular Essays: Mysore Hiriyanna, *Popular Essays in Indian Philosophy.* Mysore: Kavyalaya Publishers, 1952.

Post-Samkara Dialectics: Ashutosh Bhattacharya, *Studies in Post-Śaṃkara Dialectics.* Calcutta: University of Calcutta, 1936.

Prakasananda: The *Vedāntasiddhāntamuktāvalī* of Prakāśānanda, ed. and tr. A. Venis. Reprint from *The Pandit.* Banaras, 1890.

Prasastapada: The *Padārthadharmasaṃgraha* of Praśastapāda with the *Nyāyakaṇdalī* of Śrīdhara, tr. Ganganatha Jha. Reprint from *The Pandit.* Banaras, 1916.

Purva-Mimamsa: Ganganatha Jha, *Pūrva-Mīmāṃsā in Its Sources.* Banaras: Banaras Hindu University, 1942.

Quest After Perfection: Mysore Hiriyanna, *The Quest After Perfection.* Mysore: Kavyalaya Publishers, 1952.

Raghunatha: The *Padārthatattvanirūpaṇam* of Raghunātha Śiromaṇi, tr. K. H. Potter. Harvard Yenching Studies Series No. 17. Cambridge, Mass.: Harvard University Press, 1957.

Ramanuja's Theory of Knowledge: K. C. Varadachari, *Śrī Rāmānuja's*

Theory of Knowledge. Śrī Venkateśvara Rao Oriental Institute Studies No. 1. Tirupati: Tirumalai-Tirupati Devasthanams Press, 1943.

Robinson: Richard Robinson, "Some Logical Aspects of Nāgārjuna's System," *Philosophy East and West* VI, No. 4, 291–308 (1957).

Saksena: S. K. Saksena, *The Nature of Consciousness in Hindu Philosophy.* Banaras: Nand Kishore & Bros., 1944.

Samkhyakarika: The *Sāṅkhyakārikā* of Īśvara Kṛṣṇa, ed. and tr. S. S. Suryanarayana Sastri. Madras: University of Madras, 1948.

Samkhyakarikabhasya: The *Sāṃkhyakārikā* . . . with the commentary of Gauḍapādācārya, ed. and tr. H. D. Sharma. Poona Oriental Series No. 9. Poona: Oriental Book Agency, 1933.

Samksepa: The *Saṃkṣepa Śārīraka* of Sarvajñātmā Muni with *Tattvabodhinī* of Nṛsiṃha Āśrama, S. N. Sukla, ed. Princess of Wales Saraswati Bhavana Texts No. 69. Banaras, 1936.

Santaraksita: The *Tattvasaṇgraha* of Śāntarakṣita with the commentary of Kamalaśīla, tr. Ganganatha Jha. Two volumes. Gaekwad's Oriental Series 80, 83. Baroda: Oriental Institute, 1937, 1939.

Sarvajnatman: *The Teachings of Sarvajñātmā Muni,* by Satya Narayan Sharma. LL.D. thesis, Utrecht, 1954. (Unpublished.)

Self and Falsity: A. K. R. Chaudhuri, *Self and Falsity in Advaita Vedanta.* Calcutta: Progressive Publishers, 1955.

Sen: Saileswar Sen, *A Study on Mathuranātha's Tattva-cintāmaṇi-rahasya.* Wagenigen: H. Veenman en Zonen, 1924.

Sengupta: B. K. Sengupta, *A Critique on the Vivaraṇa School.* Calcutta: the author, 1959.

Sharma: Chandradhar Sharma, *A Critical Survey of Indian Philosophy.* London: George Allen & Unwin, Ltd., 1960.

Siddhantabindu: The *Siddhāntabindu* of Madhusūdana with the commentary of Purushottama, ed. and tr. P. C. Divanji. Gaekwad's Oriental Series No. 44. Baroda: Oriental Institute, 1933.

Siddhantalesasamgraha$_1$: The *Siddhāntaleśasaṃgraha* (of Appaya Dīkṣita), ed. and tr. S. S. Suryanarayana Sastri. Publications of the Department of Indian Philosophy of the University of Madras No. 4. Madras, 1935.

Siddhantalesasamgraha$_2$: The *Siddhāntaleśasaṃgraha* with *Krishnālāṅkāra-vyakhyā,* V. S. Aiyer, ed. Advaitamanjari Sanskrit Series No. 5. Kumbakonam, 1894.

Siddhitraya: The *Siddhitraya* by Yāmunāchārya, ed. and tr. with notes by R. Ramanujachari and K. Srinivasacharya. Annamalai University Philosophy Series No. 4. Reprinted from *Journal of Annamalai University* 11, No. 1 (1943).

Singh: R. P. Singh, *The Vedānta of Śaṅkara: A Metaphysics of Value.* Volume I. Jaipur: Bharat Publishing House, 1949.

Sinha: Jadunath Sinha, *Indian Psychology: Cognition.* Volume I. Calcutta: Sinha Publishing House, 1958.

Source Book: A Source Book in Indian Philosophy, Sarvepalli Radhakrishnan and Charles A. Moore, eds. Princeton, N.J.: Princeton University Press, 1957.

Stasiak: Stefan Stasiak, "Fallacies and Their Classification According to the Early Hindu Logicians," *Rocznik Orientalistyczny,* Tom VI, 191–197. (Lwow, 1929.)

Stcherbatsky: Th. Stcherbatsky, *The Central Conception of Buddhism and the Meaning of the Word 'Dharma.'* 2nd ed. Calcutta: Susil Gupta (India) Ltd., 1956.

Suresvara: The *Sambandha-Vārtika* of Sureśvarācārya, ed. and tr. T. M. P. Mahadevan. Madras: University of Madras, 1958.

Tatia: Nathmal Tatia, *Studies in Jaina Philosophy.* Banaras: Jain Cultural Research Society, 1951.

Tattvakaumudi: The *Tattvakaumudi,* Vācaspati Miśra's commentary on the Sāṃkhya-Kārikā, ed. and tr. Ganganatha Jha. 2nd ed. Poona Oriental Series No. 10. Poona: Oriental Book Agency, 1957.

Umasvati: The *Tattvārtha Sūtra* of Śrī Umāswāmi with the *Sukhabodha* of Śrī Bhāskaranandī, A. S. Sastri, ed. University of Mysore Oriental Library Publications, Sanskrit Series No. 84. Mysore, 1944.

Upadesasahasri: Upadeśasahasrī: A Thousand Teachings in Two Parts—Prose and Poetry, by Sri Sankaracharya, tr. Swami Jagadananda. Madras: Sri Ramakrishna Math, 1949.

Upanishadbhasya: Works of Shaṇkarāchārya. Volume II, Parts I and II, H. R. Bhagavat, ed. 2nd ed. Poona: Ashtekar & Co., 1927–28.

Vadavali. The *Vadāvalī* by Jayatīrtha, ed. and tr. P. Nagaraja Rao. Adyar, Madras: The Adyar Library, 1943.

Vaisesika Sutras: The *Vaiśeṣika Sūtras* of Kaṇāda, tr. N. Sinha. Sacred Books of the Hindus No. 6. Allahabad, 1923.

Vedantaparibhasa: The *Vedāntaparibhāṣā* by Dharmarājā Adhvārin, ed. and tr. S. S. Suryanarayana Sastri. Adyar, Madras: The Adyar Library, 1942.

Vedantasara: The *Vedānta Sāra* by Sadānanda, ed. and tr. M. Hiriyanna. Poona: Oriental Book Agency, 1929.

Vidyaranya: *Pañchadaśī,* A treatise on Advaita metaphysics (by Vidyāraṇya), tr. H. P. Shastri. Second impression. London: Shanti Sadan, 1956.

Vigrahavyavarttini$_1$: Nāgārjuna's *Vigrahavyāvarttinī,* E. H. Johnston and A. Kunst, eds., *Melanges Chinois et Bouddhiques* IX, 99–152 (1951).

Vigrahavyavarttini$_2$: "Pour Ecarter les vaines discussions," French translation of Nāgārjuna's *Vigrahavyāvarttinī* by S. Yamaguchi, *Journal Asiatique* 215: 1–86 (1929).

Visnutattvavinirnaya: Śrīmad-Viṣṇu-Tattva-Vinirṇaya of Śrī Madhvācārya, tr. S. S. Raghavachar. Mangalore: Sri Ramakrishna Ashrama, 1959.

Vivarana: Vivaraṇam (Pañcapādikāvyākhyānam) of Prakāśātman with *Tātpāryadīpikā* of Citsukha and *Bhāvaprakāśika* of Nṛsiṃhāśrama, S. Srirama Sastri and S. R. Krishnamurti Sastri, eds. Part II. Madras Government Oriental Series No. 155. Madras, 1958.

Vivarta: Paul Hacker, *Vivarta: Studien zur Geschichte der illusionistischen Kosmologie und Erkenntnistheorie der Inder.* Akademie der Wissenschaften und der Litteratur in Mainz: Abhandlungen der Geistes- und Sozialwissen-schaftlichen Klasse. No. 5. Wiesbaden, 1953.

INDEX

A

Abhāva (absence, negative entity), 103, 201–203, 209, 221
Abheda (non-difference, identity), 122–123, 127, 148, 233
Abhidharmakośa, *see* Vasubandhu, author of *Abhidharmakośa*
Absence, *see Abhāva*
Accuracy, criterion of, 28, 30–31, 53–55, 89
Adequacy, criterion of, 28, 30–31, 53–55, 89
Adhikārin (person ready to get on a path), 37–38, 43, 99
Adṛṣṭa (the "unseen"), 112, 120, 202, 206, 248
Advaita Vedānta (*see also* Bhāmatī Advaita, Vivaraṇa Advaita, Śaṃkara, Maṇḍana, Sureśvara), 44, 98, 100, 103, 109, 111, 121, 140, 157–183, 189, 199–200, 208, 238, 242–244, 251–254
Āgama, see Śabda
Ahiṃsā (non-violence), 21, 214
Aims of life, *see Artha, Kāma, Dharma, Mokṣa*
Ajātivāda, see Leap philosophy
Ajīva (non-living matter), 146–147
Ājīvikas, 50, 103
Ajñāna, see Avidyā
Ākāśa (space, ether), 135, 148, 217
Akhyāti (Prabhākara's theory of error), 103, 197–200, 207–208
Ālatacakra (wheel of fire), 112
Ālayavijñāna (abode-consciousness, "storehouse" of consciousness), 138–139, 195–196
Amalānanda (13th-century Advaitin), 180
Anādi (beginningless), 102, 140
Ānandabodha (11th-12th-century Advaitin), 181, 246
Anavasthā (infinite regress), 55, 82–83, 126–128
Anekāntavāda (Jain theory of ontology), 103, 114–115, 129, 145–150
Anirvācanīya (False), 163–164, 221–222, 226–228, 232, 244
Anirvācanīyakhyāti, see Advaita Vedānta
Annambhaṭṭa (17th-century Naiyāyika), 249
Antaḥkāraṇa (internal cause), 171, 176–179
Anumāna, see Inference
Anyathākhyāti (Nyāya-Vaiśeṣika theory of error), 103, 203–210
Anyonyāśraya (reciprocal dependence), 81
Apoha, 103, 142, 152, 187–195, 197, 201–203, 221, 233
Appaya Dīkṣita (16th-century Advaitin), 180–181, 248
A priori, 52, 54, 66–67
Aquinas, St. Thomas, 2
Aristotle, 2, 112, 126
Arjuna, *see* Bhagavadgītā
Artha (minimal concern, material prosperity), 5–10, 14–15, 258
Arthakriyātva (efficiency, character of doing something), 141–142, 191–193, 196
Asamavāyikāraṇa (non-inherence cause), 112
Asaṃskṛtadharma (non-forceful elements), 131–132, 134–135, 144, 188
Asaṅga (14th-century Yogācārin)
Asat (non-Being), *see* Reality
Asatkāryavāda (theory that effect does not pre-exist in cause), 103, 107–108, 111–114, 117–142, 150
Asatkhyāti (Mādhyamika theory of error), 103, 241, 246
Asymmetrical relations, *see* Relations, asymmetrical
Ātmakhyāti (Yogācāra theory of error), 103, 195–196
Ātman (unconditioned Self):
  Brahman identified with in Advaita, 175–178, 221–222, 233, 243, 252
  compared with *ālayavijñāna,* 138
  distinguished from *jīva,* 13
  in Nyāya-Vaiśeṣika, 82–83, 120–121, 124–125, 206, 248
  object of intuition, 42–43
Ātmāśraya (self-residence), 79–81, 126
Ātreya Rāmānuja (13th-century Viśiṣṭādvaitin), 183
Aum (sacred syllable), 160
Aurobindo (20th century), 254
Avacchedakavāda, see Limitationism
Avidyā (ignorance, "Nescience"):
  in Advaita, 109, 242, 246
    concealing, 161–162, 164, 179–180
    as *māyā, see Māyā*
    number of, 161, 170, 174–175, 179, 244
    primary (*mūla*), 169, 176
    projective, 161–164, 179–180
    seat of, 160–164, 168–171, 173–175, 244
    secondary (*tula*), 169
  in Bhedābhedavāda, 155
  in Buddhism, 102, 130, 188, 196
  as source of bondage, 12

B

Bandha (bondage), 11–13, 17, 21, 23, 38, 106, 114, 121
Beginningless, *see Anādi*
Being, *see Reality*
Berkeley, George, 195
Bhagavadgītā, 3–4, 12, 16–21, 39, 248–249, 254
Bhakti (devotion), 134, 247–253
Bhaktiyoga (path of devotion), 40, 42–43
Bhāmatī Advaita, 102–103, 168–174, 180, 183, 189, 225, 243
Bhartṛhari (7th-century grammarian), 159–160
Bhartṛprapañca (Bhedābhedavādin), 103, 110, 155–157
Bhāskara (8th-century Bhedābhedavādin), 44, 110, 155, 209, 220
Bhattacharya, Kalidas (20th century), 209–210
Bhāṭṭa Mīmāṃsā, *see* Kumārila
Bhāvaviveka (5th-6th-century Mādhyamika), 190, 239–240
Bheda (difference), *see Abheda*
Bhedābheda (identity-in-difference), 103, 121–122, 143, 154–157, 211–212
Bhedābhedavāda, 101, 103, 110–111, 114–115, 154–157, 183, 208–209, 211, 220, 233–234, 238
Bhedāgraha, see Apoha